Report to the
Global Marshall Plan Initiative

Global Marshall Plan

balance the world
with an Eco-Social Market Economy

Wolfgang Eichhorn, Dr. rer. nat. Dr. rer. pol. h.c. mult., is a professor at the University of Karlsruhe (KIT). He published numerous books and scientific papers, e.g. at Econometrica, American Economic Review, Aequations Mathematical. Visiting professorships e.g. in Berkeley, Los Angeles, Vancouver and Vienna.

Dirk Solte, Dr. rer. pol., PD (Priv.-Doz.) for Business Economics at the University of St. Gallen, Director "Economics and Financial Markets" of the SdW - Senat der Wirtschaft (Economic Senate Germany, Global Economic Network), Deputy Director of the FAW/n - Forschungsinstitut für anwendungsorientierte Wissensverarbeitung /n, Ulm (Research Institute for Applied Knowledge Processing). The institute is a think tank for globalization, sustainability and ecosocial market economy; it has developed the principles of a Global Marshall Plan.

Wolfgang Eichhorn / Dirk Solte

Swellmoney and Sustainability

Unriddle our Destiny

Originally published as:
FORUM FÜR VERANTWORTUNG,
Das Kartenhaus Weltfinanzsystem. Rückblick – Analyse – Ausblick,
by Wolfgang Eichhorn and Dirk Solte. Ed. by Klaus Wiegandt

1st edition, January 2015

Copyright © 2009 Fischer Taschenbuch Verlag in der S.Fischer Verlag GmbH, Frankfurt am Main

English translation copyright © Dirk Solte 2010/2011
with special thanks to Peter Lawrence

Cartoons copyright © Paolo Calleri, Ulm

ISBN: 978-3-9811841-5-0

Remark:
Quotations from "FAUST: the first part of the tragedy" by Johann Wolfgang von Goethe are taken from the English version of Bayard Taylor, available through www.gutenberg.org/etext/14591

Contents

Foreword	7
The Sustainability Project	11
Preface	23
Introduction	25
Part 1: Retrospect	**33**
1. Wealth and startvation in biblical times	35
2. Excursus: Money, Credit, Bank, Interest-rate, Inflation, Markets	38
3. Reasons for financial crises	87
4. Financial crises in retrospect: coursing through history	91
Part 2: Analysis	**97**
5. Houses of Cards and Circular Flows of Money	99
6. The Great Depression 1929 - 1932/1932	112
7. In the Aftermath of the Great Depression	117
8. Limits of Money: About Leverage and Legerdemain	130
9. Beyond the Limits: In the Aftermath of the World Financial Crisis 2008	164

Part 3: Outlook 197

10. Crisis as Opportunity 199

11. Way out of the Crisis 230

12. A Seven-Point-Plan towards Balance 235

Appendix 255

Glossary 257

Further Readings 286

Foreword

The aftermath of the financial crisis of 2007-08 changed for many people the understanding of how the economy works. For many years, the Global Marshall Plan Initiative, the Club of Rome, the Eco-Social Forum Europe and other well-respected organisations have advocated for adequate global governance and more regulation of markets, specifically financial markets. On the contrary, market fundamentalists have argued that no policymaker can outsmart markets, with their alleged self-healing powers. The eruption of the financial crisis was no surprise to us, whereas the market fundamentalists were dumbfounded by what had happened and shocked that their models did not hold.

After the fall of the Berlin Wall in 1989, market fundamentalism, driven by huge ambitions of power, became the leading paradigm: free-flow of capital, minimal state control and deregulated business and -trade were positioned as the framework conditions needed to solve all societal problems. This dogma is based on the idea that totally free markets inherently guarantee the best allocation of resources, hence securing the path for growth, in terms of GDP, jobs, income, and even sustainability.

The financial sector and its "spin doctors" were successful in terms of manoeuvring the political debate in their favour, positioning themselves as relatively neutral economic catalysts; similar to a casino, where net gains and net losses compensate each other. Such seemingly harmless economic players, they argued, should not be burdened by taxation and regulations for transparency, but instead should be granted unlimited freedom in order to maximize net wealth.

This was indeed a compelling "narrative" and many even believed it to be fact. Hence, it is all the more astonishing that a major player in the global financial market like George Soros claimed since a long time that it was a fairy tale. He generated huge market gains using his superior knowledge of the financial system. Soros's work focuses mainly on the concept of reflexivity: investors' understanding of the dominant- or the supposedly dominant economic paradigm and participation in the capital markets may at times affect economic performance.

Once an insight is out of the box, it changes the situation and might then not be true anymore. This is a complicated form of feedback and adds to the fact that actors in the economy generally lack foresight. Situations in financial markets therefore often may change heavily and unexpectedly. Insiders use and feed this volatility to their advantage. Their "special" know-how enables them to tweak the system in ways that generate profit. Due to the lack of transparency, these dubious activities go largely unnoticed. As long as they can get away with the "casino metaphor", they can even avoid paying taxes.

Before 2007, there were hardly any publications available that provided in-depth insights into the workings of the economy. Only few people knew what was going on and were able to predict the crisis ahead. One of these economic forecasters was **Dirk Solte** from the FAW/n in Ulm, Germany. Using the institute's expertise on globalization and deregulation, as well as his own research results, Solte forecasted the financial crisis; his scientific argumentation was in line with that of the Eco-Social Forum Europe, the Global Marshall Plan Initiative, the Senate of the Economy, the Club of Rome, to name a few.

Another expert on market regulation is **Wolfgang Eichhorn**. For decades, Eichhorn has analysed market controls, macro-economic scenarios and impossibility results to devise adequate market regulations. Some years ago, Eichhorn came up with the idea that the so-called "magical quadruple" of German economic policy (adequate- and constant economic growth – price level stability – high rate of employment – balance in foreign trade) needs to be extended to nine economic parameters, including two that focus on the environment and the nature of the income distributions. Since the last financial crisis, the theories of Solte and Eichhorn have been broadly debated. Nevertheless, it is noteworthy, that the theories described in this book are anything, but mainstream. More importantly, their theories are scientifically reliable. Prior to the fall of Lehman Brothers, Dirk Solte published a book in which he drew up a prognosis for the economic turmoil that lay ahead. Together with Franz Josef Radermacher, he worked on several projects related to the economic crisis, including teaching material for the general public.

The book "Swellmoney and Sustainability" was originally part of a series published by the Foundation "Forum für Verantwortung" under the guidance of **Klaus Wiegandt**. It gives a comprehensive overview of the authors' analysis work as well as those of other esteemed economists. We hope that it finds many readers and that those readers will benefit from the insights on a highly important issue for our common future. Especially the young generation should learn that today money is quite different from what it was a decade ago. Unfortunately it is still taught the old way at many places.

Franz Josef Radermacher	Frithjof Finkbeiner
Club of Rome	Global Marshall Plan Foundation

Sustainability Project

Sales of the German-language edition of this series have exceeded all expectations. The positive media response has been encouraging, too. Both of these positive responses demonstrate that the series addresses the right topics in a language that is easily understood by the general reader. The combination of thematic breadth and scientifically astute, yet generally accessible writing, is particularly important as I believe it to be a vital prerequisite for smoothing the way to a sustainable society by turning knowledge into action. After all, I am not a scientist myself; my background is in business.

Shortly after the first volumes had been published, we received suggestions from neighboring countries in Europe recommending that an English-language edition would reach a far larger readership. Books dealing with global challenges, they said, require global action brought about by informed debate amongst as large an audience as possible. When delegates from India, China, and Pakistan voiced similar concerns at an international conference my mind was made up. Dedicated individuals such as Lester R. Brown and Jonathan Porritt deserve credit for bringing the concept of sustainability to the attention of the general public, I am convinced that this series can give the discourse about sustainability something new.

Since the time the first books of the series have been published in 2007, unsustainable developments on our planet have come to our attention in ever more dramatic ways. The price of oil has more than tripled; for the value of industrial metals has risen exponentially and, quite unexpectedly, the costs of staple foods such as corn, rice, and wheat have reached all-time highs. Around the globe, people are increasingly concerned that the pressure caused by these drastic price increases will lead to serious destabilization in China, India, Indonesia, Vietnam, and Malaysia, the world's key developing regions.

The frequency and intensity of natural disaster brought on by global warming has continued to increase. Many regions of our Earth are experiencing prolonged droughts, with subsequent shortages of drinking water and the destruction of entire harvests. In other parts of the world, typhoons and hurricanes are causing massive flooding and inflicting immeasurable suffering.

The turbulence on the world's financial markets, triggered by the US sub-prime mortgage crisis, has only added to these woes. It has affected every country and made clear just how unscrupulous and sometimes irresponsible speculation has become in today's financial world. The expectation of exorbitant short-term rates of return on capital investments led to complex and obscure financial engineering. Coupled with a reckless willingness to take risks everyone involved seemingly lost track of the situation. How else can blue chip companies incur double-digit billion dollar losses? If central banks had not come to the rescue with dramatic steps to back up their currencies, the world's economy would have collapsed. It was only in these circumstances that the use of public monies could be justified.

It is therefore imperative to prevent a repeat of speculation with short-term capital on such a gigantic scale.

Taken together, these developments have at least significantly improved the readiness for a debate on sustainability. Many more are now aware that our wasteful use of natural resources and energy have serious consequences, and not only for future generations.

Few years ago, who would have dared to hope that WalMart, the world's largest retailer, would initiate a dialogue about sustainability with its customers and promise to put the results into practice? Who would have considered it possible that CNN would start a series 'Going Green'? Every day, more and more businesses worldwide announce that they are putting the topic of sustainability at the core of their strategic considerations. Let us use this momentum to try and make sure that these positive developments are not a flash in the pan, but a solid part of our necessary discourse within civic society.

However, we cannot achieve sustainable development via a multitude of individual adjustments. We are facing the challenge of critical fundamental questioning of our lifestyle and consumption and patterns of production. We must grapple with the complexity of the entire earth system in a forward-looking and precautionary manner, and not focus solely on topics such as energy and climate change.

The authors of the thirteen books examine the consequences of our destructive interference in the Earth ecosystem from different perspectives. They point out that we still have plenty of opportunities to shape a sustainable future. If we want to achieve, however, it is imperative that we use the information we have as a basis for systematic action, guided by the principles of sustainable development. If the step from knowledge to action is not only to be taken, but also to succeed, we need to offer comprehensive education to all, with the foundation in early childhood. The central issues of the future must be anchored firmly in school curricula, and no university student should be permitted to graduate without having completed a general course on sustainable development. Everyday opportunities for action must be made clear to us all – young and old. Only then can we begin to think critically about our lifestyles and make positive changes in the direction of sustainability. We need to show the business community the way to sustainable development via a responsible attitude to consumption, and become active within our sphere of influence as opinion leaders.

For this reason, my foundation Forum für Verantwortung, the ASKO EUROPA-FOUNDATION, and the European Academy Otzenhausen have joined forces to produce educational materials on the future of the Earth to accompany the thirteen books. We have set up an extensive program of seminars, and the results are very promising. The success of our initiative "Encouraging Sustainability", which has been awarded the status of an official project of the UN Decade "Education for Sustainable Development", confirms the public's great interest in, and demand for, well-founded information.

Taking Action – Out of Insight and Responsibility

»We were on our way to becoming gods, supreme beings who could create a second world, using the natural world only as building blocks for our new creation.«

This warning by the psychoanalyst and social philosopher Erich Fromm is to be found in »To Have or to Be?« (1976). It aptly expresses the dilemma in which we find ourselves as a result of our scientific-technical orientation. The original intention of submitting to nature in order to make use of it ("knowledge is power") evolved into subjugating nature in order to exploit it. We have left the earlier successful path with its many advances and are now on the wrong track, a path of danger with incalculable risks. The greatest danger stems from the unshakable faith of the overwhelming majority of politicians and business leaders in unlimited economic growth which, together with limitless technological innovations, is supposed to provide solutions to all the challenges of the present and the future.

For decades now, scientists have been warning of this collision course with nature. As early as 1983, the United Nations founded the World Commission on Environment and Development which published the Brundtland Report in 1987. Under the title "Our Common Future", it presented a concept that could save mankind from catastrophe and help to find the way back to a responsible way of life, the concept of long-therm environmentally sustainable use of resources. "Sustainability", as used in the Brundtland-Report, means "development that meets the needs of the present without compromising the ability of future generations to meet their own needs."

Despite many efforts, this guiding for ecologically, economically and socially sustainable action has unfortunately not yet become the reality it can, indeed must, become. I believe the reason for this is that civil societies have not yet been sufficiently informed and mobilized.

Forum für Verantwortung

Against the background, and in the light of ever more warnings and scientific results, I decided to take on a societal responsibility with my foundation. I would like to contribute to the expansion of public discourse about sustainable development which is absolutely essential. It is my desire to provide a large number of people with facts and contextual knowledge on the subject of sustainability, and to show alternative options for future action.

After all, the principle of "sustainable development" alone is insufficient to change current patterns of living and economic practices. It does provide some orientation, but it has to be negotiated in concrete terms within society and then implemented in patterns and behaviour. A democratic society seriously seeking to reorient itself towards future viability must rely on critical, creative individuals capable of both discussion and action. For this reason, life-long learning, from childhood to old age, is a necessary precondition for realizing sustainable development. The practical implementation of the ecological, economic, and social goals of a sustainability strategy in economic policy requires people able to reflect, innovate and recognize potentials for structural change and learn to use them in the best interests of society.

It is not enough for individuals to be merely "concerned". On the contrary, it is necessary to understand the scientific background and interconnections in order to have access to them and be able to develop them in discussions that lead in the right direction. Only in this way can the ability to make appropriate judgements emerge, and this is a prerequisite for responsible action.

The essential condition for this is presentation of both the facts and the theories within whose framework possible courses of action are visible in a manner that is both appropriate to the subject matter and comprehensible. Then, people will be able to use them to guide their personal behaviour.

In order to move towards this goal, I asked renowned scientists to present in a generally understandable way the state of research and the possible options on twelve important topics in the area of sustainable development in the series "Forum für Verantwortung". All those involved in this project are in agreement that there is no alternative to a united path of all societies towards sustainability:

– »*Our Planet: How Much More Can Earth Take?*« *(Jill Jäger)*
– »*Energy: The Worlds Race for Resources in the 21st Century*« *(Hermann-Joseph Wagner)*
– »*Our Threatened Oceans*« *(Stefan Rahmstorf and Katherine Richardson)*
– »*Water Resources: Efficient, Sustainable and Equitable Use*« *(Wolfram Mauser)*

- »*The Earth: Natural Resources and Human Intervention*« *(Friedrich Schmidt-Bleek)*
- »*Overcrowded World? Global Population and International Migration*« *(Rainer Münz and Albert F. Reiterer)*
- »*Feeding the Planet: Environmental Protection through Sustainable Agriculture*« *(Klaus Hahlbrock)*
- »*Costing the Earth? Perspectives on Sustainable Development*« *(Bernd Meyer)*
- »*The New Plagues: Pandemics and Poverty in a Globalized World*« *(Stefan Kaufmann)*
- »*Climate Change: The Point of No Return*« *(Mojib Latif)*
- »*The Demise of Diversity: Loss and Extinction*« *(Josef H. Reichholf)*
- »*Building a New World Order: Sustainable Policies for the Future*« *(Harald Müller)*

Those twelve books habe been published in spring 2009. As a thirteens book the topic "Swell money and sustainability" has been addressed by Wolfgang Eichhorn and Dirk Solte.

The public debate

What gives the courage to carry out this project and the optimism that I will reach civil societies in this way, and possibly provide an impetus for change?

For one thing, I have observed that, because of the number and severity of natural disasters in recent years, people have become more sensitive concerning questions of how we treat the Earth. For another, there are scarcely any books on the market that cover in language comprehensible to civil society the broad spectrum of comprehensive sustainable development in an integrated manner.

When I began to structure my ideas and the prerequisites for a public discourse on sustainability in 2004, I could not foresee that by the time the first books of the series were published, the general public would have come to perceive at least climate change and energy as topics of great concern. I believe this occurred especially as a result of the following events:

First, the United States witnessed the devastation of New Orleans in August 2005 by Hurricane Katrina, and the anarchy following in the wake of this disaster.

Second, in 2006, Al Gore began his information campaign on climate change and wastage of energy, culminating in his film "An Inconvenient Truth", which has made an impression on a wide audience of all age groups around the world.

Third, the 700-page Stern Report, commissioned by the British government, published in 2007 by the former Chief Economist of the World Bank Nicholas Stern in collaboration with other economists, was a wake-up call for politicians and business leaders alike. This report makes clear how extensive the damage to the global economy will be if we continue with "business as usual" and do not take vigorous steps to halt climate change. At the same time, the report demonstrates that we could finance countermeasures for just one-tenth of the cost of the probable damage, and could limit average global warning to 2˚C – if we only took action.

Fourth, the most recent IPCC report, published in early 2007, was met by especially intense media interest, and therefore also received considerable public attention. It laid bare as never before how serious the situation is, and called for drastic action against climate change.

Last, but not least, the exceptional commitment of a number of billionaires such as Bill Gates, Warren Buffett, George Soros, and Richard Branson as well as Bill Clintons work to "save the world" is impressing people around the globe and deserves mention here.

An important task for the authors of our series was to provide appropriate steps towards sustainable development in their particular subject area. In this context, we must always be aware that successful transition to this type of economic, ecological, and social development on our planet cannot succeed immediately, but will require many decades. Today, there are still no sure formulae for the most successful long-term path. A large number of scientists and even more innovative entrepreneurs and managers will have to use their creativity and dynamism to solve the great challenges. Nonetheless, even today we can discern the first clear goals we must reach in order to avert a looming catastrophe. And billions of consumers around the world can use their daily purchasing decisions to help both ease and significantly accelerate the economy's transition to sustainable development – provided the political framework is there. In addition, from a global perspective, billions of citizens have the opportunity to mark out the political "guide rails" in a democratic way via their parliaments.

The most important insight currently shared by the scientific, political, and economic communities is that our resource-intensive Western model of prosperity (enjoy today by one billion people) cannot be extended to another five billion or, by 2050, at least eight billion people. That would go far beyond the biophysical capacity of the planet. This realization is not in dispute. At issue, however, are the consequences we need to draw from it.

If we want to avoid serious conflicts between nations, the industrialized countries must reduce their consumption of resources by more than the developing and threshold countries increase theirs. In the future, all countries must achieve the same level of consumption. Only then will we be able to create the necessary ecological room for maneuver in order to ensure an appropriate level of prosperity for developing and threshold countries.

To avoid a dramatic loss of prosperity in the West during this long-term process of adaption, the transition from high to low resource use, that is, to an ecological market economy, must be set in motion quickly.

On the other hand, the threshold and developing countries must commit themselves to getting their population growth under control within the foreseeable future. The twenty-year Programme of Action adopted by the United Nations International Conference on Population and Development in Cairo in 1994 must be implemented with stronger support from the industrialized nations.

If humankind does not succeed in drastically improving resource and energy efficiency and reducing population growth in a sustainable manner – we should remind ourselves of the United Nation forecast that population growth will come to a halt only at the end of this century with a world population of eleven to twelve billion – then we run the real risk of developing eco-dictatorships. In the words of Ernst Ulrich von Weizsäcker: »States will be sorely tempted to ration limited resources, to micromanage economic activity, and in the interest of the environment to specify from above what citizens may or may not do. "Quality-of-life" experts might define in an authoritarian way what kind of needs people are permitted to satisfy« (Earth Politics, 1989, in English translation: 1994).

It is time

It is time for us to make stock in a fundamental and critical way. We, the public, must decide what kind of future we want. Progress and quality of life is not dependent on year-by-year growth in per capita income alone, nor do we need inexorably growing amounts of goods to satisfy our needs. The short-term goals of our economy, such as maximizing profits and accumulating capital, are major obstacles to sustainable development. We should go back to a more decentralized economy and reduce world trade and the waste of energy associated with it in a targeted fashion. If resources and energy were to cost their "true" prices, the global process of rationalizations and labor displacement will be reversed, because cost pressure will be shifted to the areas of materials and energy.

The path to sustainability requires enormous technological innovations. But not everything that is technologically possible hast to be put into practice. We should not strive to place all areas of our lives under the dictates of the economic system. Making justice and fairness a reality for everyone is not only a moral and ethical imperative, but is also the most important means of securing world peace in the long term. For this reason, it is essential to place the political relationship between states and peoples on a new basis, a basis with which everyone can identify, not only the most powerful. Without common principles of global governance, sustainability cannot become a reality in any of the fields discussed in this series.

And finally, we must ask whether we humans have the right to reproduce to such an extent that we may reach a population of eleven or twelve billion by the end of this century, laying claim to every square centimetre of our Earth and restricting and destroying the habitats and way of life of all other species to an ever greater degree.

Our future is not predetermined. We ourselves shape it by our actions.

We can continue as before, but if we do so, we will put ourselves in the biophysical straitjacket of nature, with possibly disastrous political implications, by the middle of this century. But we also have the opportunity to create a fairer and more viable future for ourselves and for future generations. This requires the commitment of everyone on our planet.

Klaus Wiegandt

Preface

The Chinese ideogram for crisis - wēijī - does convey the notion of danger and of a cruicial point of change. That reflects deep insight to the systemic character of life. A crisis denoter a system in a "near-chaotic" situation; it is highly unstable and even abrupt changes are possible; changes that would be considered unrealistic in "normal", calmer times. We find ourselves in such a "near-chaotic" situation with the window of opportunity wide open to solve the most important global problems together. If we look through this window in the right direction it would provide us with the greatest prospect of a sustainable future. It is like a "stargate", a "wormhole", appearing to us: Will we dare to step through to grasp at the chance to us: Will we dare to step through to graps at the chance to achieve a world in balance?

Global problems call for global answers. In medical terms, vorrect diagnosis is the essential prerequisite for an effective remedy. Otherwise in the chosen treatment will at best alleviate the symptoms without actually curing the illness. Likewise, in considering the "disease" afflicting us, it's vital that we first grasp how the global financial system works and how its operations impact on our society and the real economy.

We want to stimulate a wide-ranging public devate on the mechanics behind the crisis, to highlight some possible ways forward, and to motivate people from all walks of life to ponder on the problems facing us an get involved in working out solutions.

That is why we wrote this book.

> Anyone who travels the world - hopes for it,
> Anyone who experiences other cultures - senses it,
> Anyone who looks into other peoples's hearts - knows it:
> A common future is what we all want and need.
> It won't be easy - but we can achieve it.

Wolfgang Eichhorn &
Dirk Solte

Introduction

It is a riddle wrapped in a mystery inside an enigma:
but perhaps there is a key.

Winston Churchill, 1939

This famous remark by Churchill is also an appropriate opening quotation for this book. Admittedly, the British statesman was not speaking about the global financial system, when he uttered these words. However, it's tempting to speculate that, if he were alive today, this might well be how he would characterize the current economic crisis and its possible outcomes. In the spirit of Churchill's insight, in the pages that follow we try our best to unravel the mysteries of money creation. We explain how to gain high profits even in times of crisis by using magic tricks, and finally suggest a way out of this disaster.

The current world financial system came into being after the Great Depression of 1929 – 1932/33, which began with a "Great Crash" (the title of J.K. Galbraith's seminal work of 1954). At least in part, this system is a very real entity made up of imposing (rarely even aesthetically pleasing) buildings, computer centres, infrastructures, telecommunication networks and so on. On the human level, it comprises owners, bosses, employees and customers. Beyond all this there are other, less tangible but even more important constituent elements of this system: ideas and legislation.

How has this become a collapsing house of cards? In this book we answer this question. Before going into details, one can summarize: the world financial system has developed into a house of cards because of a shift in the focus of its operation. Since about 1970 it resorts to figments of imagination from worthwhile and necessary services and intermediate inputs to the real economy. These designed figments of imagination are in part fancy and highly inventive – arcane financial instruments. In using them, small bets could result in immensely high gains. Like in a gambling house these games are by no means economically justified. On the opposite side high bets could lead to a total loss. One example is financial derivatives. In most cases derivatives are unsecured debt obligations whose values depend on the values of their so-called underlying instruments they refer to (these could be precious metals, commodities, shares, bonds, stock indices or currency exchange rates). Small changes of the market value of these underlying instruments could result in exorbitant changes of the amount of debt which is "securitized" by the derivative. Maybe one could ignore this gambling, if only a few gamblers would have these high gains or losses and only from time to time, but this is not the case. M. Gburek (2007, p. 243) figures out that »the worldwide volume of credit derivatives only has reached more than the eighteen-fold of the market value of all shares traded at the New York Stock Exchange in the second half-year 2005«. Although this high volume of estimated $ 600 Trillion ($ 600'000'000 Million) sums up the value of all referenced underlying instruments, it figures out how voluminous the figments of illusion have become. What a gambling house! Who benefits? Those betting right are the profiteers. They gain from all those who bet wrong. However, even those lucky profiteers could become unlucky, if the debt obligation they own could not be paid back by the debtor.

By the end of this book, readers will hopefully have come to realize one basic fact, namely that the global financial system –

the vital cardiovascular system of the world's economy – is anything but stable. To continue the analogy, at the heart of the economy its task should be to keep the blood in circulation around the body, thus ensuring that it neither overheats nor cools down unduly. It should, like the heart, be the most important factor in maintaining the health of the entire body, the world economic system. We aim to show, however, that this is sadly far from the truth. In actual fact, global finance is a complex system of pumps that only really operate efficiently in "calmer times" – in other words, on those rare occasions when the economic body is not under stress. The fundamental problem is that this particular heart is not geared to the most important factor of all, namely the well-being of its body. Despite being an integral part of the whole economic body, it has started to behave like a self-serving entity. In this respect, it can be likened to a disruptive adolescent child in a family: a growing body in and of itself, following its own aims. Yet even this behaviour could be endured if the economic heart, like a real heart, proved elastic and resilient. Unfortunately this is not the case. The heart that is global finance has long since begun to pursue its own agenda, growing out of all proportion to the wider economy that it should actually be serving. Instead of being a stable basement of the economic system it has become a growing house of cards. Indeed, it is now a multitude of the economic house it should serve. It will continue to be a house of cards as long something extraordinary doesn't happen.

We have been inspired by all the good intentions and resolutions from politicians and some academic commentators that promoted the idea of an economic rethink as a cure-all. This bullish approach was encapsulated in the slogan of Barack Obama's 2008 presidential campaign: »Change – yes we can!« Yet it remains to be seen whether these good intentions will result in concrete action, and whether the restructured global financial system that emerges from the shake-up will really be a rock-solid edifice. Many suspect that the changes will be little more than cosmetic. There seems scant ground for optimism. Political action and public discourse make us ruminate and we are afflicted by doubts. It causes despair. The world financial system of the world economic body still remains a vulnerable and fragile heart. There is a concrete danger of witnessing the economic body collapsing at the next infarction of the financial system. To run with the metaphor of a house once more, we haven't even yet settled on what the best foundations or underpinnings for the building might be. It is still a house of cards, but should be the stable basement of our economy. There is a very real danger that the whole structure of our economic house could come tumbling down when the next earth tremor hits the financial system. Plus, by then, countermeasures to ensure the stability of the financial system will have become even more difficult and costly. In such an eventuality, should national governments – and more importantly, taxpayers – find themselves unable or unwilling to intervene a second time in order to prop up financial institutions of systemic importance and save them from collapse? Then the main building – the wider economy – will also come crashing down.

Yet don't precisely the lessons that we have learned from the near-collapse of the global financial system in late 2008 make such a scenario highly unlikely? Unfortunately not! Writing in the German newspaper Die Zeit (4 June 2009), economic commentator Uwe Jean Heuser summed up the problem: »Soon the window of opportunity for rewriting the rulebook governing the financial markets will close. Privately owned banks have already set the tone, with the Deutsche Bank boasting about their immense quarterly profits. Meanwhile, brokers and dealers from other banks are already raking in bonuses from currency speculation once more; and where states have banned bonus payments, banks have simply hiked up their employees' fixed salaries. Hedge funds are expanding their business and many banks are wooing their customers with promises of high rates of return. The gamblers are rolling the dice in the casino again, and most are still playing by the old rules. What really should be happening instead is for banks to be forced to retain higher equity, especially during the boom times. If they gamble, this should not be based on credit and if they provide others with credit for speculation they should not be able to simply abrogate responsibility by pointing to a credit rating from some dubious agency. We need a centrally appointed board to act as an early-warning system for when financial markets threaten to overheat. In other words, we need to put in place measures to guard against this increasingly frequent cycle of boom and bust, which bankers are evidently far more comfortable with than the rest of us.« To echo Heuser's assessment: there should be an immediate ban on credit-based speculation on property or shares in value added. On the other hand, so long as ecological limits are not reached, credit should be readily available if it is used to generate added value.

Let's draw one more analogy here – the obvious one of an ill person. In order to prescribe the most appropriate remedy, a doctor must first correctly diagnose what's wrong with the patient. For instance, if a husband or wife goes to the doctor complaining of severe headaches, it would be negligent to simply prescribe aspirin and send them away. There may be underlying reasons for these symptoms – say, a severe marital crisis, for which the most appropriate and effective therapy would be relationship counselling. Likewise with the global financial system. The deep-seated causes of the crisis must be identified and their impact on the economy and society clearly understood. In particular, it's essential to really get to grips with the concept of money. What is money? What different kinds of money are there? How exactly is money created and how can money disappear? Only a comprehensive grasp of the monetary and financial system equips a person to sort the wheat from the chaff in statements like: »Governments spend Billions to combat recession«, or »The bank has secured itself a new injection of funds as equity«. What do such statements actually mean? Do governments really spend money or is there something else going on here? Of what kind are those "new funds", which the bank has secured as equity? One of our chief endeavours in this book has been to demystify the business of money and money creation. In doing so, we have consciously set our face against gridlock, clichéd patterns of thought, which much of the press coverage and political discourse on the subject only serves to reinforce. One upshot of this is that we deliberately revisit certain key aspects of the operation of the global financial system (and the "diseases" affecting it) throughout the text, by way of stressing just how important they are. It is only through a proper understanding of these aspects of finance and a fundamental grasp of the concept of money that we will be in a position to draw the right conclusions and lessons from the situation facing us.

The book is in three parts: Retrospect, Analysis and Outlook. A glossary explains some technical expressions and terms from finance an economics that may be used in the book.

The first part consists of a lightning tour through the history of booms and busts, bubbles and depressions experienced by the global economy and its monetary and financial systems. This historical overview begins in Biblical times and runs up the present day. Along the way, we take time to explain such terms as money, money supply, deposit money, interest rates, currency, Central Bank, commercial bank, inflation, deflation, debt obligations, securities, markets, the market economy and invent the term swell-money / leverage-money. The main conclusion of part 1 is the insight that monetary and economic crises – whether in individual nations, groups of nations or on a global scale – have throughout history been the rule rather than the exception.

Part 2 is given over to an analysis of these phenomena. Answers are given, or at least attempted, to a wide range of questions. For example: what causes the underlying instability in the global financial system and the circulation of money? How did the Great Depression of 1929 – 1932/33 come about, and what were its consequences? Does money actually disappear as the result of a crash in a financial market, or is it just redistributed? How is it possible to use "sleight of hand" to exploit anticipated future values in the here and now? Who are the winners and losers in a financial crisis?

Part 3 looks to the future. We emphatically do not predict what the world economy and the global financial system will look like in years to come – for the simple reason that nobody can possibly know. However, what we can say with certainty is this: if the near-collapse of the global financial system that we witnessed in late 2008 – and whose aftershocks are still rippling through the real economy and society – does not result in a root-and-branch overhaul of the system, then humanity is sleepwalking to its own destruction. Instead of looking to the future with fear and trepidation, it is down to us to use all our creative efforts to shape our own destiny. In this spirit, this book puts forward a seven-point programme for a possible way out of the crisis and makes some practical suggestions on how to manage the current state of affairs. Behind all these guidelines and action plans is one overriding aim – a sustainable recovery of all societies on the planet and of the planet itself! The essential prerequisite for this is a shift of the collective mindset, a move away from a counsel of despair that claims nothing can be done. What will happen in the future, if we do not even attempt to take the first step and investigate wishful scenarios for our future and debate on them?

Following the delightful deliberation of the Swiss theologian and poet Kurt Marti we should ask ourselves:

> »Where would we be
> if everyone simply said: »Where would we be?«
> And if no-one ever dared
> to go and discover where the first step might actually lead us?
> If no-one would dare
> to become aware of what could be next century?«

Part 1: Retrospect

1. Wealth and starvation in biblical times

Well favoured fatfleshed and ill favoured leanfleshed kine,
seven plenteous years follow seven years of famine
Genesis 41, 1-4 and 34-36

»And it came to pass at the end of two full years, that Pharaoh dreamed: and, behold, he stood by the river. And, behold, there came up out of the river seven kine, well favoured and fatfleshed; and they fed in the reed-grass. And, behold, seven other kine came up after them out of the river, ill favoured and leanfleshed; and stood by the other kine upon the brink of the river. And the ill favoured and leanfleshed kine did eat up the seven well favoured and fat kine. So Pharaoh awoke.« (Genesis 41, 1-4) Joseph interprets this dream that seven years of wealth and abundance are followed by seven years of famine in Egypt. Joseph suggests to the pharaoh to take precautional measures in good times. »Let Pharaoh ... appoint overseers ..., and take up the fifth part of the land of Egypt in the seven plenteous years. And let them gather all the food of these good years that come, and lay up corn under the hand of Pharaoh for food in the cities, and let them keep it. And the food shall be for a store to the land against the seven years of famine, which shall be in the land of Egypt; that the land perishes not through the famine.« (Genesis 41, 34-36)

This narration from the Bible principally explains all that mankind is occupied with in the following centuries, even millennia in economics or to say it more precisely: it quickens, worries, disturbs, constricts and harasses mankind. Abundance and famine both cause early death for millions of people until this very day – year after year it causes the death of thousands of people even if abundance and famine is meant not physi(ologi)cally but economically.

The seven years of abundance and the seven years of famine can be seen as a metaphor describing that the economic development is following a continuous up and down. Meanwhile economics think to have more insight into this up and down and explain it using professional words instead: the economic trend is following business cycles. Short term, middle term and long term cycles interfere with each other. They can be affected through political measures. Choosing bad political measures frequently lead to economic crises that could be given the attribute "abundant". It could lead to economic overheating with inflation, rising interest rates and the request for growing yields. Choosing bad economic measures could as well lead to crises of the "famine" kind. The crisis we witness currently since 2008 is of such kind: permanently decreasing orders, the danger of insolvency for companies, bankruptcy of private households and an increasing level of unemployment.

The metaphor in the Bible does not (yet) talk about money, interest rates, returns, yields or the like. To avoid that Egypt »perishes through the famine« they collect and store corn in the good years. Corn should not perish fast if it is soundly preserved. That is how corn becomes a "store of value". Corn is an asset that could be eaten in the bad times of famine. Corn is in and of itself carrying a capability. If there is a famine it really can be eaten. In good times for sure it will be accepted as "medium of exchange". Nevertheless, to use corn as a medium of exchange is somehow inconvenient and uncomfortable. If corn often goes from hand to hand it will perish soon. It is much better if it is preserved soundly in a common silo. That is why it is obviously better to use "corn vouchers" as money. The corn vouchers can be used as a medium of exchange instead of using corn. One is using - as one would call it in the words of today's world financial system – "a chartered right on an asset", "an asset backed security". Money – the voucher – is a "claim on corn" of the money owner against the money issuer. The issuer has created the voucher, has created the money. Basically if everybody believes that they will receive corn in case of a famine in exchange for the money, this money serves "as good as corn". As long as good faith prevails to receive corn in case of famine in exchange for money, it is accepted by everybody as a means of payment. To exchange all money into corn needs more corn in the silo than money in circulation. Unfortunately, in bad times, in times of famine, the corn stock is shrinking because corn is being eaten. As a result the money stock also has to shrink. The amount of money in circulation that is needed as a medium of exchange is decreasing.

Do we always have to couple money to food or any other kind of valuable goods as for example: gold? In a modern, developed economy this is not necessary and will be explained in the following section.

2. Excursus: Money, Credit, Bank, Interest-rate, Inflation, Markets

The Phoenicians invented money- but why so little?!
Johann Nepomuk Nestroy

Obviously Nestroy had wished for a lot of money – wishful thinking that is shared by the majority of people. Johann Wolfgang von Goethe in his famous drama Faust let Gretchen (Margaret) say unvarnished this focal point of human endeavour: »To gold still tends, on gold depends, all!«

Oscar Wilde states something similar in a sarcastically way: »When I was young I thought that money was the most important thing in life. Now that I'm old I know that it is.« What does Seneca say? »It is not the man who has too little, but the man who craves more, that is poor.« Does money rule the world? Gerhard Uhlenbruck answers this question: »Money does not rule the world but the rulers of the world.«

That hits the mark. It's the government and their rulers that are governed by money – national governments and corporate governments. Money often precipitates them without heed into upmost misery. It's curiously something which they invented by themselves or delegated to produce that is putting them under high pressure and – as Goethe wrote in a poem – like sorcerer's apprentices they call helplessly for the lord and master:

»Lord and master, hear me crying! -
Ah, he comes excited.
Sir, my need is sore.
Spirits that I've cited
My commands ignore.«

Johann Wolfgang von Goethe has illustrated marvellously the principle and the complex of problems that lie in money creation. Around 180 years ago Goethe has described in his "Faust: The Second Part of the tragedy" lures and perils of an economy based on fiat-money made available as (bank)notes. (In his poem, Goethe denotes the fiat-money not as "notes"; he used the German term "Zettel" which has a negative connotation; throughout the book we translate "Zettel" as a mere "slip of paper"). What happens if not too little but too much money has been created?

> **How Goethe explains money and money creation**
>
> In "Faust: The second part of the tragedy" Goethe describes the precarious situation of the public finances at a medieval emperor's court in two scenes. Chancellor, Commander-in-chief, Treasurer and Steward have met the emperor to deliberate on the disastrous financial situation. ... Mephistopheles enters the scene ... and first asserts: »Where in this world does not some lack appear? Here this, there that, but money's lacking here.« He oraculates mystically about new possibilities to raise money. Confronted with scepticism he retorts the chancellor: »What you don't touch, for you lies miles away; What you don't grasp, is wholly lost to you; What you don't reckon, you don't believe is true; What you don't weigh, that has for you no weight; What you don't coin, you're sure is counterfeit.« Emperor, loosing his patience, responds: »That is not the way to help or aught determine. What do you mean now with this Lenten sermon? I'm

sated of this endless "If" and "How". There is no money. Well, then, get it now!« Mephisto: »I'll furnish what you wish and more.« Mephisto now explains that since roman times …up to now … people have hidden gold …»It all lies buried in the earth, to save it; The earth's the Emperor's, and he should have it.«

The Commander-in-chief is a realist, so that he perceives: »Shrewd fool to promise each what will befit; Whence it may come, no soldier cares a whit.« Day's later …money creation is already in full operation. Steward reports the emperor: »…Bill upon bill has now been squared; The usurers' talons have been pared. From hellish worry I am free! In Heaven life can not happier be.« Commander-in-chief adds: »Arrears are paid as they were due, And all the army's pledged anew; …« …

Chancellor now uncurtains the secret behind this whirligig: »So hear and see the fateful, solemn leaf, Which into joy has transformed all our grief.« He reads the text on a banknote: »To all whom it concerns, let it be known: Who hath this note ("Zettel" = "slip of paper"), a thousand crowns doth own. As certain pledge thereof shall stand, Vast buried treasure in the Emperor's land. Provision has been made that ample treasure, Raised straightway, shall redeem the note at pleasure.« The emperor … was convinced by the chancellor to sign consent for printing money by the words: »A lofty festal joy do for thyself attain: Thy people's weal - a few strokes of the pen!« Emperor is wondering: »My people take it for good gold, you say? In camp, in court, sufficient as full pay? Although amazed, still I must give assent.« Chancellor refers swiftly on it and explains the inexorable transition mechanism: »The fugitives (banknotes) we could nowise capture; Like lightning they were scattered on the run. The changers' shops open wide to everyone; And there all notes

> are honoured, high and low, With gold and silver - at a discount, though. From there to butcher, baker, tavern hasting, One-half the world seems thinking but of feasting, The other in new raiment struts and crows; The draper cuts the cloth, the tailor sews. In cellars "Long live the Emperor!" is the toasting; There platters clatter, there they're boiling, roasting.«
>
> Mephistopheles' plan works. He summarizes the new monetary policy dictum: »Nor gold nor pearls are half as handy as such paper. Then a man knows what he has. There is no need of haggling or exchanging; In love and wine one can at will be ranging. If you want metal, changers are at hand; If lacking there, dig for a while the land….« Undiscovered and therefore imaginary gold has been successfully turned into money. (Frank Schumacher, in: P. E. Anders, 1995, pp. 33–35)

»The interchange between the deficitarian fiscal policy and an inflationary monetary policy in an economy in recession« (Frank Schumacher) can nowhere else in the world than here be read with such clearness, descriptiveness and sprinkled with humour.

Goethe lets the chancellor herald the new constitution of money in the first act of "Faust: The Second Part of the tragedy", in the pleasure garden scene. Money is a "mere slip of paper" that should be valued with what is written on it. "Who hath this note, a thousand crowns doth own." This little sentence explains marvellously the essential nature of modern money. Money is nothing else than a voucher, a slip of paper with a value ascribed. Today money is nothing else than a voucher one can get something for. And the question is: What can I get for the voucher? The answer is partially given by legislation of the monetary system. It is given only for a very particular kind of money, for slips of paper issued by the Central Banks (and with restrictions issued by government either) as "legal tender". And this is one important aspect that has to be kept in mind. "Money" is not the term that is regulated by legislation, but "legal tender". "Money" is only a word given to slips of paper that are produced from very different drawer, the so-called issuer. The drawer of a slip of paper, the issuer of money can ultimately be every player in the economic game.

Is it enough for a robust and steady monetary system to have slips of paper, vouchers or notes that have a natural number like 1, 2, 3, 4, 5, 10, 20, 50, 100 etc. as its securitized monetary value written on it and (besides other things) decorated with the signature of a high-ranked person and backed by something valuable, imperishable? Is this enough to provide a Nation or a group of Nations with a fine-working and sustainable, robust monetary system or will this become a house of cards that is collapsing whenever winds are blowing stronger? This book is devoted to give answers to these and associated questions.

To understand the basics is essential. That is why we have to explain some fundamental terms and concepts. What is money? How does it come into circulation? Why are notes, why are mere slips of paper accepted by everybody (at least in calm times)? What is the role of a bank, a banker or a financier? Why and for what is interest charged and paid? Are economic cycles and crises, inflation and deflation mainly affected by the financial system – meanwhile globally by the global financial system? Are free markets the cause of most economic crises or rather to say: is it market failure, market fundamentalism, turbo capitalism? Libraries are filled with answers to these questions. Our answers fill this book. We start with some explanations.

What is money?

Money is a special medium of exchange. We characterize it as "special" since it does not satisfy the concrete "real" needs of an exchange partner. Money can (only) be used for further exchange transactions. Broad acceptance is a prerequisite. This is achieved mainly by the government but it is restricted to a very particular kind of money. It concerns money only issued by the Central Bank (or the government). The government has obligated itself by legislation to accept this money without limitation to settle a tax debt. The government also suggests the acceptance of Central-Bank-money to settle all (money-)debts in general. Money issued by the Central Bank is legislated as "legal tender". Money comes in very different forms, e.g. coins, (bank-) notes, book money, deposit money, check money and much more.

Every market participant is recommended by government to accept legal tender to settle the payment of goods and services. Government itself is obligated to the market participants to accept legal tender to settle any kind of debt. Money is a unit of account and a measure of value since money provides a mean to compare goods and services via their prices. Thus money covers the following functions: medium of exchange and legal tender, unit of account, measure of value and a store of value.

> **Money and legal tender**
>
> In legislation the frame is set for general terms and conditions. Laws and provisions define as standard which kind of means of payment cannot be refused in settling of a debt. As long as nothing else is fixed in a trade agreement, a creditor is forced to accept legal tender to settle a debt at maturity. That means law sets legal tender as a standard for all pay-

ments since the buyer of a good or service owes the seller the price of the purchased good or service as money. This monetary debt can be settled by legal tender. In the European currency zone legal tender is all the money issued by two different issuers. One of them is the national government. In Germany e.g. the Federal Government has the right to produce coins. Coins are within the European currency zone only limited legal tender. Nobody except the emitting government is forced to accept coins in unlimited value to settle a debt. In general that means unlimited legal tender are all notes only emitted from the Central Bank. The Central Bank does not emit coins but only notes. They emit slips of paper. Central-Bank-money/Central Bank notes are money vouchers signed by the president of the Central Bank. Coins are emitted and brought into circulation by the national government. National government sells the coins to the Central Bank and is paid for them with Central Bank notes. The volume of coins that can be brought into circulation has to be authorized by the Central Bank in advance. That is defined by the laws of the European currency zone. In Germany e.g. these details are regulated in the "coinage act" (Münzgesetz) and the "Deutsche Bundesbank act". The Deutsche Bundesbank (German Central Bank) is not allowed to emit coins. Only the Federal Government is allowed to do so. Since the 1st of January of 1999 the European Central Bank (ECB) is the only emitter of Central Bank notes within the Euro currency zone. The European Central Bank is responsible to define and exercise the single monetary policy. Until 1998 the Deutsche Bundesbank was allowed to emit notes – slip of paper money – a "paper of value" (the German language reflects in a very direct manner the main characteristic of a banknote. The German term "Wertpapier" has two parts: "Wert" meaning "value" and "Papier" meaning "paper").

This leads us to the question: what is the value of these coins and slips of paper? To give the answer we describe briefly the two different alternatives for the principle design of a monetary system. Here two variants are possible.

The first is based on commodity money and representative money, the second is based on fiat-money. In the first variant the money is backed by naturally scarce commodities. These could be precious metals like gold or silver. In such a monetary system coins are or are made of the scarce resource. The value of the scarce resource used to produce the coin determines the value of the coin. (Central-Bank-) Notes are representative money in such a system. They are debt obligations. They are commodity vouchers for a well-defined amount of the commodity (e.g. a special amount of gold) which is held on trust at the Central Bank. In such a system the value of all (Central-Bank-)notes in its total volume cannot be higher than the total value of the deposited scarce commodities held at the Central Bank. In a system based on commodity money and representative money the owner of a coin holds a real value in his hands. If he owns a note, what he holds in his hands is a pledge of the Central Bank: »certifying that there is on deposit the guaranteed value in gold, payable to the bearer on demand.«

In a system based on fiat-money it's different. The value of the material that a coin is made of is quite low. If one owns a note the only claim against the Central Bank is to get a brand new note if the one owned is soiled by usage. There is no claim on gold or other real values connected to the note. It is fiat-money made from nothing ("fiat lux" in Latin means "let there be light", fiat-money means "let there be money"). Coins and notes in a system of fiat-money will be given a value by those who are willing – voluntarily – to give something in exchange. Whatever number is written on the note or the coin, its "real" value is what you can get for it. The characteristic of such a monetary system is that legislation defines as standard that money debt can be settled by those notes and coins defined as legal tender (as long as nothing else has been fixed by contract). A system of fiat-money is backed by "good faith". Everybody in an economy or society with such a monetary system assumes and expects that one can buy goods and services with this money. It is confidence that today and in the future enough members of the society will accept the money in exchange with goods and services. There is no claim against the issuer of fiat-money that is legal tender. E.g. in Germany neither Federal Government (the issuer of coins) nor the Deutsche Bundesbank/European Central Bank (the issuer of notes) can assure that legal tender is always accepted in normal business. Federal Government only commits itself to accept legal tender to settle a tax debt. Today most of the monetary systems in the world are fiat-money-based.

Why does such a system work if legal tender has no value in its own? The answer is: it works as long good faith and general acceptance is given. As long as it is commonly usual to settle money debts with legal tender and that means to buy goods and services paying with legal tender. Whenever somebody buys goods and services the result is a money debt that can be settled by legal tender. As long as it is accepted and as long as everybody is confident that it will be possible to buy something with the slips of paper one owns, these slips will usually be accepted. However, there should be no inflation. There should not be the situation where what you can acquire in the future will be less than today. This could happen if too many slips are in circulation. This is the main reason why the total money stock, the total amount of notes and coins, the total amount of currency in circulation, is limited. There should be no or at least no high inflation.

So far we described the most important but not all aspects of money. There is more, which B. Hardorp (2009) comprehensively describes as the manifested consciousness of people and the entire society about the mutual networking of activities to produce goods and services: »Money is society's stream of consciousness enabling to clear the societal stream of capacities or added value. It flows as laws and provision towards capacities and added value reaching all the concrete places of consumption or investment.«

Money together with the monetary organization (the system of rules and regulations to organize the monetary system) is called currency. As an example one talks about the Euro currency, the US Dollar currency or the Yen currency etc.

What is a credit?

A lot of people may think that a credit is a loan of money. It is the prevailing opinion of people which can also be found broadly in scientific literature. From a commercial banks' (a credit institutions') point of view this would mean: the bank lends money to the borrower. Granting a credit would than mean that money has been given away for a time and the creditor charges interest for the time he gives the money to the debtor. A result of this mistaken perspective is the assertion that a kind of basic interest rate would inhere in money. This prevailing opinion does not fit the economic truth, but it can be seen as a reason for some difficulties one could have to understand the monetary system, the financial system and in consequence the whole economic system.

What is actually a credit and what is the difference if somebody does provide a loan? To loan something to somebody does not mean to grant a credit. To make this point clear take the following example: if I lend a pushcart to my neighbour he could lend a hedge trimmer to me. In this small example there is absolutely no granting of any credit and money is also not used. Of course it is obviously possible to lend money. This could be done as is or against a reward or a return service, but this is not a must as a basis to grant a credit. To grant a credit does not mean to lend something. To grant a credit is an exchange transaction. It is a sale and a purchase. One could say it clearly: a (money-)credit is a short sale of money, a short sale of legal tender. The borrower, the debtor, sells money that he does not have. He promises to settle this money at an agreed upon date in the future (at maturity of the credit). That means: one should look to a credit generally from the point of view of the debtor (and not the creditor). Then one gets the right understanding for what a credit is. The debtor makes the promise to deliver a certain amount of money at an appointed point of time in the future. The owner of the debt obligation, the owner of the slip of paper where the promise has been written and signed (in finance this is usually called "security") will get this amount of money at the appointed future point in time. A money credit is nothing else than a promise of money in the future. To make this promise one does not get necessarily money as a loan. That means the newly created and then sold debt obligation is not necessarily paid with money. Or take it the other way round: the debtor buys with his newly created money voucher not necessarily money. The first purchaser of the money voucher does not pay money for it necessarily. The purchaser may pay for it a bottle of milk. If this is done the milk is not lend, the milk is sold. The new owner of the milk is allowed to do, and will do, with the milk whatever he or she wishes to do. This kind of process one knows from antecedent times, if somebody has gone to the Mom-and-Pop store around the corner to buy something and forgotten to take cash with her. When she bought what was needed the amount she had to pay was "put on the slate". In exchange for the goods a promise was made. The money was promised to be delivered in the future. One said: »I will come next week and clear my debt.« This should be clearly seen in this example: in case of a credit not necessarily money is in the game. The debtor only gives a promise to settle money in the future. The price to be paid to get the credit depends on the creditor's request. That means the one who accepts the money voucher as good as money will specify which return service the debtor should offer to get acceptance. This could be an interest to be paid because the risk is taken that the debtor will not fulfil his promise. It could also be an interest for going without the money for some time because the creditor will have the money only in the future at his disposal. Other requirements could be stipulated by the creditor to accept the money promise as well.

How does money come into circulation?

The answer to this question depends on the concrete organization of the monetary system of the currency zone. In the following description we assume that our exemplary currency zone has exactly one Central Bank. Besides other responsibilities the Central Bank is the only institution in this currency zone which is allowed to create new notes and bring them into circulation. The Central Bank is essentially self-governed but is not the only bank in this currency zone. There are – we assume – a couple of commercial and governmental banks as well. These are financial institutions operating in the field of monetary transactions and the credit business. They grant credits (that is why they are often called credit institutions), they manage savings, insurance premiums etc. They are trading financial instruments like bonds, securities, shares and other "financial products". They provide custody services in order to administer such instruments and often provide a complete range of services. If such an institution offers a very broad set of products and services it is called a full-service bank or universal bank. An example for such a currency zone is the "Euro land", with the European Central Bank being responsible for the unified monetary policy of all European countries that are part of the Euro zone.

To describe the principle of money creation and how money is brought into circulation we do not take a concrete currency zone as an example. Instead we construct a fictive and idealized country "Thaland". In Thaland initially all business should be barter business, the direct exchange of goods and services. They neither have money nor a monetary organization. Commodities and scarce resources are not available in Thaland. They also don't have any precious metals in storage. In addition Thaland is isolated: there is no foreign trade with other countries. The citizens of Thaland are diligent and hard-working people. They are well educated and highly inventive. Production and distribution of goods and services is excellent. There is nothing left to be desired – with one exception: prosperity and – more importantly – the amount of leisure time free of work could be higher if not so much time and joie de vivre would be lost for all the needed bartering. That is why Thaland decides in a democratic process to invent a currency. Those who are against this decision are arguing that Thaland has no possibility to back a currency. Thaland does not have gold or other precious commodities at its disposal. When the decision was put to the vote won those who supported it. They convinced the majority perhaps with their thesis: much more important than a backing by precious material is to inspire the physical and mental potential in us, to stimulate ideas and endeavours to produce much sought-after products and services following the principle »to render for each other with each other« (G.W. Werner, 2008).

After the decision has been made it was fixed the following:

the name and the unit of the money is "Thaler". Only the Central Bank has initially the right to produce (paper-) banknotes as much forgery-safe as possible. These slip of paper notes with different denominations like 1, 2, 5, 10, 20, 50, 100, 200 and 500 Thaler were brought into circulation the following way only: together with the Central Bank the government of Thaland provides each citizen (adults and children) uniquely 100 Thaler in banknotes. Government acts on the assumption to get this money back later when taxes will be paid. After this initial step the Central Bank is allowed to provide commercial banks with newly created banknotes only if there is demand. If commercial banks demand new money the Central Bank decides the amount and period of time newly created Thaler will be given to the commercial banks and fixes the fee to be charged. The new money will be given in exchange to a debt obligation. The commercial bank has to sign an obligation to pay back the received money in the future. Usually a commercial bank gets less newly created Thaler than requested. The banknotes are lent short time only (some days, weeks or months) in this credit transaction. In everyday language this transaction is named a loan. The Central Bank lends the money to the commercial bank; the commercial bank borrows the money. In fact the commercial bank is allowed to use the money for whatever purpose it decides. Strictly speaking this means this money has not been borrowed but purchased on credit. The Central Bank has sold money against a debt obligation. After this transaction the commercial bank has the new Thaler as an asset and on the other hand the obligation to pay it back in the future as liability. The new Thaler are on the asset side on the commercial bank's balance sheet. The debt obligation is on its liabilities side. The balance sheet of the Central Bank looks quite the opposite. The newly created Thaler in circulation represent a debt (that is why they are on the liabilities side). The debt obligation from the commercial bank represents a receivable, being thus an entry on the asset side. It's an asset of the Central Bank.

In the following we assume that in our idealized economy Thaland ten different commercial banks are founded and accredited which have only one business activity: the granting of credits (to make this point clear again: these banks grant credits, they do not lend money; they are credit institutions and not loan institutions).

Further we assume that the citizens will use the initial receipt of 100 Thaler prudently and with a level of caution. The citizens value the money and they tend to hoard rather than spend.

First prices for goods and services occur depending on supply and demand. The prices represent the initial assessment of the value of goods and services measured in Thaler.

> ### Money and markets
>
> Our Thaland should have ten Million inhabitants. Initially each inhabitant receives 100 Thaler. The total initial volume of money – the initial money stock – is 1 Billion (1'000'000'000) Thaler. We assume that the 10'000th part of the total volume, which is 100'000 Thaler, is ready - in the citizens' brains - for purchases of meat, e.g. tenderloin. Further we assume that not more than 10'000 kg of tenderloin could be offered. The butchers don't have more. As a result the market would be cleared, if all market participants accepted a price of 10 Thaler for each kg tenderloin. The evaluation of tenderloin, at that day, would be 10 Thaler. The price of a good or a service is the number of monetary units that one has to give in exchange to one unit of the demanded good (in our example it is 1 kg).
>
> The building of prices and the clearing of markets is not that easy. For example it could happen that a lot of suppliers

or demanding citizens do not accept a price of 10 Thaler/kg. What will happen in that case? Pure economic theory supposes that – under a special set of assumptions – a so-called equilibrium price will come into existence. The equilibrium price arises within a certain period of time and is in effect in that period. The period could be a day, a certain hour, a minute, a second. The price is valid for all participants in the market that supply or demand the product in that time interval. Generally, economic theory assumes: the equilibrium price can always be found, and the clearing of the market will happen (To give an example: at a share market – e.g. the London Stock Exchange – the prices for traded shares are evaluated every few seconds. These equilibrium prices are calculated on the basis of all current offers and demands and are used for all share transactions in this short period).

If the initially provided amount of money in Thaland was not 100 Thaler but 200 Thaler for each participant we could guess the following would have happened: Because of the (nominal) higher purchasing power – measured in Thaler – a (nominally) higher equilibrium price in Thaler would have been established. The swelling of the initial money stock would have resulted in a swelling of the prices. One talks about inflation. The word inflation originates from the Latin word "inflare"; it means "blow into", "tough up" and "blow up". The building of prices is even more complicated since it is even possible to buy something "on tick". Instead of immediate payment, the payment could be deferred. The amount of money owed is put on the slate. One buys on credit. That means: as long as postponed payment is accepted, and thus credits are granted, the demand is not necessarily restricted by the available money.

We explained these ideas to introduce the term inflation, but never in history has the process of inflation had its origin

> in the initial equipment of an economy with an equal amount of money for each participant. Nevertheless, even that could be imagined. The following could happen: after the citizens receive the initial money, a lot of them do not work or they work only very little. As a consequence the supply of goods and services is decreasing and the prices are rising. Or something else might happen: all of the citizens are working as much and as good as before and the initially issued money stock is kept constant. It could happen that the buying behaviour is changing in a way that the so-called circulation velocity of money is increasing. For instance in the second week the total volume of emitted money would pass from hand to hand ten per cent faster than in the first week. In the third week it will be again ten per cent faster etc. One should be aware that behind any payment there is a demand. Thus a higher frequency of payments means higher demand. If the supply – and therefore the production of goods and services – cannot follow this rapid growth of the demand swiftly, a so-called hyper-inflation – a galloping inflation – could be the result. The growth rate of the price-level increases from one digit inflation rate to two digits, three digits inflation rate and so on. Not only in this thought experiment but also in the real world galloping and hyper inflation have happened. Take this as an example: Hyper inflation in Germany between World War I and World War II resulted in postage for one letter which was 1 Billion Mark in November 1923.

In our idealized, isolated Thaland with its ten Million citizens the transition from the era of bartering into the era of a monetarized economy had to be mastered. The initial emission and distribution of hundred Thaler for each citizen was sufficient only for the first few days (quite similar to the situation of (Western) Germany in 1948 due to the monetary reform: every German citizen got initially 40 "Deutsche Mark". The "Reichsmark" became worthless). Purchases of goods with high value require higher amounts of Thaler. One gets the salary for work usually only at the end of a month. In consequence one could pay all one needs only at the end of the month. The result is that demand and needs of goods and services and the possible settlement of money to pay, do not time wise coincide. The requirement for credits is evolving. We ask again: what exactly is a credit – or more precisely – what is a money credit? Answer: a credit is a promise of money. That is why debentures are sometimes called – "promissory notes". A credit is not the borrowing of money. It is a promise to settle a debt at a specified date in the future to the one who has granted the credit (or who owns the promissory note) at that time. This aspect is all important. Very often it is not seen. Instead the prevailing opinion is that granting of a credit is a lending (and borrowing) of money. This understanding looks at credit falsely. To understand a credit one has to look at it from the debtor's point of view – then the difference between a credit and a loan will become clear. If I buy tenderloin on tick, if I buy it on credit, the granting of the credit is performed when the butcher accepts deferred payment. The customer makes a promise to the butcher to settle the debt sometime in the future. The butcher does not lend money to the customer but he gives tenderloin in exchange for a promise of money. The promise of money is accepted by the butcher instead of actual money. Money is required only if the butcher does not accept this credit-based deal. This could be the case if, for example, the butcher is unwilling to take the risk that his customer will keep his promise in the future and thus insist on cash payment. In such a case the customer has first to obtain money to go shopping. Eventually he obtains this money from any creditor who accepts to exchange money that he owns against the debtor's promise of money. Interest is charged not for the money lent but for the acceptance of the promise of money. With the interest the "purchased" acceptance is paid. Summarizing this means: in case that there is not enough of generally accepted legal tender in circulation there could be a gap that has to be filled by the granting of credits. If some of the people who offer goods and services cannot sell enough to cover their own needs with their earnings - because of not sufficient turnover caused by missing money in circulation – there is a danger of an economic break-down. Legal tender must be available at a sufficient volume and has to circulate at a reasonable speed. Credits could fill the gap between the total volume of necessary payments and timely available legal tender. As a prerequisite to grant credits the willingness to take risk is needed. If a supplier accepts "purchases on tick" she takes the risk that the customer does not or cannot keep his promise to make the future payment. This leads to the important question: who should take the risk of a possible credit default? Who should grant credits and in which form? Does everybody have to grant credits? Should the granting of credits be a public service, for example offered by the Central Bank? Should the government grant credits to everybody who needs them? In our Thaland the system of banks is responsible for granting credits. As mentioned before, the system of banks consists of one Central Bank and ten commercial banks (we denote these commercial banks with: G1, G2, ...G10).

We assume that all ten Million citizens owning 100 Thaler each have other needs and aims than to invest their money in the banks. The commercial banks do not have the possibility to raise capital in form of money by creating and selling shares. In our fictive Thaland neither commercial banks nor the Central Bank possesses equities. When the era of their monetarized economy begins they do not have equities in any form – especially not in the form of money. That is why we assume that the banks have the needed branches and state-of-the-art work place equipment

Money, Credit, Bank, Interest-rate, Inflation, Markets

initially put at their disposal by the government free of charge.

There is Zero money at the beginning of the money-era in Thaland except those Thaler that have initially been emitted and distributed to the citizens. The banking system in Thaland has initially Zero Thaler and Zero energy – unless something happens. What could happen? An inventive idea could come up; an idea not destructive but affecting something very positive: economic improvement that is coupled with a qualitative and quantitative growth of prosperity and welfare for the population of Thaland. It is not an explosion of energy or mass like in the beginning of the universe (Big-Bang theory of physics). Where, all of a sudden, time and space were created out of nothing. The inventory idea in Thaland is something different: Thaland has ten Million capable and industrious citizens. The banking system with its Central Bank and its ten commercial banks (G1, G2, …, G10) is formally established but there is Zero energy. Suddenly a very soft sound is heard, a very small noise, almost imperceptible, triggered by a flash of inspiration: produce as many Thalers as needed by swelling the Zero. Inflate the Zero, a dot without any dimension, a Thaler-nothing, to a bubble that looks like a written Zero. Create money, in our example Thaler, by blowing up an infinitely small Zero to a continuously increasing Zero. The bigger the bubble of this inflated Zero is, the more money circulates in the economy. This is shown in the following, but already here a warning should be given: the bubble should not grow over-sized. That means: the money stock, the volume of money, which is blown into the economy through the banking system, should not overflow. The monetary expansion should not lead to a burst of the bubble. The result would be a collapsing system of banks and a collapsing of the economy and the government with a bang. It will not be the Big Bang (like in the beginning of the universe) but perhaps a final bang – hopefully only a collapsing house of cards leaving the chance open for reconstruction with better ideas for stabilization and strength. Is it possible that a swelling Zero becomes fertile without becoming horrible?

Let now the Zero of money grow in Thaland! We assume that the demand of additional Central-Bank-money (legal tender) from the commercial banks (G1, G2, ..., G10) exceeds the amount of 20 Billion Thaler at the historically first "auction". Central Bank decides to allot only some 20 Billion Thaler to the commercial banks. There are different terms when the allotted money has to be paid back – depending on the banks requirements. We do not address the issues of "auction", deadlines, apportionment formula, etc. and how the government is able to bring coins into circulation. The total volume of coins is negligibly small compared to the total value of circulating Thaler banknotes.

It is important to know that the commercial banks do not get the Central-Bank-money at their disposal for free. The Central Bank levies fees for the granted credits. More precisely, the Central Bank has defined key interest rates which are fixed depending on the current economic situation. Let us say, for example, the key interest rate is three per cent. In our example this would mean:

If a commercial bank obtains 1 Billion Thaler for a year, 0.03 times 1'000'000'000 Thaler = 30 Million Thaler interest has to be paid to the Central Bank. If the duration of the credit is only one month and the commercial bank has to deliver the obtained money already after one month, an interest of 1/12 of a year has to be paid, 2.5 Million Thaler.

Key interest rates of central Banks

As one activity the Central Banks lend Central-Bank-money to their customers which are mainly commercial banks. They lend this – usually newly-created – Central-Bank-money for various periods of time which could be overnight, one day, a week or a month. The Central Banks charge interest for their service. It is important to mention that interest rates are not related to the money lend. The interest charged depends on the terms of the credit contract that a commercial bank is signing in exchange for the money. That means the Central Bank defines interest rates depending on the concrete form of the promise to re-pay the money. There are different key interest rates, for instance an interest rate for overnight credits. These are promises of money with the maturity of one night only. A commercial bank will get Central-Bank-money at the end of a trading day that has to be paid back to the Central Bank at the beginning of the next trading day. This sounds somehow funny but it is the truth. Commercial banks can sleep better if they fulfil the requirements of legislation to have at least a well-defined amount of Central-Bank-money at their disposal (the so called minimum required reserve ratio) at the time they have to report. And they have to report at the end of the trading day. Interest rates vary depending on the duration of credits but on the kind of credit backing as well. The interest rates are lower if the commercial bank gives collateral against the Central-Bank-money they borrow. In the past it was even possible to deposit commodities as collateral. Those credits are called "Lombard credits". The interest charged is thus not depending on the (Central Bank) money lent but it is to reward the acceptance of a promise of (Central Bank)money with special terms for a defined period of time. The terms of the credit define the amount of interest to be paid to get its acceptance from the Central Bank.

What is the reason for charging this interest? Mainly there are two aspects that should be mentioned. The first aspect is risk. There is a risk to be taken by the Central Bank because it gives away Thaler getting a promise on Thaler as trade-off. Although there is an obligation of the commercial bank to settle the received Thaler and interest at a later time, but what if at that time the commercial bank has no or not enough Thaler at its disposal; if the promise is neglected or if the Thaler cannot be delivered? If this is the case the Central Bank does not get back their lend Thaler. The credit defaults, a loss occurs. That is why a debtor has to fulfil a set of imposed conditions to reduce the risk of credit default. There is a second, important aspect to be considered when asking why Central Banks are charging interest when lending their money. This aspect is of fundamental nature. The essential question behind this is: should there be in a society the right to own property and should it be allowed to request a payment or another trade-off if the right to use the property is relinquished to somebody for some time. If I can borrow money for free I could for instance buy a house and let it. In this case I would gain income by relinquishing the right to use the house to somebody. The earnings that I get could be used to pay back the credit granted to me at no charge. Why should anybody rent a house if this is possible? Everybody could borrow money for free to build houses. What should then be the criteria to lend money? It should be clear: As long as a society legally stipulates and protects the ownership of property this should hold true for money being property as well. In consequence one has to accept that interest is charged on granted credits.

Easy money policy

In times of a crippling economy Central Banks usually try to give a stimulus via monetary policies. If, for instance, the growth rate measuring the Gross Domestic Product (GDP) is

> decreasing over time, eventually becoming negative as well, Central Banks could choose the easy money policy. By lowering the key interest rates the borrowing of money becomes cheaper. The hope is that the market participants' willingness to make credit-based investments is rising. That is why it is not astonishing that in the current crisis (June 2009) of the world economy the US Fed (Federal Reserve Bank), which is the Central Bank of the USA, has brought down their key interest rates towards zero per cent. This has been done by the Central Bank of Japan as well. The interest rates at the British Central Bank are at 0.5 per cent and at the European Central Bank at 0.5 to 1 per cent.

How does the balance sheet of the Central Bank of Thaland look like in the evening of the day after the auction of 20 Billion Thaler? As liabilities we see at the position "currency in circulation" an amount of 20 Billion Thaler. On the asset side of the balance sheet, where owned properties and claims are listed, we find a "claim on money" valuing 20 Billion Thaler. This is the position "credits to commercial banks". In addition, there is more on the asset side. If we assume that the first interest to be paid on the granted credits (let's say 3 per cent) immediately becomes due, this will result in an amount of 600 Million Thaler booked to the "accounts receivable" (which are open claims on the commercial banks). In consequence the total sum of assets is more than all liabilities. This is the first balance sheet profit ever made in Thaland. It is 600 Million Thaler and constitutes the first equity (listed on the liability side) of the Central Bank. Of course this profit corresponds to a book loss at the commercial banks of the same amount. In total the balance sheets of the commercial banks mirror the Central Bank's balance sheet. The added value to cover the Central Bank's profit without loss at others has not yet been generated. We visualize this situation with a number line, as shown in Figure 1:

Figure 1: Number line representing the balance sheet of the Central Bank. Right from zero-point (representing the number Zero) are all positive numbers ordered in size. Left from zero-point are the negative numbers. With a well-defined distance of the numbers Zero (0) and One (1) the position of all other numbers on the number line is well defined. A number on the number line here represents an according amount of Billions of Thaler.

As one can see, the total amount of all liabilities (Central-Bank-money and equity), which is 20.6 Billion Thaler on the positive side of the number line, equals the total amount of 20.6 Billion on the negative side representing the assets of the Central Bank (incl. balance sheet profit). Both total values are adding to Zero.

The following idea suggests itself! The whole trick inventing money is the idea that seems natural: to spread out the Zero horizontally to the left and to the right like an infinitely small string or rubber strap stretched horizontally gaining more and more tension but hopefully no fraction. Actually it is still a Zero – a stretched Zero. It is somehow mystic. The magic of stretching the Zero provides us with 20.6 Billion Thaler for a period of time. The impact this trick has for the development of economy and society is seen positively from almost all in Thaland. Niall Ferguson (2009) writes in "The Ascent of Money":

»Today's financial world is a result of four millennia of economic evolution. Money – the materialized relationship between debtor and creditor – begat banks, clearing houses for ever larger aggregations of borrowing and lending …..Economies that combined all these institutional innovations – banks, bonds, markets, share markets, insurances and property owning democracies – performed better in the long run than those that did not, because financial intermediation permits a more efficient allocation of resources than for instance feudalism or central planning. For this reason it is hardly surprising that the Western Financial Model tended to spread around the world – first in the guise of imperialism then in the guise of globalisation.«

The fresh money created at the Central Bank from nothing (fiat money: meaning "let there be money") is allotted to the ten commercial banks (G1, G2, …, G10). For instance the commercial banks get from these 20 Billion Thaler the following amounts:

commercial bank	G1	G2	G3	G4	G5	G6	G7	G8	G9	G10
Billions of Thaler	2.5	2.5	2.2	2.2	1.9	1.9	1.8	1.9	1.6	1.6

After getting the Central-Bank-money each commercial bank has this amount of Thaler at its disposal (it's an asset of the commercial bank) but there is a liability too. Liability amounts to the volume of Thaler they received adding the interest to be paid. The liabilities of the commercial banks are thus more than the total amount of Thaler available in Thaland. There are more promises of Thaler than there are existing Thaler. That is why those promises going beyond the total volume of existing Thaler have to be paid back (directly or indirectly) with something other than Thaler. Otherwise it would be simply impossible to deliver all the promises. There is a need for additional value added. The creation of money, or rather, the granting of credits opens a gap to value added to be filled with not yet generated added value. Let us assume now that in Thaland there is a high demand for credits that enterprises and private households are requesting. After due diligence, where the debtors requesting possible credits come under scrutiny, the commercial banks decide whether they are willing and able to grant a loan.

The "ability" is limited since the commercial banks only have a limited amount of Thaler at their disposal (as described above).

If they trade these in total against promises on Thaler they would risk their ability to pay (liquidity). How could they, for instance, pay the interest at maturity to the Central Bank if they do not have any Thaler at their disposal? They would have no Thaler if they have given all of them away to grant loans (or rather: if they spend all their available Central-Bank-money to buy promises on money). Commercial banks will receive repatriation of credits granted and they will make some profits if they levy higher interest than the Central Bank, assuming low default level, but one can see that an effective risk management is inevitable. In addition we can also see that the interest charged, which should be seen as a price to be paid for the service to accept a promise on money for some time, has to cover several aspects. Interest payments have to cover losses resulting from defaults and serve as income to pay wages and other liabilities. Nations or economies that prohibit interest charges are permitting to collect fees by the credit business instead.

In our example we have seen that because of the key interest rates charged, a value of 600 Million Thaler popped up as asset on the balance sheet of the Central Bank. The Central Bank possesses more claims on money than Central-Bank-money has been brought into circulation. These 600 Million claims on money have been created at the same time and in addition to the 20 Billion Thaler Central-Bank-money. There are 600 Million of promises on Thaler more accounted in the books (balance sheet, statement of profit and loss, giro account) of the Central Bank than Thaler in circulation. These promises on money are called book money, check money or deposit money. From the Central Bank's point of view book money is a Thaler deposit, a claim on money that has to be settled by the commercial banks at maturity. All receivables to commercial banks are such claims on Thaler. They are book money. In exchange with Thaler the commercial banks gave Thaler "vouchers" to the Central Bank.

These vouchers are promises on Thaler to be settled in the future. As a result there are 20 Billion Thaler emitted and brought into circulation by the Central Bank. Additionally there are 20.6 Billion book money (claims on Thaler, Thaler vouchers, credits), which have been issued by the commercial banks. That is bank money. More precisely: Commercial-bank-money. Commercial-bank-money is a credit granted to a commercial bank. In the process of credit granting – as described above – the commercial bank is buying Thaler "on tick" from the Central Bank. Those Thaler received are not paid for with Thaler. They are paid with a newly created promise on money – a money voucher. It is a promise to pay interest and the credit amount at the agreed time in the future to the Central Bank. Book money emerges in other situations as well. For instance in a purchase on credit if the owed price is put on the slate. The selling merchant takes the amount owed as receivables "in his books". As a result there is a claim on money against the customer in the books. It is book money. And the issuer of this type of money is the customer.

Let us contemplate flexibility for decisions: Which options do commercial banks have to grant credits to their customers and what does it mean to grant a credit? The customer likes to buy money "on tick". The customer asks the commercial bank to put the purchase price on the slate. He gives the commitment to pay back the amount of money he gets from the commercial bank along with interest at a future point in time. The commercial bank gets a promise on money if a credit is granted. This promise on money is book money as well. A claim against the customer is taken as an account receivable into the books. The question however is: What kind of money does a commercial bank give to the customer? Does the customer really get Central-Bank-money or does he get something different? Something that is accepted by all market participants – more or less the same as a real Thaler, as real Central-Bank-money is. What could it be? Could it be commercial-bank-money? That would mean it is not a real Thaler but a promise on Thaler that the commercial bank gives, "Thaler vouchers" which are accepted by everybody as "as good as" Central-Bank-money; as good as a real Thaler. Exactly that is what commercial banks most often do if they are granting a credit. They provide the customer with newly created commercial-bank-money – a promise on money – in exchange for the customer's promise on money. The customer takes this promise of the commercial bank as an account receivable in his own books. As a result of a granted credit, book money has been created twice. It is firstly the promise on money that the customer gives - that is customer money in the books of the commercial bank. Secondly at the same time the commercial bank has given a promise on money – that is commercial-bank-money – that is taken to the books of the customer. This commercial-bank-money comes disguised in very different costumes. It could be an account deposit, a certificate of deposit, a bank debenture, a convertible bond and a lot more. What so ever, it is commercial-bank-money – a promise on money that the commercial bank gives. It is nothing else than a Central-Bank-money voucher!

From now on we do not use the terms "book money" or "check money" – as they are normally used in relevant literature. We talk about "swell-money" (another term introduced in D. Solte (2007) is: "leverage-money"). Swell-money is not the Central-Bank-money; it is not legal tender. Swell-money is every promise on money - securitized by a contract. The owner of the contract owns the promise that a specified amount of money, usually Central-Bank-money – as the only legal tender – will be paid now or later. The term "swell-money" encompasses the term "book money" (check money). As its most general description, the term "swell-money" covers all contractual securitized claims on anything that can be accomplished by even settling an equivalent amount of legal tender (Central-Bank-money). This definition considers that there are more than only money credits. It is possible to have granted credits on oil, gas and a lot of other kinds of commodities. In your personal environment you could even have a credit for dancing. You could have made the promise to dance with the owner of the dance voucher (evidencing the dance credit) somewhere and sometime. In its most general form a credit is nothing else than a short sale. The debtor sells today something in form of a promise to settle this something "later" at a certain point of time in the future. This point of time could be – as it is the case if the promise comes as a share – in perpetuity.

It its easy to imagine what could happen if the amount of swell-money in the currency zone or globally would be a multitude of the nominal value of all Central-Bank-money (legal tender) in circulation. If the swell-money exceeds legal tender by factor 2, 3, 50 or more there will be a bubble swelling – the flatulence of the Zero – and there will be a big danger for inflation.

There are some professors in Thaland that foresee this immanent danger in a monetarized economy. With high personal engagement they fight successfully to fix the following rule in the legislation: there is a minimum required reserve ratio of ten percent that commercial banks always have to fulfil. They need to have at least ten percent of Central-Bank-money at their disposal in relation to the total sum of all committed promises on Central-Bank-money they made. Or the other way around: the amount of credits they can take could be no more than ten times the amount of Central-Bank-money at their disposal. The minimum (required) reserve ratio then is ten percent. That means: if a commercial bank like G1 got 2.5 Billion Thaler from the Central Bank, the maximum promises on money given by that bank could be 25 Billion Thaler as long as all the Thaler borrowed from the Central Bank are retained at its disposal. If this bank has to give Thaler to somebody else, fewer promises on money can be made. These own promises made, can be "lend" (sold). They can be given for instance in exchange of a customer's promise on money. This is what usually is called "grant a credit" or "lending money". But what happens in reality is: both, customer and the commercial bank, are granting credits one to each other. Both make a promise on money. Swell-money is created twice – customer swell-money and commercial bank swell-money – and exchanged.

We restrict our considerations of money creation in Thaland to a monetary system that only has banknotes, bank or giro accounts and a very small number of coins with Thaler as the only unit of account. Debt securities, debt obligations as tradable "securitized money claims" should not (yet) exist. What are securities? Securities are claims on money evidenced by a document. That does not mean that there is a security backing the money claim. The document is a security in and of itself. That is why we prefer to name them debt obligations. Securities/debt obligations can be of various kinds: shares, bonds, notes, bills, shares in a fund and certificates. Also cheques and mortgages for instance are securities. All the number of today existing derivatives are not yet existing in Thaland. Derivatives are a special form of securitized claims. The claim is derived from the value of a so-called underlying instrument (or underlying asset). Underlying instruments could be for instance shares, debt obligations, commodities, interest rates or stock indices. The securitized claim could be very different. It could be the right to buy an underlying instrument later at a specified price. It could be the right to get an amount of money in a time in the future that corresponds to the price of the underlying instrument at that time and much more. All those slips of paper are essentially swell-money. In Taland we assume all these kinds of swell-money do not yet exist. For our further consideration we assume that swell-money can be created only in the way described above. However, already in this situation it is possible that the amount of the existing swell-money is rising, it can grow indefinitely in the absence of effectively limiting and controlling rules and regulations fixed by law.

In economic text books on monetary theory – for instance O. Issing (2007) – the minimum required reserve ratio is mentioned as such a rule. Usually in such text books it is demonstrated what is caused through introducing (and controlling) the requirement of a minimum reserve ratio: the swelling of swell-money is seen to be limited. More precisely: if the minimum reserve ratio is about ten percent and if a set of assumptions is complied with, the whole amount of swell-money created in an economy cannot swell to more than the ten-fold of the total sum of available Central-Bank-money in circulation. Generally: a higher minimum required reserve ratio leads to a lesser swell-money supply, a lesser total amount of swell-money. However, this requires that the reserve ratio is related to any kind of swell-money. It should not depend on e.g. the maturity and kind of swell-money, but exactly that is not given today. The intended limitation of money creation should be considered as not effective as it is shown in D. Solte (2007) "world financial system at its limits – insights to the 'Holy Grail` of globalization" (Weltfinanzsystem am Limit).

Let us come back to our fictive Thaland with its ten commercial banks (G1, G2, ..., G10) and let us have a look to their balance sheets after the first (and before the second) auctioning and distribution of Central-Bank-money. Until that point in time the banks should have made promises on money among each other and against enterprises and personal households as well. The customers of the commercial banks have borrowed these promises on money by taking a credit. Meanwhile a multiple of promises on money – swell-money – in relation to Central-Bank-money has been created. Even the interest to be paid to the Central Bank has been "paid" with promises on money, since the needed added value to fill the gap between the first made promises on money and the available Central-Bank-money has not yet been generated. We want to assume that the commercial banks have created seven times as much commercial bank swell-money than they got Central-Bank-money to their disposal in the first auction. All the numbers are listed in the following chart 1.

The relevant accounts in the commercial banks balance sheets are the following: Assets: cash, receivables from other commercial banks, receivables from customers and as Liabilities and owner's equity: debts and obligations to the Central Bank, other commercial banks and all customers. Depending on the type of the client and maturity these debts and obligations are summarized in different accounts. On the liability side of the balance

(a) Commercial bank	(b) Thaler-promises to the Central Bank	(c) Thaler-promises to customer	(d) Commercial bank swell-money
	allotment + interest		
G1	2.5 + 0.075	17.5	20 + 0.075
G2	2.5 + 0.075	17.5	20 + 0.075
G3	2.2 + 0.066	15.4	17.6 + 0.066
G4	2.2 + 0.066	15.4	17.6 + 0.066
G5	1.9 + 0.057	13.3	15.2 + 0.057
G6	1.9 + 0.057	13.3	15.2 + 0.057
G7	1.8 + 0.054	12.6	14.4 + 0.054
G8	1.8 + 0.054	12.6	14.4 + 0.054
G9	1.6 + 0.048	11.2	12.8 + 0.048
G10	1.6 + 0.048	11.2	12.8 + 0.048
Sum of the columns	20.0 + 0.6	140.0	160.0 + 0.6

Chart 1: Allotment of Central-Bank-money and creation of swell-money by the commercial banks (fictitious example; all values in Billion of Thaler)

sheet would be the position owner's equity (or equity for short) if there is any.

In case of an accumulated profit that is not distributed to the owners it would increase the value of equity at the liability side of the balance sheet. In case of an accumulated loss there would be an account "negative or missing equity" on the asset side.

In our example the balance sheet total of the commercial banks are the values listed in column (d) in chart 1. As we did in the number line above (Figure 1) to visualize the situation of the Central Bank, we do the same for all commercial banks and their balance sheets. As positive numbers we mark the total sum of their assets and as negative numbers their liabilities. The reason for this mirroring is that receivables from commercial banks on the Central Bank's balance sheet (assets) are liabilities of the commercial banks.

In the next step we arrange all of these eleven number lines in a rectangular system. We do it the following way: the number line representing the Central Bank's balance sheet overlaps the axis of ordinate (y-axis) of the system. The number lines representing the balance sheets of the ten commercial banks have the zero-point of the system in common, but are oriented in different directions: north-east (NO) or north-west (NW) with the following angles formed with the vertical axis of the system (axis of ordinate): the direction of the number lines are

G1 to NO, G2 to NW with an angle of 15° to the ordinate
G3 to NO, G4 to NW with an angle of 30° to the ordinate
G5 to NO, G6 to NW with an angle of 45° to the ordinate
G7 to NO, G8 to NW with an angle of 60° to the ordinate
G9 to NO, G10 to NW with an angle of 75 to the ordinate

In figure 2 we connect all the noted points in an obvious manner.

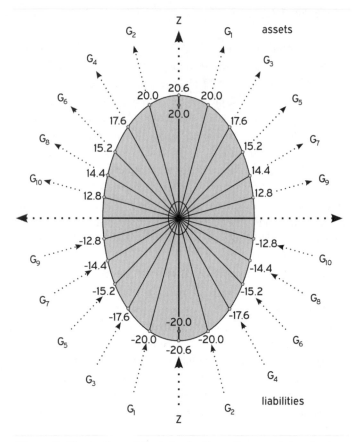

Figure 2: Illustration of the introduction of money into a barter economy by "swelling of the zero"

What we can observe is a "huge Zero". This puffed up and bloated Zero appeared from nowhere. It evolves from the zero-point of the system (the situation with Zero money) through the "genesis of money"! Ballooning the zero-point of the system to a small but bigger Zero is the first step. This small Zero connects some points marked on the numbered radials which represent the balance sheets of the commercial banks. All points referencing their allotment of Central-Bank-money (cf. chart 1, column (b)). The "genesis of money" starts with nothing – what should one do with nothing even if it is a central point, the zero-point, of a Cartesian Coordinate System?! What follows is similar to what is written in the Bible: "fiat lux – let there be light, and there was light". A Big Bang of money creation occurs, however it doesn't happen quite so fast but expands continuously: fiat money – let there be money, and there was money. One starts to produce and distribute slips of paper, beautiful coloured so that everybody should believe the declarations of value (for instance 100 Thaler) that are printed on these notes. The truth? Is this a boast, a fraught with hocus pocus or a delusion? Should the values printed on the slips be backed by a scarce resource like gold? What does "backed by a scarce resource" mean?

Before answering these questions let's have a further look to the "lean Zero" and the "fat Zero" in figure 2. The lean (inner) Zero gives us an impression how much legal tender (Central-Bank-money) has been brought into circulation by lending it to the commercial banks: 20 Billion Thaler. These 20 Billion Thaler are marked on the number line representing the Central Bank's balance sheet. The fat (outer) Zero does not go through this point. Instead its outmost points are 20.6 and -20.6. The reason is that there is a first book profit of the Central Bank increasing the total sum of its assets. All these assets are promises on money made by the commercial banks. They have to pay back this amount of money in the future. The fat Zero illustrates how many Billions of money and swell-money (promises on money) are now available because of all those business activities of enterprises and citizens, activities which are now supported and evaluated with money: 327.6 Billion. Starting from Zero and an initial step of producing 20 Billion Thaler there are now 327.6 Billion. Wow, how does one get this? How are these 327.6 Billion composed of? To get this one has to consider attentively all balance sheets, for instance all assets, in Thaland. First of all there is the Central Bank. What are the assets that are owned by the Central Bank? All assets are promises on money made by the commercial banks. These are all promises to pay back the borrowed Central-Bank-money plus the interest of 3% charged. The total sum is 20.6 Billion swell-money Thaler. What are the assets of the commercial banks? First of all there are 20 Billion Thaler that have been borrowed from the Central Bank. This is Central-Bank-money, not swell-money. It is 20 Billion Thaler of legal tender. Further assets of the commercial banks are the promises on money that the customers made. These are all the promises on payments in the future that result from granted credits. In addition to the Central-Bank-money the commercial banks own customer swell-money. The customers have given promises on payments in the future. Its total sum is the volume of all credits granted by the commercial banks and these are 140 Billion swell-money Thaler. And if we assume that the customers should have to pay an interest of let us say 5% to get the acceptance of the commercial banks to grant the credits, we have another 7 Billion of customer swell-money. And what are the assets of the customers? They own money claims against the commercial banks. They own commercial bank swell-money. It is the money on account – as one says – but it is nothing else than a debt of the commercial banks. The customers own liabilities of their banks. The situation for all is quite similar. The commercial banks own the liabilities of their customers and the Central Bank. The Central Bank owns the liabilities of the commercial banks. Now it becomes clear: the total sum of money and swell-money is nothing else than the total sum of all debts, of all made promises on payments to be made in the future. Let's try to realize what that means. Let's compare the balance sheets and the consolidated balance sheets of the commercial banks and all customers with each other. We mark in the balance sheets the corresponding positions. That means: which assets equal which liabilities?

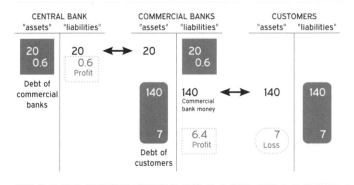

Figure 3: money / swell-money and book profit / book loss
money + swell-money as assets: 20.6 + 167 + 140 = 327.6
money + swell-money as liabilities: 20 + 160.6 + 147 = 327.6

The Central Bank has as assets the liabilities of the commercial banks. These are in total 20.6 Billion. Commercial banks have as assets 20 Billion Central-Bank-money and the promises on money of their customers. The total sum is 140 Billion plus 5% interest of 7 Billion which in sum is 147 Billion. The resulting total sum of assets of commercial banks is 167 Billion. The customers do have as assets the volume of all granted credits (without interest) which is 140 Billion. In total this is an entire volume of money (legal tender) and swell-money of 327.6 Billion (20.6 + 167 + 140). What else you can see in figure 3 is that the customers' liabilities of 140 Billion plus 7 Billion for interest to be paid exceed their assets. That means the customers do have a book loss, negative equity. It is a profit or effort hoped for to be made in the future. It is a gap of value added that has to be filled somewhere by somebody at sometime in the future. Only if the customers do produce or gain this added value in the future is it possible to realize all book profits through a real transaction. There is a risk of an accounting loss in the amount of 7 Billion Thaler. This risk results from the gap of value added, the necessity to produce further added value to fulfill the promise on money indirectly via value added since that money simply does not exist.

Now it is easy to imagine how fast the Zero is further expanding if at a second auction of Central-Bank-money the total sum of legal tender at disposal of the commercial banks will be more than those 20 Billion Thaler allotted at the first auction. From auction to auction the Central-Bank-money stock – our lean Zero – is swelling. (We do not want to go into details like the fact for instance that there will be different credit durations and maturities in our Thaland which will result in quite a huge number of transactions that create or delete money and swell-money.)

Swell-money and inflation

What could happen if the total amount of money in circulation (in Thaland) consisting of Central-Bank-money and swell-money is growing faster than the production of goods and services? We will focus our consideration to those goods considered in the consumer price index. If the money stock grows the following could happen: the consumer price index is rising, which means the price level is rising. It is a sign for inflation. Money, these slips of paper, is loosing value. This could happen but does not necessarily happen. If for instance the velocity of money decreases and if the monetary stocks grow there could be no effect on the price level. The consumer price index is also not affected if the new money injected to the economy is used only for payment processes, which have nothing to do with all the goods and services forming the index (example: in the middle of 2009 the price index remains constant even though the Euro money stock was rising or better to say was increasing continuously perhaps in a worry about economic consequences of the world financial crisis). The growth of swell-money neglects the consumer price index. More and more money does not purchase consumer goods but swell-money instead – securities of different kinds (derivatives and so on). As long as slips of paper are buying other slips of paper or real estate the consumer price index will be calmer. There will not be much volatility affecting the consumer price index.

The situation is quite different if

- the money stock is growing
- the growth of value added (production of goods and services) is less than the growth of the money stock
- warehouses are depleted
- the velocity of money does not decrease
- significant parts of the money stock will be suddenly used to buy goods that are considered in the consumer price index

Inflation will be the result. In this situation we can state the following: if money stock – especially the amount of swell-money – is swelling, if the bloated Zero grows, then the consumer price level swells as well. The monetary system, the economy is blooming when inflation begins, and will bloom further.

What are possible means to prevent inflation or at least to keep it low? The answer is: economic policy instruments and monetary policy means that empower Thaland and the Cen-

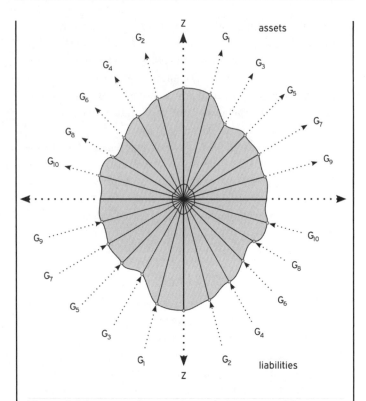

Figure 4: Money stocks are constantly in a state of flux

tral Bank to keep the growth of value added (the growth of the Gross Domestic Product) and the growth of the money stock in balance. Thaland could e.g. reduce the overall money stock if at the second auction less Central-Bank-money is allotted to the commercial banks than they have paid back up to that point of time. Due to the set minimum required reserve ratio the commercial banks have to reduce the created volume of swell-money. In consequence the total amount of swell-money is reduced twice since the customer swell-money, the credits granted to customers, have to be reduced as well. By the way swell-money (or legal tender) disappears whenever a credit or part of it is paid back. Principally that means that the one who created the swell-money got it back into his own ownership. This is a situation in which the money can disappear. In addition the monetary policy via key interest rates has to be mentioned. The demand on Central-Bank-money can be repressed to a desired level by increasing the key interest rates. This makes Central-Bank-money expensive. In real economies the Central Banks have much more instruments to fine control the money supply, more than the Central Bank in our fictive Thaland. Examples are the instruments of the so-called open market policy: debt obligations like fixed income securities, treasury bonds, covered bonds (like mortgage bonds), asset backed securities – all of which is swell-money – today's existing Central Banks can purchase with Central-Bank-money. That means swell-money disappears from the market, kept safe at the Central Bank. Since the same amount of fresh Central-Bank-money comes under disposal of the commercial banks, a multiple volume of new swell-money could be created. That is the transfer mechanism behind the measures of the Central Bank to give a positive stimulus to the real economy or if a deflation – a declining price level – is to be averted. Conversely today's Central Banks could sell swell-money under their ownership, requesting Central-Bank-money as payment. With these transactions Central-Bank-money disappears from the markets being replaced with swell-money. In order to comply with the minimum reserve requirement the swell-money in the markets has to be reduced up to a multiple. Through such a politic an economic slow-down should be achieved. This could be a reaction to a predicted danger of inflation e.g. in times of "economic overheating" when the

> productive capacity of an economy is unable to keep pace with the growing aggregate demand that could result from too much money being active in the markets. The back and forth of monetary politics can lead - already in our fictive Thaland with its small set of monetary instruments - to a rising and ebbing of the lean and the fat Zero. The monetary Zeros lasse could be deformed as illustrated in figure 4.

What threatens the stability of such a system? As we have seen one effect of the creation of new swell-money is the resulting gap of value added. The risk of the entire economic system, derived from the need to generate further value added in the future, is increasing. And there are two factors determining how high this risk is. Besides the newly created swell-money (the granted credits) it is the payment behavior in an economy. It is the so-called (circulation) velocity of money that multiplies the newly created swell-money with respect to its possible aggregated purchasing power. Since the velocity of money has to be considered as being larger than one, the creation of new swell-money affects a gap on value added which is a multiple of the granted credit. In consequence there is a risk of inflation that is on top of the already mentioned gap on value added, resulting from the interest being charged to accept the credit. If promises for payments in the future are made this necessitates a multiple growth in the value added to avoid inflation. The total amount of money and swell-money has to be balanced to the capacities and capabilities of an economy to produce goods and services. This also has to consider the aspect of ecological sustainability, especially concerning the total input and all waste of the value added process that should never over-exploit the limited resources on our planet and thus should always be compatible to all of our environmental needs and limitations. Growth and the total volume of money and swell-money have to be in a reasonable relation to growth and volume of value added – in a global perspective.

There is another important aspect concerning the amount and availability of the basis for money creation in an economy. In our Thaland this basis is all legal tender, which is all Central-Bank-money in circulation. Rules and regulations have fixed in a minimum reserve ratio requirement that all swell-money created requires a certain amount of Central-Bank-money under disposal. We have seen that a commercial bank can only make ten times as many promises on money (commercial bank swell-money) than it has Central-Bank-money under its disposal, if the minimum reserve ratio is set to ten percent. A customer's account is such a promise on money, since the commercial bank gave a warranty to the customer to receive Central-Bank-money up to a positive account balance if requested. What is the risk if a commercial bank has ten times as many promises on Central-Bank-money than she has under disposal? This risk is quite obvious. The commercial bank could loose the required basis for all the created commercial bank swell-money if a customer who has a positive account balance requires Central-Bank-money. The customer needs e.g. to remit an amount of money to somebody who has an account at another commercial bank. In that case Central-Bank-money has to be transferred to the other commercial bank. The customer's commercial bank is obliged to obtain enough Central-Bank-money up to the required minimum reserve ratio. Somebody has to be found willing to give (lend) Central-Bank-money in exchange to a promise on money made by the commercial bank. The stream of Central-Bank-money should never come to a standstill. It should always be ensured that Central-Bank-money can flow to where it is necessary. The necessity could result for instance from legislation (requirements like the minimum reserve) but also if liabilities to settle money mature. With respect to the latter another problem is obvious: if a multiple of promises to pay than money exists, it should never come to a situation where the total amount of all liabilities simultaneously becoming due is higher than all available Central-Bank-money. If there are more vouchers for soup than soup is available and all the owners of the vouchers like to redeem them, there obviously is a problem. Is it possible to solve that problem by "backing" Central-Bank-money? Should currency be backed by scarce and precious goods or commodities like gold? For instance: if Thaland would have a treasure trove of one thousand tons of gold which is one billion grams, if the relation 1 gram of gold equals 20 Thaler is fixed, the Central Bank would be not allowed to create more notes than a total nominal value of 20 Billion Thaler. Thus a maximum of 20 Billion Thaler being injected into the economy should not be exceeded. Since the 1'000 tons of gold cannot be increased fast, the Central Bank's ability to create Thaler is limited under a short or medium term perspective. Even if a lot of rationales would make it reasonable to expand the volume of money in circulation, this cannot happen. (Theoreticians in the field of monetary theory, who are in favour with these restrictions, have always been disappointed. Real existing Nations simply changed the stipulated relations between the backing commodity and the money. If Thaland needs more Central-Bank-money they could decide on the fly: 1 gram of gold equals 30 Thaler.)

All those believing that the Central Banks will not be able to take care of a reasonable, balanced and "lean money supply" will opt for "backing". Those who are confident like us that it is better for a Nation and an economy to have a money containment through a sophisticated monetary system with deliberate rules and regulations, rather than a backing through gold, will opt as said for "awakening". Awakening means: awaken, reasoning, inspiration, creation and organization (especially a stable and quite elastic and responsive economic and monetary system) to produce (eco-friendly), distribute (reasonable, sensible and judicious) and to keep the »stream of societal value added and performance« (B. Hardorp, 2009) in balance with the stream of money.

Which kind of money can be used to pay?

What we have seen is that there are more kinds of money than coins and banknotes only. Ultimately every slip of paper, every voucher, every securitized claim on legal tender, should be understood as money. From this perspective money is every debenture, certificate of debt or promissory note, every promise on money evidenced by document, which is accepted in an exchange transaction. If somebody buys in a Mom-and-Pop store around the corner a bottle of milk and the merchant accepts a promise to give him the money later by putting the purchasing price on the slate, such a slip of paper has been produced. Figuratively the slate is the slip of paper. The slip of paper, signed by the debtor, is for its owner a securitized claim on legal tender. The slip is the security. And it is only the question of acceptance and thus a question of "good faith", whether this slip of paper could be circulating as good as (legal tender) money in the economy. As long as everybody is confident that the underwriter of the slip will settle the promised money at maturity, it should be possible to buy and to pay with the slip instead of legal tender. It's like in a big family. The children will probably accept money vouchers of the parents among each other. They deeply believe that their parents will redeem the vouchers if "real" money is needed. Legal tender is probably required only if payments have to be settled outside the family. We have experienced such a situation in the real world day by day. It worked many decades but with some disturbances. The basis has been the "good faith" on the banks that have created these slips of paper, these money vouchers. The special form has been book money/credit money of the commercial banks. What we name (positive) "deposit account balance", is this money? The answer is yes, because it is money in our very general view to money as slips of paper. A positive deposit account balance at a commercial bank is a securitized claim on legal tender. In fact it's a voucher or more precisely a Central-Bank-money voucher. It is not Central-Bank-money directly. The commercial bank owes the customer legal tender in the amount of the (positive) deposit account balance. On request the commercial bank has to hand out banknotes (that the bank's customer has to accept unlimited) or coins (that have to be accepted at least in small amounts). The (positive) deposit account balance is a credit that the customer has granted to the commercial bank. If a customer brings cash to a commercial bank to "put it on the account", he will get in exchange a certificate of debt from the commercial bank. One accepts this slip of paper in "good faith" that whenever one needs legal tender the debt of the commercial bank will be redeemed. Whenever the slip is presented to the commercial bank one gets legal tender in exchange. The question is: is this always ensured? Only in part legislation takes care. Laws and regulation require that commercial banks have only a fractional amount of legal tender under their disposal in relation to all promises on legal tender made. This is the so-called minimum required reserve which works under the assumption that in a given period of time only a small amount of all customers will ask for legal tender instead of holding a (positive) deposit account balance.

To summarize, there is a real economy, the production of goods and services. There exists a lot of real estate and properties of "real value", tangible assets and the opportunity to trade. Legal tender as money could be used for trade but it shouldn't be seen as mandatory. Anchored in the legislation is the freedom of contract principle. The partners of a trade are free to negotiate service and return service. It is up to them to specify how a bottle of milk is rewarded, whether it should be paid for with money like legal tender or whether somebody has to dance for it. This trade has also to be considered in reverse concerning the question: how should the sale of money be rewarded? Will it be the settlement of money in the future, a credit? Will somebody dance for it and the money is rewarded with a ticket for a ballet or will it be a hoped for price in the future? The reward in that latter case would be a lottery ticket; or will it be a company share? A legal compulsion to accept legal tender is given if there is nothing else negotiated. In "normal times" there is confidence in the monetary system. In most cases it will be possible to pay with legal tender to settle a debt with it. Even today in most cases of trade contracts there will be no other form of settlement be stipulated. However, there are examples: employment contracts stipulating that the wages are remitted to a bank account. That means the work will be paid with commercial-bank-money instead of legal tender. The employee has no right to demand legal tender from his employer. The employer has no obligation to settle the wages in cash at request of the employee.

A further complex of problems in the monetary system is liquidity. All that kind of money that is needed to settle negotiated transactions should be available. It has to be in circulation for those who promised to settle that kind of money at a specified point in time to avoid their inability to pay. The problem has its origin in the existence of debt (monetary liabilities). If a monetary liability becomes due, the debtor has to settle money. Each liability is owned as an asset by somebody else. All financial assets, all claims on money, balance the sum total of all debts. Let us think experimentally the following: our "Mom-and-Pop store around the corner" could for instance have sold a lot of milk on credit. It got a corresponding amount of promises on money. In addition the store should have sold a lot of other goods for money. Now let us assume that our store has gained such a high surplus that it has collected all available money (especially all available legal tender) in the till. He owns the total stock of Central-Bank-money and some promises on money in addition. If now this store is hoarding its money, all of the legal tender under disposal, it is simply impossible for all the debtors to keep their promise to settle legal tender. All the legal tender is under disposal of the store. So a debtor should first have to obtain legal tender from the owner of the store in exchange with something, to be able to settle his debt. Only if the owner of the store accepts anything else in exchange to legal tender, there is a chance for the debtor to redeem the liability resulting from the promise on money that was made.

Liquidity denotes the special characteristic of money to be accepted as one part of an exchange transaction. Money of high liquidity opens the opportunity to get something of value or use in a one-step exchange transaction. Money with high liquidity can be used to settle a debt. More precisely: to settle a monetary debt.

3. Reasons for Financial Crises

I can feel it coming, …, a whole new round of disastrous speculation, with …blue chip boom, then a fad for secondary issues, then an over-the-counter play, then another garbage market in new issues, and finally the inevitable crash. I don't know when it will come, but I can feel it coming, and damn it, I don't know what to do about it.
Bernard J. Lasker, Chairman of the New York Stock Exchange in 1970

Financial crises do not appear from nowhere. Often they can be found when the economic cycle has reached a level that afterwards will be seen as a peak. What is called a financial crisis? Raymond Goldsmith defined a financial crisis as »a sharp, brief, ultra-cyclical deterioration of all or most of a group of financial indicators – short-term interest rates, asset prices, commercial insolvencies, and failures of financial institutions.«

Are weaknesses of markets and the involved market participants, the humans, reasons for financial crises? What is a market? A market is where supply and demand for goods and services, commodities, properties, real estate etc. meets. There are markets where no real goods and services are traded but financial products: swell-money like company shares, bonds, asset backed securities and the most different forms of financial derivatives as well. The coincidence of supply and demand is essential for the functioning of markets and gives economy a meaning and substance. "Market" is a term shrouded in mystery. Wishes and hopes are connected to the term "market". But also, curse and despair of those investigating blessings, trials and tribulations of the economy. Looking at the above definition initially one would suspect a market or the market (epitomizing the universe of all markets) to be something harmless, banal and innocent.

A market isn't that harmless! By no means, if in a national economy or in parts of the global economy, acting free or better to say acting moderately free is allowed for all humans as market participants. There would be no supply and demand without economic participants like producers or entrepreneurs producing and offering goods and services and consumers and entrepreneurs requesting goods and services, and without brokers and dealers like bankers, merchants, insurers, stock brokers. Without all these people or groups of people with subtle economic ambitions it would still be complicated that supply and demand coincide. All these economic entities, the "players" of a "game" we call economy, are oriented towards their own advantages in their actions. They could strive for maximizing their profits. Advantages achieved could entail disadvantages for others. Making a profit could result in losses in the economic environment even if it is not directly involved. Quite often the ecological environment has to suffer the loss to make a profit. That is why one problem is of outmost importance: what are the rules and regulations (organisation of the market) that have to be fixed as mandatory, so that the market's operation and hopefully "the" market is doing well in the following sense: national markets – opening up step by step – will increase economic
wealth and prosperity of the society, not only prosperity of very specific Nations but the prosperity of the overall global community of all societies as well. More than that, this should not only be true for a short period of time but sustainable, with an always sound ecological environment!

Do the currently existing organizations of markets solve that problem? Do the markets of the world with their interdependencies in their current organization accomplish these goals? The answer is: markets are operating quite orderly in certain stages of the business cycle. The nearer it comes to a peak there could be a sudden disruption where markets are not or bad operating (catch words: crises, financial crises, crash, stock market crash, collapse, market failure, breakdown, panic, turmoil). What we have seen is that in the long run the current markets are everything but stable. They do not solve the above mentioned problem at all. Given the current organization of markets the wishful aim for the global community and ecology cannot be reached. That is why a better organization of the market, that means a balanced system of rules and regulations, adjusted optimally, with given differences being harmonised in globally crucial aspects, has to be invented, investigated, introduced and implemented. That has to be accomplished on each and every national and especially on the international level.

Occasionally there have been some positive changes of the organization of markets within the past thirty years, but neither concerning the "prevention of (financial) crises" nor a "sustainable prosperity of the world community of societies" we managed the breakthrough. There has been growth in the world's Gross Domestic Product. If we define prosperity and increasing wealth as an economic growth that reduces poverty, we have to state a systemic fault: poverty has been increasing. The part of the global population living in poverty increased in the last decades. Even in (wealthy) Nations poverty has been rising. Repairing the organization of markets were not enough to reverse this process; cf. F.J. Radermacher & Bert Beyers (2007).

With respect to financial crises all attempts to find rules and regulations aligned to prevent, avert or master such crises, are of no avail – on the international and the national level either. What is the reason for this deficit? One thing is obvious: the scientific reasoning did not come to results that are seen as confident and reliable. Nevertheless we agree with G. Scherhorn (2009, p. 81) who explained reasons of the critical developments starting from around 1980: »It is the escalating potential of money creation that has led the world into the financial crisis. Its origin is liberalization and deregulation of financial markets enabling the financial capital to gain excessive profits disguising risks, using leverage effects of credit financed investments and finally it enabled to compel tax privilege. The rising demand on high yields on financial capital has accelerated the serious exploitation of ecological and social capital.« Could this be the key to unriddle the secrets of the world financial system? It explains the systemic transition mechanism leading to systemic changes.

4. Financial Crises in Retrospect: Coursing through History

> Major default episodes are typically spaced some years (or decades) apart, creating an illusion that "this time is different" among policymakers and investors. A recent example of the "this time is different" syndrome is the false belief that domestic debt is a novel feature of the modern financial landscape. ... crises frequently emanate from the financial centers with transmission through interest rate shocks and commodity price collapses. ... often accompany default: including inflation, exchange rate crashes, banking crises, and currency debasements.
>
> *Carmen M. Reinhart and Kenneth S. Rogoff (2008)*

Thanks to C.P. Kindleberger (1978), C.M. Reinhart/K.S. Rogoff (2008), (2008a) and some other authors we can get a sound and systematic overview about all regional, national and international financial crises of the last four centuries. Quite many of the historic crises are described and investigated elaborately. Notably commendable is the very new work of C.M. Reinhart and K.S. Rogoff (2009). They did a survey on a large number of banking crises in the 20th century. They investigated the effects and aftermaths of these crises to the real economy. They tried to expose the interdependencies between the duration of a banking crisis and how (real) prices of domiciles, unemployment and (real) Gross Domestic Product per capita developed in the years of economic downturn. An aspect particularly to be mentioned is that these two authors found out that there has always been a new and additional indebtedness of the Nations (real after inflation adjustments). In the three years following a banking crisis all contemplated Nations had on average a new additional indebtedness of 86%.

The book of C.P. Kindleberger (1978) contains in the fourth edition (2005) after twelve masterly written chapters a chart overview about all the financial crises in the world from 1618 till 1990. It is interesting to mention that only seven attributes are sufficient to characterize all the 46 financial crises that are listed by Kindleberger. The tabular overview starts with:

Year:	1618 - 1623
Countries (City)	Holy Roman Empire
Related to	Thirty Year's War
Preceding speculation in	Subsidiary coin, exchanging bad for good
Monetary expansion from	Debasement of coins by weight, fineness, denomination
Speculative peak	Feb. 1622
Crisis (crash, panic)	Feb. 1622
Lender of last resort	None

Lender of last resort means the institution as part of the organization of the financial market that in times of a crisis could provide the market participants with legal tender by granting credits. Today these are for instance all Central Banks, the International Monetary Fund in Washington D.C. and to some aspect the Bank for International Settlements in Basel as well. If the world financial system, this house of cards is wobbling, the lender of last resort can (hopefully) give help to avoid the collapse.

About Kindleberger and his book Peter L. Bernstein wrote in the foreword: »Underneath the hilarious anecdotes, the elegant epigrams, and the graceful turns of phrase, Kindleberger is deadly serious. The manner in which human beings earn their living is no laughing matter to him, especially when they attempt to do so at the expense of one another. As he so effectively demonstrates, manias, panics, and crashes are the consequence of an economic environment that cultivates cupidity, chicanery, and rapaciousness rather than a devout belief in the Golden Rule. In truth, Kindleberger is a seducer. By bringing colourful individuals to life, … his goal is to employ history to demonstrate theoretical ideas of primary importance. … he points out that "History is particular; economics is general." The lively blend between the two is Kindleberger´s unique contribution to the literature of both disciplines.«

Kindleberger considers each century on average eleven to twelve financial crises. If we have to assume that this is a typical ratio for the appearance of financial crises we would be faced with ten more economic disasters within this century – if there is not ultimately a real effective change. It's not exactly glad tidings! Detailed compilation of financial crises like the one from Kindleberger show that the following holds truth for almost all Nations: generations that have not been hit by financial crises are rather exceptions. The general rule is that each generation experiences at least one crisis.

A financial crisis has not always been triggered by speculations on money, shares and securities or real estate. There could be quite other things which form the basis for speculation, Kindleberger pinpoints in his survey of a second crisis. He analyzed what speculative areas were the origin of the crisis that hit the Republic Holland in 1636 and 1637. It was shares of the Dutch East India Company (Vereeniged Oost-Indische Compagnie), real estates, water ways and – unbelievably – tulip bulbs; of both kinds, exotic and ordinary. The prices for all exotic tulip bulbs were swelling like share prices. Also the prices for ordinary tulip bulbs as well had suddenly the desire to swell. Everybody cherished an illusion. These days made history as the era of tulipmania. Tulip bulbs became swell-money. At the end all these speculative bubbles burst: shares, real estates, water ways and tulip bulbs. The crisis began.

The most severe financial crisis in the last century was the "Great Crash" of 1929. J. K. Galbraith (1954) has written a whole book dedicated to all those "black days" happening in that era trying to investigate the reasons and interdependencies. We will give an explanation of this crisis in Part II Analysis. Kindleberger has described the Great Crash briefly with the following characteristics:

Year:	**1929**
Countries (City)	United States
Related to	End of extended post-war boom
Preceding speculation in	Land to 1925, stocks 1928-1929
Monetary expansion from	Stocks purchased on margin
Speculative peak	Sept. 1929
Crisis (crash, panic)	Oct. 1929
Lender of last resort	FRBNY (Federal reserve bank of New York) open market operations (inadequate)

The last crisis that Kindleberger explains in his overview is Japan 1990. The objects of preceding speculations were the Nikkei Index and real estate. Reduction of interest rates in 1986 resulted in an extension of the monetary aggregates. Speculation came to its peak in the first half year of 1989. The crash followed in January 1990. The lender of last resort at that time was the Central Bank of Japan. The measures – taken together with the government's treasury department in reaction to the crisis – were tardy. Reviewing the aftermath one can notice that a recession of more than a decade followed. All those having the opinion that this long recession was a result of the tardiness of the actions taken, will compliment the United States of America and the President on promptly taken actions in the current world financial crisis. Perhaps they will get laudation for doing things in a big way rather than digging with spoons. In a few years we will see whether it was the fast action that leads to a fast recovery of the seriously injured and sick patient. Whether all these thousands of Billions US Dollar, money and swell-money, whether a big syringe was a successful remedy for the financial system and the real economy.

Part 2: Analysis

5. Houses of Cards and Circular Flows of Money

Poem (translated): The Fundament
Be true, throw far away
the veil that shades your day.
Take a look at yourself,
and assess your behaviour.
What have you done
for all and your neighbour?
Truth – a sword so powerful –
directly moves into your soul.
Magic disappears, illusions fade,
Buildings in the air, disintegrate.
When dust is worn away so far,
accept yourself the way you are.
Then build again and bring to end
onto this humble fundament.

Conrad Ferdinand Meyer

Whether a fast reaction in face of a crisis – from both politics and Central Banks – will be successful, depends on whether the real problems are tackled. Measures taken have to counteract the objective reasons for the crisis to avoid them in future or – at least – to be able to master their impact. A precise and correct diagnosis is a prerequisite for an effective therapy. Dealing only with observed symptoms could merely induce the impression that the disease has been conquered. If the deeper reason for the disease is a severe problem – a systemic problem – the observed symptoms will be much worse the next time. We have to consider: the world's financial system is figuratively often compared to be the heart of the real economy. It is the heart of the "body economy" with money as blood – and blood should circulate all the time. If we aim at avoiding "infarction" or "strokes" we should not think that it is sufficient to dilute the blood (by creating more money). We need to understand the most important interdependencies and operational patterns. The systemic structure has to be considered to invent and implement effective improvements. We have tried to unravel the mystery of money in Part I of this book - up to a degree that we can now dare to strive for a deeper insight. We will endeavour to show a revealing look at the houses of cards and circular flows of money in the last century. We analyse and depict their "constructional deficits" and distortions. Then we investigate and explain the current situation.

The monetary system is of vital importance if we wish to understand the processes on the way to the great depression of 1929 until 1932/1932. What were the main characteristics of the monetary system in the years preceding that crisis? What were the potentials of risk? The basis of the monetary systems at that time was representative money, backed by precious metals. The Central Banks received from their Nations a treasure of gold (silver in case of China) as a backing commodity. Legal tender, created and brought into circulation by the Central Banks, was backed by gold. Legal tender has been a claim on gold – a gold voucher. A banknote – this slip of paper – documented the ownership of some gold, deposited at the Central Bank. A bearer of legal tender has had the right to get gold (silver in case of China) in a well-defined ratio in exchange for that money on request. Central-Bank-money was the only money this right was attached to. Legal tender money was a gold debenture – a gold voucher, a "securitized right" evidenced by a document (banknote) to redeem the slip of paper at the Central Bank in the holder's favour. The Central-Bank-money was at that time a promise also to alternatively receive gold. The attractive basis of Central-Bank-money, representing a real value – precious gold – was safeguarded in the most secure safes of the Central Bank. It was under deposit for those requesting gold in exchange for Central-Bank-money. Central-Bank-money as legal tender has been as good as gold. Or rather to say: the owner of that money regarded it as good as gold, as long as they had good faith to receive gold in exchange whenever requested. A further prerequisite for that trust was that the exchange ratio of money to gold was a legally set fix. In addition to the backing with gold, the imputed value of money arose from market inspection. The valuation of money was by answering the question: what can be purchased with it? To say it in other words, the value of legal tender money backed by gold is at least a fix ratio of the value of gold, or how much of the "real values" (for instance goods and services) one can get for in exchange.

Here a potential of danger is given. It is deflation: If prices for real values, for goods and services decline, the value imputed to money rises. In the course of deflation more can be purchased with the same amount of money since prices for goods and services are going down. This can lead to a situation where owner of money prefer it against real values, keeping the money instead of making purchases. One thinks: »I gain a profit by hoarding money. To maximize the profit I will wait as long as I get the most in exchange for goods and services.« Unfortunately no one can foresee at what point in time this will be.

If the volume of "active" legal tender in the market is decreasing and a deflationary tendency is seen, one possibility of action to avert this is to bring more Central-Bank-money into circulation. As already mentioned only the Central Banks are allowed to do that. The overall volume of Central-Bank-money being created is limited by all the gold at their disposal. Furthermore it depends on the exchange ratio – the legally set ratio of gold to Central-Bank-money (c.f. Chapter 2).

In Chapter 2 we have described the principles of granting credits in interplay with Central-Bank-money and promises of money made by the commercial banks. According to the same principle everybody can take out a credit – each market participant, each individual person, each company and also the Government. When taking out a credit one makes a promise to pay, one does not borrow anything. A new credit is nothing else than producing swell-money that could come into circulation for instance as a securitized debt obligation. Everybody can create a slip of paper documenting a debt. The slips of paper are called "securities" and represent debentures that – to some extent – can be traded at exchanges or other trading environments. Today these debentures are administrated in electronic form in so-called security settlement systems. It is not only shares that can be traded but also debt obligations of Governments and companies. The potentiality of companies and Governments to create these promises on money are merely limited by insolvency legislation and governmental decisions. This is a question of the level of debt. There is bankruptcy if all regular or expected earnings are not even enough to pay interest for all credits. This situation is called over-indebtedness. Another situation of bankruptcy is illiquidity, the inability to pay. This is a situation where a company does not have enough money and is not able to obtain enough money to pay all liabilities when they become due. Market participants should always have to fulfil their payment obligations at maturity. A company – also Government – has to ensure sufficient liquidity at any time. Therefore they need to possess enough legal tender – Central-Bank-money – or any other medium of exchange that is accepted as a means of payment. If a market participant does not have enough accepted means of payment and is not able to sell some of its assets to receive (liquid) money in exchange, it has no possibility to meet its obligations. This can happen independently from the question of over-indebtedness. Even if a company's net worth is a positive equity, which means the assumed value of all assets exceeds the amount of all debts, there can be illiquidity.

How long will such a system remain stable? How long will such a system be well-functioning? Essentially it's a question of acceptance. How long will a promise on money be accepted as good as money – as good as legal tender? Promises on money should be seen, or should be, as good as Central-Bank-money. As long as everybody believes that promises on money are as good as money, the monetary system can be regarded as comparatively stable. As long as there is confidence and "good faith" there should be no problem of liquidity. Everybody who needs could obtain Central-Bank-money, since everybody requiring Central-Bank-money could give in exchange a promise on money to those who have it, and pay interest. There is a flow of Central-Bank-money in such an economy. If somebody needs (Central Bank) money but has none, he buys Central-Bank-money "on tick" paying with a promise on money – "put it on the slate". The question is: How long will a promise on money be accepted? The possible answer is: firstly if those accepting the promise are of good faith that they can obtain Central-Bank-money whenever they need it. This is a question of their own liquidity. Secondly as long as those accepting promises are of good faith that those making the promise will really settle their debt when it becomes due; or if the interest charged for accepting the credit is so high that it is attractive to take the risk of a payment default. This is the aspect of solvability that has to be considered in making any kind of forward business. What is a forward business? A forward business is a purchase on credit. One purchases something on credit today assuming – or hoping – to gain benefits. This would be the case if the advantages (for instance getting earnings from) during owning and using what is purchased, plus the price achieved when re-purchasing it in the future, exceeds all paid interest plus the re-payment of the credit. These businesses are also called leveraged businesses. The higher the credit in relation to the already available capital in use is, the higher the leverage. If one owns – for instance – one Dollar in cash and purchases something at a cost of ten Dollars (taking nine Dollars as a credit) the leverage is 1 : 10. Somebody purchases for example company shares but has to make a money promise (a credit) to pay for in the future. This forward business, this leverage business, is done in the hope that the value (price) of the company share will be higher in the future. The amount of money obtained in re-purchasing the share in the future together with the dividends paid should exceed the total debt service – all paid interest plus what is needed to redeem the promise on money made. Or – as another example – it may be profitable if real estate is purchased on credit. There would be a profit if all the rent one saves living in one's own house, plus the amount of money one gets selling the real estate, exceeds the pay back of the credit plus all interest to be paid. Leveraged businesses are at the core of all commercial deals of credit institutions. Credit institutions – for instance – go into short-term debt, when they make promises on money with short-term maturity, e.g. the account deposit of a customer. On the other hand customers are granted credits most often with a more long-term maturity. The interest to be paid on account deposits is usually less than the interest charged to customer credits. The difference is what the credit institution gains. The commercial bank's leverage is the ratio of the sum total of all these businesses to the equity.

The World Financial System House of Cards previous to 1929

What were the constructional components of the world financial system and the world economy house of cards in the years previous to 24 October 1929? Most of the economically leading Nations built up their monetary system after the end of World War I with representative money. For instance legal tender in the US, Great Britain and France were backed by gold (as already mentioned, the Chinese monetary system was backed by silver). The following "playing cards" were in the game building up the house of cards:

– Gold
– (Central Bank) money, at that time representing promises on gold
– swell-money (leverage-money), that means promises on money (c.f. Chapter 2)
– goods and services (added value)
– tangibles an intangibles ("real" values like, for instance, industrial and residential properties, real estate, land, patents, production facilities, artworks or commodities)

Money as playing cards was in number and volume limited through the available volume of gold on deposit. In all currency zones the amount of money brought into circulation via the Central Bank was restricted, since its overall value should not exceed the total value of gold at their disposal. The price of gold is derived from the set ratio to a unit of legal tender. "Real value cards" could be added to the game when they were created. That means if the value added process creates a durable good like a house, an office building, a factory or a farm, this results in a new "real value card" brought into the game, added to the house of cards. Like gold and all legal tender money (Central-Bank-money) backed by gold, this added value was of durable existence and as such a sturdy stone in the house of cards. On the contrary all swell-money, all promises on money made, had a limited duration. When they became due those promises had to be redeemed - the promised money had to be settled. Shares are a very special kind of promise on money since there is no fixed duration. These promises on money, or rather, the promise to own something, will be settled only the day after "judgement day" – if there is one. What does it mean? The slip of paper named share documents the ownership of a part of the net worth of a company. The value of a share results from subtracting all debt (the liability side of the balance sheet without the equity position) from the total sum of all assets (c.f. B. Hadorp 2008, pp. 189-204). Only in the case of liquidation of the company and after all the debt has been serviced, is that which remains distributed to all share holders pro-rata. From this perspective, shares could be seen in principle as a special kind of backed swell-money. It is swell-money backed by an underlying value (net worth of a company), but unfortunately this value can decline to zero, it even could become negative.

How and when does swell-money come into the game? In principle everybody, each market participant, could make a promise on money. Everything that has to be done is: take a card and write down »I owe 100 US Dollar to the owner of this card. It has to be paid as Central-Bank-money plus 10% interest a year. The whole amount of money will become due after duration of ten years starting at subscription«. The only question is: when will this card be part of the game? First the newly created swell-money is a card up one's sleeve. There has to be another gambler, the counterpart, accepting the new card in exchange for something different. That something could be money, it could be a real value as well; money or a real value would be purchased "on tick". The counterpart could also pull an ace out of his sleeve, offering to exchange swell-money against swell-money. A credit institution could grant me a credit, booking it on my bank account. It gives me book money in exchange to my credit contract – this slip of paper, this swell-money. Book money is a bank debenture. Booking a positive value into my bank account is nothing but producing new swell-money by the credit institution. It is the credit institute that makes the promise to redeem it on request. The amount somebody has on his account is nothing but a liability of the bank. It becomes due whenever the owner of the account makes a request to obtain Central-Bank-money. This form of swell-money has thus duration of one day or shorter. Other swell-money – like a saving account or mortgage loan – has in general longer duration. Why is it attractive to create swell-money? The creator of swell-money may be lured to go into debt, in order to make a leveraged investment that dangles the prospect of profit. In short, the credit based investment should gain more earnings than there are credit costs. At least the total sum of all earnings, plus the revenue on a re-sale if needed, should exceed the amount of debt plus the total debt service. The same examination should be done at the credit institution. The bank has to consider that besides deposit account balances and the operating costs, dividend payments have to be made to all share holders. All these payments together specify the minimum interest to be charged to granted credits. In addition to setting the interest rates, the risk of credit defaults – if a credit will not be redeemed by the debtor – has to be considered.

The instability of this house of cards is increased, if money and/or added value cease to flow! This could happen, if promises on money are not delivered or cannot be delivered. The willingness to hold swell-money as a playing card, the desire to own promises on money as assets, could decrease or even vanish as a consequence. In this case those swell-money cards have to be taken out of the game. They should be removed from the house of cards, with no chance for replacement. Neither by Central-Bank-money cards, added value cards nor a value card of any other kind. The house of cards will start to totter.

All cards of our house of cards are assets – they are in and of themselves valuable possessions, components of wealth and fortune. What is the main characteristic of assets? Assets carry a capability. They possess ability. What are these cards able to do? These asset cards are able to gain earnings in the future. Asset cards represent a claim on a promise to get a share in wealth and value added in the future. Holding a debenture as asset one assumes a positive outcome to make purchases. The bearer receives interest payments and repatriation of the debt amount of a promise on money held as an asset as it becomes due. A company share held as asset will result in a dividend payment instead of interest. If a company is owned, goods and services for self-consumption can be produced. In a house the owner's benefit comes in the form of free residency. The world financial system and world economy house of cards is thus the complex construction of all components of wealth and fortune that are competing for future shares in value added and property. All tangible assets and (Central Bank) money are the stable cards of this house, or rather, they are comparatively stable. Real estate, gold, durable products and commodities, production facilities and the like promise their owner at least some material benefit. They can be used in and of themselves. They are raw material or they could produce goods and services – for the owner and for others. Whether there is a need to release or re-sell an asset is determined by the owner's liability to pay and his liquidity (ability to pay). Figuratively: each card of the house of cards should have a guaranteed flow of incoming money, since on the other hand this card also has a compulsory outflow of money. The output side determines the needed liquidity as the minimum required flow of money in a stable house of card. Each card representing the ownership of a real value like a company with its production capacity is a stable binding tie in the house of cards as long as the least required inflow of money can be assured in order to settle all compulsive payments and liabilities as and when they become due. Liquidity is a must. Liquidity has to be assured at all times – otherwise the card is tilting. Which part does swell-money play in this game? Swell-money can be created for a limited period of time as a substitute to a missing income stream if there is the expectation to reinstate this currently unavailable income stream timely. Then swell-money is added as a card to the game. It is attached to a growing house of cards. However, this happens only if a counter-player is accepting the new card.

Water is needed to flow – money, too

To explain the interrelationships and the interdependencies of money, other financial assets, properties and the economy, we will choose a metaphor: let us imagine the real economy as a kind of perfect oasis – a fertile and flourishing oasis of happiness with a proper functioning water circulation, representing money and its circulation. For all that is growing and blooming in the oasis water is a necessity. Care has to be taken that water, in the proper amount, should reach the roots of all the plants. Water has to flow. All sound and wholesome growing plants evaporate most water taken out of the ground at their leaves. In a closed system the resulting humidity will find its way back as condensed water – as rain – to the springs of this circular flow of economic life. There are people in this economic oasis carrying water taken from a well to the fields to assure that an all benefiting harvest will occur. Everybody renders something of use for others. Everybody is producing some goods or services required or requested by others. This economic oasis is sustainably balanced. There is no excessive amount of water which could endanger land and people with floods. Water is not swelling. There is no water inflation. What is swell-money in this oasis? Answer: it is a promise on water – a water voucher. Let us imagine: one unit of swell-money is a well-defined part of a huge glass dome spanning the whole oasis; the more swell-money the larger the glass dome. At the bottom around the dome sit the owners of the swell-money, the owners of all water vouchers (representing financial assets). Those who emitted the vouchers are promising to give the bearer water at a later point in time. Up to that point the evaporating water will condensate on the inner surface of the glass dome. This is the interest to be paid to the owners of the water vouchers. The bigger the glass dome the more water vapour has to ascend (assuming a constant interest rate being charged). The condensed water is firstly collected by the owners of the water vouchers outside the oasis. It has to be brought back into circulation to assure further fertility in the oasis. This water should be used for consumption. It has to be exchanged for fruits and other goods and services. What could be an alternative to this exchange instead? Answer: to trade the water for a newly created, a further water voucher. The result would be a growing dome – and with the dome grows the total sum of all interest to be paid. Ever more water has to evaporate. A further alternative could be to give the water in exchange for components of real value (tangible properties). Whatsoever, there is a strong necessity that water flows to assure that all business deals that have already been agreed upon can be conducted with water. One should try to imagine what happens if faith is lost in water vouchers being as good as water – if there is growing uncertainty to get water by redeeming the water voucher, if it is really needed. If those emitted the vouchers do not have enough water at their disposal to honour all presented vouchers. More and more market participants in the oasis will refuse to accept water vouchers. Everybody insists on water to get it safely isolated and controlled. It will be filled in canisters – thus withdrawn from circulation. What are the consequences? There will be not enough water to irrigate the fields. The plants will wither – less harvesting and less water is evaporating. At the same time water will always be more valuable because of high demand and low supply. Water becomes a scarce, a precious resource. Now more and more fruits or other goods and services are to be given in exchange for one unit of water. The value, or rather, the valuation of money is rising. To say it the other way round, the valuation of fruits (goods, services), their price in (let us say) gallons of water, declines. There is deflation – water deflation. We have to mention: deflation does not only affect the market of goods and services, but also all non-financial assets, those tangibles and intangibles as well. Who controls the water rules the oasis! Those who have privileged access to water can acquire the very best crop land, plantations and all other valuable properties with just a sip of water. What happens to those who issued the water vouchers and are now confronted with the necessity to redeem the vouchers for water? In order to obtain water they must offer whatever will be accepted – they perceive themselves as being lost in a desert suffering of thirst, begging greedy spring tycoons coming across for water. The oasis is threatened into a desert.

6. The Great Depression 1929 – 1932/1933

The problems are not the oases but the desert around.
Guido Westerwelle, 2009

The problems are neither oases nor the surrounding desert but the big camels of oases, sucking-up the others out of house and home.
Renate Künast, 2009

At the end of World War I the "European oasis" was destroyed – devastated – in part turned into a desert. Too much time all the people's energy and attention was devoted to weapons and other deathly tools of war. All too much effort was wasted in battles, lacking enough attentiveness to attend to vegetables, plants, trees and fruits. This caused a shortage of food. In the years after World War I "oasis USA" thus expanded the production of food. Part of the production was meant for exporting it to Europe. "Water" was needed to finance this expansion. First increasingly, but afterwards soaring, people were lured to invest in new production facilities on credit. Everybody expected further and continuous growth, not being aware that the growth happened in the aftermath of World War I was mainly a result of devastated – and thus missing – production capacities in Europe. A lot of people were investing (credit-based), since it seemed and was assumed that more and more was produced and sold with a profit. As a result of this broadly shared estimation more and more "water vouchers" were accepted to drive the further extension of "oasis

USA". The water to pay interest and to redeem the water vouchers later was intended to come from Europe. Countries like Great Britain and France were highly indebted and Germany, highly indebted as well, was put under pressure for reparation. Those reparations should settle the debt of France and Great Britain to the credit granting Americans. It should be obvious that this could only work if the European desert will be re-constructed into an oasis to possess enough production capacities. Europe should be enabled to produce added value, that enough "water vapour" would soar to be collected and transferred to America.

On both sides of the Atlantic Ocean the economic development, the expansion of production capacities, was through heavy leveraged investments. More and more promises on money lead to more and more payments of interest – it started to become foggy under the swell-money domes spanning both oases. These leveraged investments, especially at a later stage the purchasing of shares, was planned and accomplished with a speculative expectation of rising value. The payback of credits plus interest should be achieved from the proceeds when re-selling the shares in the future. More than that, a profit was expected to be achieved. Dazzled by the high exports from USA to Europe all too many people thought that American companies could increase turnover and profits permanently. That caused the illusion that share prices will also rise continuously. It resulted in a speculative bubble. More and more people started leveraged investments in shares. Day by day higher prices were accepted in share acquisitions on tick. There was a deep promise that the prices will be even higher in the future. The dividends gathered and the desired and hoped for returns in the future when re-selling the shares should amortize the credit. Dividends and other future earnings should be enough to repay credits and cover all interest to be paid. Figuratively spoken, there was a speculation to get enough money from selling fruits and, if needed, selling the plant bearing those fruits to honour all water vouchers at their maturity. The glass dome, made by swell-money, this "bloated Zero", became bigger and bigger.

The reconstruction of production capacities in Europe was needed actually to get a chance to pay back all credits taken for the reconstruction. The revival of the "oasis Europe" was a needs-must in order that credits granted could be paid back with money, goods or services.

The world saw two houses of cards emerging after World War I. The European house of cards was built up in an oasis that was, to a large extent, lying in ruins. Devastations of war were the reason why Europe was not able to produce as many goods and services as in the times preceding World War I. A huge amount of water vouchers has been brought into circulation to finance the costs of war. A lot of those credits, especially to France and Great Britain, were granted by the USA. Europe had bought the needed tools of war from Americans "on tick". They had paid the US with money vouchers. The oasis USA, the second house of cards, was built up mainly driven by the creation of swell-money used for speculation. There were a growing number of leveraged investments in full confidence that there are no limits of growth for the US economy. There was no doubt about it. However, it has to be seen that the key driving force of the growth that was mentioned in the beginning of the "Roaring Twenties" was the reconstruction of Europe, devastated by war damages. The time needed for reconstruction was limited. In the USA a speculative bubble was emerging. At the stock exchange the prices for most company shares climbed to incomprehensible levels. At the same time Europe's economic system was partly restructured: The swell-money bubble that emerged during World War I with threatening size caused Great Britain to abandon the gold standard and led to hyper-inflation (especially in Germany). As a positive outcome most European currencies were, more or less, properly reformed. What persists was a threatening swell-money bubble in the USA. Its disastrous potential onto the monetary system and the flow of money became effective when the speculative share market bubble burst in October 1929.

What are the operational patterns behind these processes? Figuratively it can be described as follows: more and more trees have been planted in the oasis USA. To irrigate these new trees more water was needed. That is why water was borrowed from the "spring tycoons" of the oasis. Even those were increasingly obliged to borrow water from other springs. The flow of swell-money became ever faster until being a torrential stream, since the all available volume of Central-Bank-money was limited by the available amount of gold. For a while the exports to Europe provided the oasis USA with new water. In paying the debt service for the huge amount of water vouchers that had been emitted, there was a flow of money, respectively gold as a backing of Central-Bank-money, from Europe to the USA. As a result less and less water remains available in Europe. When the flow of water from Europe to America runs dry the growth was stopped. Just growth was a prerequisite that all these credit based speculative businesses could be successful. In consequence a lot of these businesses – leveraged businesses – failed. The companies' share holders had to sell their shares. They needed water to pay back their credits. They had to deliver water on their promises made. More and more shares were offered for sale and prices deteriorated as there was no purchasing power left to be able to purchase shares at higher prices. As a consequence those who had water were hoarding it instead of making trades. Water vouchers were not anymore being accepted. Nobody knew who would be able to keep the promise to deliver water when a voucher was presented at maturity. It was not possible to "draw" fresh water. It was not possible to create new Central-Bank-money, since it was bound to gold and the amount of gold was limited. People hoarding gold caused a shrinking of the overall volume of Central-Bank-money. The circulation of water – the circulation of money – stopped. Prices declined and with them the possibility to earn as much money as was necessary to cover all expenditures. That is why expenditures had to be reduced. Companies had to fire employees because they were no longer able to pay the wages. Those without employment had no income, they were not able to purchase. It was a downturn spiral into depression. The house of cards collapsed. The world economy was in a sorry state. As a result the world saw a small group of big profiteers and a big group of losers. The profiteers were those that stashed away the water right in time, those who took off money liquidity from the system.

Franklin D. Roosevelt, the President of the United States, was facing that problem with his New Deal. His approach was redistribution, enhancing the social balance, but also protectionism and thus a focus on a strong isolated national economy. Isolation and protectionism induced problems unseen at that time. Import duties being set reduced the export from Europe to the USA and in consequence the flow of water from USA to Europe. This led to a dry-up of the European oasis. Here, meanwhile considerable good and sizable production capacities had been re-built, there was an increasingly lack of water. That is why now in Europe the flow of water stopped. Again, the not sufficiently adjusted "swell-money bubble" had unfolded its disastrous potential. The world economy was disrupted, suffering and in a sorry state. The world economy hit rock bottom.

7. In the Aftermath of the Great Depression

Learn the past,
watch the present,
and create the future.

Jesse Conrad

Most of us know how history was continuing. An extreme radicalization of society in all countries of Europe was soaring – most of all in Germany. It finally ended in World War II. To face the Great Depression and the disastrous economic situation in Germany, governments started programmes to restore and expand the countries infrastructures. Unfortunately, that was only one part. Massive investments were also made for rearmament in order to regain military power. At the end of World War I Germany already was heavily indebted. In addition to that, Germany was burdened with immense requests for reparations. That is why governments investigated new and "innovative" ways to finance their national investments and they were successful. It would be no exaggeration to say: they invented the "mother of all conduits"; they invented the mother of all special purpose vehicles. Her name was "Metallurgic Research Company Ltd." (MEFO Metallurgische Forschungsgesellschaft mbH). The principle of this innovative financing approach used MEFO as a dummy company creating swell-money vicarious of the Government. This slip of paper money was named "MEFO-Bills" (MEFO-Wechsel). This newly created swell-money was used to pay all purchases of the German Government. To assure that all suppliers accepted these MEFO-Bills – this swell-money – as good as money, to assure that they accept MEFO-slips as medium of exchange, they were provided with a governmental guarantee. This guarantee was off-balance. Legislation did not demand for full disclose of off-balance guarantees in the governmental budget. It did not need to be accounted for as expenditures or liabilities. That is how the German government became (indirectly) deeper and deeper indebted than was allowed by the constitution, but the public was unaware of this fact. It was possible to conceal the soaring of indebtedness to the general public – at least for a while. When World War II was breaking out, the mountain of debt grew rapidly to an amazing level.

Those days before yesterday (1945-1972)

The situation after World War II looked quite similar to the aftermath of 1918. Europe was widely destroyed and devastated. The warring parties from Europe were highly indebted. America was the "saviour of the world" and it was the biggest creditor as well. Would history repeat itself? Would there be similar developments as after World War I? Truly, something was quite similar but obviously there were differences. The road followed was mainly determined by a most important issue that had been raised. It was the systemic question: what is the most appropriate organization of the society? Which economic model is the best? How can it be achieved that the financial system and national economies are robust and stable? Not being houses of cards that would collapse like in 1929? This issue held sway over the world, dividing it into blocks. The capitalist model of free markets on the one hand side, communism and planned economy on the other. In between the "Rhenish Capitalism", the economic philosophy to organize society and markets which has also been called ordoliberalism; a "Social Market Economy" with competition on markets, but operating under strict rules and regulations for fairness and to achieve a commonly agreed upon aim: "prosperity for all people".

An important aspect of those models in place, having impact on the status of the financial system, is how the social frameworks are financed. What are the main sources to finance all required or desired social balancing processes? In Anglo-Saxon regions the social systems were mainly based on the funding principle. Those employed have to accrue capital that yields enough return to live from, when unemployed or retired. Or the accrued capital will be sold to get the appropriate financing of comfortable sunset years. Probably the most convenient kind of capital for all intents and purposes is financial assets – swell-money, slip of paper money which is debts of other society members. If the accrued capital consists in this way of promises on money or promises on added value, the required amounts for consumption could be redeemed by selling the financial assets. The part not used can be bequeathed. Communism and Social Market Economy as well have been different. They follow a pay-as-you-go financing. Implicitly in those systems there is a so-called inter-generational contract. The generation, gainfully employed, gives parts of its earnings and income to those not employed. That is how those being jobless or retired will get their fair share on wealth and value added for consumption.

A further important aspect affecting the financial system, especially the size of the financial markets and their growth, is the so-called leveraged investment. Leveraged investments have direct impact on the amount of all created swell-money (slip of paper money). A leveraged investment means purchases paid partly capital-owned and partly on credit. The investment is partly paid with already existing money and partly with new debt, new swell-money, with new slips of paper. Usually the investor first has to obtain swell-money of a kind being accepted broadly from market participants. This could be, for instance, commercial-bank-money. To get the necessary swell-money, the investor will produce an obligation, for instance a credit contract (which is nothing but the investor's own swell-money). The commercial-bank-money is purchased with this newly created obligation. One could say the required type of swell-money is borrowed with newly created investor's swell-money handed over to the lending commercial bank as a security. The investor calculates as follows: the sum total of all returns from the investment plus the return when re-purchasing the investment is more than one has to pay to service the credit. All benefits resulting from the investment should be more than the volume of the credit plus interest charged. If, for instance, one intends to purchase a house but does not have enough capital, one has to transfer a part of the payment into the future. If there are 200'000 US Dollar lacking, one has to make a promise on this money to be paid in the future. 200'000 US Dollar swell-money has to be created by the investor. Usually this swell-money – the investor's promise of a payment in the future – is not accepted broadly as a means of payment. That is why it has to be exchanged against commercial-bank-money which is usually accepted broadly in the markets. Everybody accepts a payment via bank transfer. The exchange of slips of paper one typically calls "borrowing" or "to take out a loan". In fact, both parts of this transaction are taking out a loan. Both parts borrow slips of paper. Both parts lend slips of paper. It is in fact the exchange of two slips of paper. The commercial bank charges an interest for accepting the transaction. It lends its own slips of paper – self-made promises on money; it is not money, it is swell-money. More precisely: the commercial bank sells its self-made debentures. It is the bank's own slip of paper money that has been created from nothing. In the same way the investor signs the credit agreement, where he is the debtor – meaning, he is creating his own investor's slip of paper money from nothing. In those societies, which finance their social framework following the funding principle, there is a higher degree of leveraged business. There is a higher volume of swell-money.

Again, as it was in the aftermath of 1918, the world's economies found themselves in a situation of growth, leading again to a "wealth illusion". It was the illusion of a permanent rise in value. At the same time especially the members of the capitalism block were urged to take care to provide for financial security in times of unemployment or retirement by themselves. Yet, another time a considerable part of all investments were made in Europe. There was a build up of real properties as one side of the medal and the build up of financial assets on the other side, but the latter means the build up of debt. With respect to leveraged investments, one should mention that the overall economic system could stay at a comparatively stable state if the sum total of all benefits gained from a leveraged investment exceeds the sum total to service the debt. The economic system could stay robust as long as the interest charged to accept promises made to pay all debts in the future, is less than the profits gained. However, that is not enough to guarantee robustness. Why isn't it enough? There is the aspect of liquidity of slips of paper which could raise problems of stability. All debts – all money vouchers – do have duration. When a debt becomes due it has to be decided whether a so-called "roll-over" of the debt is needed or desired and whether this roll-over is accepted. The question is: will the owner of the debenture insist upon redemption of this voucher? Does the owner insist on getting what has been promised, or will he accept a new debenture which again would have a new duration date? This question is of significant importance and could raise problems, especially in case of leveraged investments. Most often, the asset one has invested in is geared to long-term profitability or amortization. For instance, usually when building or buying a house to live in, nobody likes to sell it if the credit becomes due when the first contracted credit period ends. Usually there is a need for roll-over credits – at least partly. At maturity not all of the credits should be called for redemption. The investor needs to get acceptance for new debentures from somebody else, not to be urged to re-purchase the investment. If in case of a roll-over of the credit the costs increase, it could be that the investment no longer will pay off. There will be some problems.

A fundamental historical development was of much greater importance for the situation of the world and the situation of the world financial system: the struggle concerning the "systemic question". Which kind of societal constitution is best? Which concept to organize the participation in society and markets and to get a share in the wealth and value added should come first? Which societal model should become the world-wide preferred principle, Capitalism, Social Market Economy or Communism? The systemic struggle has led even to partially malicious proxy-wars like in Korea and Vietnam. These proxy-wars entailed permanently rising national debt of those Nations supporting the warring parties. This indebtedness should in addition be seen as corresponding to leveraged investments with a negative return and negative value because in a war typically there is destruction and devastation. Productive properties are not built up. They are bombed and destroyed. As a result, these governmental leverage businesses will yield a loss. At the same time the savings ratio in the economy was not increasing. In consequence, the credits to the state could not be granted by lending saved capital to the Government. Instead of saving capital the market participants had made investments by themselves expecting attractive profits. It is a big problem if there is no new real property at the outcome of new national debts. There is no possibility to gain returns without having real properties or production capacities to create a real added value.

There is a further aspect to be considered. The European economies, and especially Germany, were re-constructed with the latest state-of-the-art technology that was supported by the amply, but not entirely unselfish, Marshall-Plan. In the following years the export champion USA turned into the world's import champion. Both developments that have been outlined here led to a turn around situation of all the world's debt positions. Over the years the biggest creditor of the world, USA, turned into the biggest debtor of the world.

Yesterday (1973-1999)

At the end of World War II the Allied Nations agreed on a meeting in Bretton Woods, New Hampshire, USA on a monetary order, with the United States Dollar as the reserve currency of the world. The United States were committed to convert Dollars to gold on request. The United States guaranteed the backing of Dollars with gold. As long as the national debt of the United States, as long as these promises on money were backed with gold, those slips of paper from the USA were mostly accepted. The more this money bubble inflated, the more its relation to all gold on deposit of the American Central Bank gets worse, the more doubts arise whether this money is of real value. Could one trust that money will be redeemed in gold on request? Will there be positive developments in the United States in order that the growing deficit in foreign trade will turn into a surplus trade balance? Finally it became obvious that "state-of-the-art" technology and advanced equipment provides the most efficient and thus highly competitive production of goods and services. This was the basis in Europe and especially in Germany as it has been used to re-construct the production capacities after the war. The older manufacturing methods and techniques used in the United States had become almost obsolete. All in all, countries like Germany or France started to demand the payment of their trade balance surpluses in gold. This raised problems for the monetary system of the United States, and their potentiality to create slip of paper money was slowly but surely reduced because of the backing on gold. It resulted in a flight out of money into gold by the trade partners of the United States. The European partners started to hoard gold. A situation quite similar to the processes in 1929, where inside the United States there was a flight out of slip of paper money into gold. Differently from 1933, when President Roosevelt prohibited the private ownership of gold by legislation, the USA did not have a possibility of that kind to influence the behaviour of its European trade partners forty years later. They saw only one possibility for action which they chose. They terminated unilaterally their obligation as it had been negotiated and committed in the Bretton Wood agreement to convert Dollars to gold at request. The United States reneged on their promise to exchange Dollar slips against gold on request. As a result the Dollar slips were losing value and this money bubble burst. The monetary system turned from a system of money backed by gold into a system of fiat money. This has been the situation of the monetary system since 1973. It should be seen as a key to allow a further growing indebtedness in the USA and world-wide. Without backing, without the limitation of underlying scarce and precious resources limiting the potential to create money, the monetary basis – the Central-Bank-money stock as legal tender – could be increased if seen necessary. The limitation of gold was no longer a limiting factor for the amount of legal tender. Furthermore the fundamental basis of saved capital became legal tender and swell-money created from nothing and not backed with real value. Real properties, real added value became less important. All this opened the door to an explosion of leveraged investments such that the national debt far exceeded the total value of gold on deposit. Again, the strong necessity for economic growth was the result. If there is not enough growth the resulting added value gap had to be filled again with new governmental debt. The debt service on governmental debentures would fill this gap. Abolishing the gold backing of money was the first "trick" to fill the added value gap of the economy. With this trick the deficit spending of Nations to fill the gap through national debt was enhanced significantly. Hand in hand with the growing national debt goes the need for increasing tax revenues. An increasing amount of interest to be paid has to be covered with additional public revenues. If tax rates were kept constant, there was a necessity for economic growth to acquire these revenues. There was as strong request for growing economic performance. At least the taxable basis had to grow. When the necessary growth was not reached, higher indebtedness was the consequence. That is why incentives had to be set to motivate economic growth – and to expand the volume of leveraged investment. This implied the expansion of granting credits. It implied the creation of more and more swell-money. At that time the commonly accepted types of money were Central-Bank-money (as legal tender) and cheque money of commercial banks. Both, but mainly the creation of new commercial-bank-money, increased and became expanded. Each expansion of the overall amount of promises on money, which should be seen as a promise for the future added value, is also an increased potential for default. Especially the problem is if the total volume of swell-money grows faster than the total economic performance, the latter can be measured in terms of the Gross Domestic Product. The vulnerability of commercial banks was growing and the leverage they used was growing. Face to face with the potential to gain profit by owning debentures was also the growing potential of losses. To bear any occurring losses, enough equity was needed to avoid bankruptcy. Otherwise bankruptcy could result, as it happened 1974 to the German Herstatt-Bank. In response to this bank failure with its impacts to economy, a negotiation process to define minimal capital requirements for financial institutes had been started on an international level. The so called Basel Agreements approved after nearly 15 years in 1988. The so called Basel Accord, defining capital requirements, narrowed the potential of credit institutions to create swell-money. By setting these limitations, problems arose to reach the required economic growth, since less leveraged investments were possible. The necessity of growth of economic performance was resulting from the further growing national indebtedness. Now, the leverage potential of the commercial banks was limited. To enlarge the leverage potential again, the Basel committee worked on "refinements" to the capital requirements. This reform had been triggered in 1999, publishing the first proposal on the "Basel II-Accord". This framework for capital requirements has been activated already in some currency zones, enabling them to expand the potentiality to create money by choosing "innovative financial instruments" and "nifty constructions".

At the time Basel / Basel II came into effect, the creation of swell-money by the commercial banks is not only limited by the minimum required reserve ratio that takes care of liquidity. Now there are also requirements concerning the liability of a commercial bank in relation to their assets. That, which the commercial banks have purchased with their own produced swell-money, is analyzed and assessed. Commercial banks are purchasing various promises on money, e.g. those created by customers. Generally this is called "granting credits". For all promises on payment that are owned by the commercial banks, the so called risk of default is assessed. It means to estimate the risk, that a promise is not kept. The party that made the promise could be unable to fulfil it. If the debtor is not able to redeem the granted credit at maturity, the bank has to write off this receivable and there is a loss. If there is no other profit made that can compensate the loss, the result is a reduction of what is called equity. Basel / Basel II accord specifies minimum required equity in relation to the total sum of all risks of default. These requirements have been internationally agreed upon and already transferred for example into European law. However, it has not yet been transferred into law in the United States. Legislation specified that commercial banks must have enough available equity to cover at least some percentage of its risk evaluated assets. Leverage business can be enhanced providing commercial banks have higher equity. Basel II does not regulate for example how profits should be used, this however is a weakness. Fulfilling the minimum capital requirements exactly, does not allow the commercial bank to cover any losses. As soon a loss occurs and no profit is made to compensate it, the equity is decreasing and thus the required ratio is not fulfilled anymore. Compliance requires asset and liability reduction. In consequence, this commercial bank has to reduce its overall business. Exactly that happened during the crises in 2008 and should be seen as a reason why commercial banks have restricted the volume of credits granted. Thus it would be reasonable to modify the existing set of rules of Basel II and the corresponding national legislation by adding another requirement: in "plenteous times" commercial banks are gaining profits. They should not be allowed to distribute the complete profit as a dividend to all its owners. A reasonable part of the profit should be retained to enhance the equity. This would lead to some additional equity exceeding the minimum required capital. It would allow an amount of additional losses that could be covered, whilst still maintaining the level of minimum capital required.

Much more important than those agreements of Basel II are the accounting rules of international accounting standards that have been developed within the same historical context. Already in the year 1991 these accounting guidelines concerning "financial instruments" had to be considered when publishing balance sheets. The "fair value principle" gave the companies a possibility, to evaluate the assets by their market value instead of their procurement or production costs (depreciated historical costs / amortised costs). The assets were permitted to be assessed for a price that similar objects have been traded at in the markets. The question is simply not asked, whether such a price could really be achieved if the asset is offered on the market. That means a much smaller amount of product seen as equivalent or comparable to an asset owned, and the given demand for such product on the market, defines the value given to quite a large number of assets. A currently observable supply and demand determines the value of a much larger possible supply of these products. Without being offered, without taking care whether demand would be there if offered, this value is attached to the asset. To say it clearly, the fair value accounting ignores a fundamental economic principle which is prevailing in all economic theories: »The equilibrium price on the markets is determined by balancing supply and demand. If the demand keeps constant or is decreasing and the supply is increasing a decrease of prices would be the result. An increase of prices will result only if supply stays constant or decreases and demand increases«. To summarize there is an enormous risk by choosing fair value accounting. This risk is especially present if the total volume of all assessed assets at their fair value in relation to all actually traded assets that are seen as similar is large. There is a "wealth illusion" which could lead to an enormous expansion of the potential to create swell-money.

Where the social balancing act followed the funding principle the capital stock consisted (and consists) of leveraged investments. In addition there are large private properties owned individually. This leads to a vicious circle. The intention of the systems based upon the funding principle is to yield sufficient earnings regularly from the built up capital stock. Over the past decades the capital stock has become slowly dominated by debentures of the public authorities. The interest to be paid should be financed by taxes. In consequence those capital based systems are turning into pay-as-you-go financing systems but are not so named. This is an "illusion of capitalism". Tax revenues are decreasing the more value added is lost in the struggle for prosperity between all nations; the struggle for jobs and components of the taxable base. Loosing value added puts the national budgets under pressure and consequently the indebtedness will be high. If a Nation is neither able or willing to increase tax rates or other forms of national revenues, nor willing or able to decrease the expenditures, can the indebtedness be reduced only if the taxable value added is increasing.

8. Limits of Money: About Leverage and Legerdemain

A magic mantle did I but possess,
Abroad to waft me as on viewless wings,
I'd prize it far beyond the costliest dress,
Nor would I change it for the robe of kings.
Faust I, Johann Wolfgang von Goethe

The Shy Wizard of Money;
Fed's Enigmatic Greenspan Moves easily in His Own World
The Washington Post, March 24, 1997, John M. Berry

Alan Greenspan, Wizard or Villain?
Business Week, June 28, 2005, Christopher Farrell

How to Become A Wall Street Wizard At Home
Forbes.com, September 09, 2009, Emily Lambert

Is there anybody who, as a child, did not have at least once the wish to become a wizard or a magician? Being a wizard one could conjure up money so that the family could always live in prosperity. What happened if one talked about this career aspiration? Parents, aunts and uncles answered the idea with a gentle smile. There was simply not enough knowledge about the job of a Central Banker and the occupational image of investment bankers. Or those we talked to about our wish to be able to conjure up money were not familiar with what hedge funds are doing.

Those funds have invented long-short strategies around the year 1950. Long-short strategies are leveraged investments of a very special kind. To start with, something is sold one does neither have nor own. The return from this sale is used to purchase something that hopefully gains some profit. This profit is needed to buy what one has to settle because it has been sold before - although one did not have it at that time. What is the most important point of this long-short strategy? Answer: the "trick" should work. What evaluates the attractiveness of a leveraged investment? Or turn this question the other way round: when will it be notably worse to make an investment by creating the needed money from nothing? The answer is: the lesser the cost to create new money for the investment, the more attractive it is. If there would be the opportunity to make any purchase by deferring the owed price to be paid indefinitely and no interest will be charged for accepting these credits, all investments would be attractive. The newly created swell-money would cost nothing. As long as everybody would accept my newly created slip of paper, there would be no limitation to leveraged investments gaining profit or benefits. Thus there are two aspects determining the attractiveness and extent of leveraged investments: (1) the interest to be paid to gain acceptance of the newly created money and (2) the total volume that could be created. Precisely these two aspects (interest rate and volume) are in the focus of laws and conditions set to or by the world financial system. Monetary policy and monetary measures of the Central Banks are aimed to affect these values. They define requirements limiting possible volumes. The set restrictions will be influenced and attenuated by potentialities of circumvention resulting from systemic lacking, as Jesse Eisinger pointed out in The International Herald Tribune, 2010: »The regulatory overhaul of the U.S. financial system that passed last summer scored a big victory: It barred investment banks from wagering with their own capital. Some cynics expect Wall Street to find a way around these rules. By "some", I conservatively estimate 99 percent of people who do not work on Wall Street and 100 percent of those who do«. In consequence the values depend and result on faith and distrust, greed, speculations and there could be stupidity as well. All these aspects impact on the limitation and attractiveness of leveraged investments and leveraged businesses. Let's have a look at an "ordinary" player. What is the situation, for instance, of the "Joe Bloggs" family that wants to build a new house? (We do not discuss aspects as – for instance – operating expenses, hire charges eventually given, property value growth or decline, inflation etc. We do not consider these aspects here in order to simplify matters.) Conceivably all that is necessary to build the house could be purchased on tick. Any kind of work that has to be done by the craftsmen (bricklayer, painter, carpenter, floor tiler, roofer etc.) could be paid, for instance, by monthly equal instalments over a period of thirty years – and we will assume – without charging interest. In this case all companies or contractors would agree to put the payment on the slate. All swell-money created by the family would be accepted without any additional costs. Money created from nothing would be free of charge. Actually there are trading platforms – so-called barter platforms – that work on this principle, and the exchange of goods and services is built on mutual trust and confidence. Everybody participating and selling goods or services has confidence to receive a return in a reasonable period of time. They all trust in those making promises on return services to be kept in a not too distant future. Those promises for rendering a return are – in principle – nothing but debentures and thus swell-money, interest-free.

There is only one critical aspect: the question of acceptance. Will all suppliers and sub-contractors accept the swell-money of our above mentioned family? Will it be accepted as a reward for all settled goods and services? If this question is answered with "yes" there could be an additional "but". There could be a further question: what are the conditions to gain this acceptance? Or to formulate it differently: what is the interest that has to be paid to the owner of my newly created swell-money so that he will accept it as a means of payment?

Three different criteria to "rate" the swell-money have to be posed:

(1) Solvency: This reflects the credit-worthiness of the issuer of the swell-money. To what degree one feels confident that the debt, "securitized" by the swell-money, will be paid in the future?
(2) Liquidity: Will there be a broad willingness of market participants to accept the swell-money as a payment instrument? The more participants are willing to accept the swell-money, the higher the level of liquidity provided by it. To evaluate swell-money with the highest level of liquidity possible, it would be enough to know at least one market participant (for instance the Central Bank) that would guarantee an exchange against legal tender. Legal tender has the highest level of liquidity attached to it. If one could always get legal tender in exchange for a swell-money, this swell-money could be seen as "as good as" legal tender. The swell-money's liquidity could be seen as "as good as" Central-Bank-money's liquidity.
(3) Supply and Demand (value): This is the most complicated issue. It concerns the assessment of the swell-money's value. It is the question: if the swell-money is used as a medium of exchange what could I get for it considering all markets? To explain this difficult question roughly, the following examples are given.

As a first example we contemplate the Central-Bank-money supply. The more Central-Bank-money that is in circulation, the more I will request in exchange against goods or services (assuming a constant level of goods and services being produced). The Central-Bank-money is losing value if its total amount in circulation is growing. One should say a little bit more precisely: if other factors, like payment behaviour (velocity of circulation), are not varying and the Central-Bank-money supply grows in relation to the overall volume of all goods and services offered and in demand on the markets, the value attached to Central-Bank-money is decreasing. As said, one talks about inflation (cf. Chapter 2). The process of inflation can lead to a galloping inflation and hyper inflation if Central-Bank-money proliferates unbridled. Central-Bank-money could lose its value completely. The opposite process could happen if the volume of Central-Bank-money in circulation is decreasing, if the Central-Bank-money, that is actively available in the markets, is restricted or even shrinking. With increasing scarcity its value rises; Central-Bank-money will be much valued. This results in a competition to obtain the scarce Central-Bank-money as property. There will be a growing willingness to give more for it in exchange; paying more goods or services to purchase Central-Bank-money. The price level denominated in units of Central-Bank-money will decrease. The result is deflation. The value of (Central Bank) money rises since the valuation of money depends on how badly the money is needed on the markets for commodities of any kind.

The impact of money scarcity, or rather the scarcity of a special kind of swell-money, was experienced for instance in the year 2008. There was an extreme price rally at the stock exchange, related to the swell-money "VW share". The shares of the company VW (Volkswagen) suddenly became scarce. The supply of VW shares offered at the exchange was suddenly desperately low. Beforehand there were a lot of so-called short sales: market participants had made promises on VW shares. They were obliged to settle this specific swell-money VW share at a later point in time. When they sold these VW shares short, they did not own them. That is why those short in VW shares were urged to purchase VW shares when their promise to settle had become due. At that time the owners of VW shares, the owners of this special swell-money were not willing to sell against "reasonable" quotations. There was an urgent demand but a reluctant supply. At that time the share quotes had soared. The price of VW shares quadrupled to more than 1'000 Euros. This example illustrates the value risk of swell-money for those who created the swell-money. If the total amount of promises made to settle whatever properties is comparably high in relation to the availability of those properties, it could be very expensive to redeem the promises. The ratio between a special property and the amount of promises for settling these properties is important and this aspect has to be considered when assessing the value of money and the value of any kind of swell-money, too. We emphasize: in principle each short sale is a credit, and also the other way round, each credit is a short sale. Here the aspect of time is most important. Banking business is business with promises on money under the aspect of time. Banks being aware of this special characteristic of their business, considering and reckoning points and periods of time, banks overlooking dynamic horizons, could expect a better future.

As said, in principle swell-money is a short sale. That means swell-money is a contract of the following kind: I get something today and make the promise to deliver well-defined commodities at a later point in time (or at some later points in time). Before accepting this contract the contracting party that has to deliver now, will pre-estimate the following risks:

Will the other contracting party, that has to deliver in the future, fulfil the contract (aspect of solvency)?

Will it be possible to re-sell the contract if necessary or intended? Will there be a willingness of others to adopt the contract if one does not want or is not able to wait until it will become due (aspect of liquidity)?

Which value performance is expected for what one will get in the future (aspect of value)?

These are the aspects determining the interest one would charge to accept the contract. A higher interest will be charged, to reward a higher level of uncertainty that the contract will be fulfilled. It will be higher if the expected potential to re-sell the contract without a loss before its maturity is less. It will be higher the less value one attaches to what one will get at a later point in time. Commercial banks granting credits analyze and determine exactly these parameters. Based on their assessments they will fix the interest to be charged for granting a credit. The commercial bank will scrutinize the credit worthiness of its customer and will estimate the future process of inflation. Those two aspects were all to be considered when credit institutions hold the credit contracts until maturity. Meanwhile this cannot be seen as a norm. Credit contracts will quite often be re-sold before maturity. That is why those granting credits have to assess how easy it will be to re-sell the contract without losses but hopefully even gaining a profit. It could be the need to sell a credit contract to obtain legal tender as payment in the case that legal tender is urgently needed because of a liquidity problem.

Now we contemplate the interaction between customer and the credit granting bank from the customer's perspective. Does the customer usually assess the solvency of the bank? Does the customer assess the level of liquidity to be seen to be attached to the bank debenture he will get? Does the customer estimate the value performance of the account balance (a special kind of bank debenture) – whether this swell-money owned can be used to get something of value that is of use in the future in the same amount than today? Usually this due diligence is not performed by the customer. Why is there trust in the swell-money of commercial banks? Why is there faith in the commercial-bank-money, for instance the money kept on a cheque account? Legislation by rules and regulations provides some safeguarding, concerning solvency and liquidity at the commercial banks. Concerning the solvency there are so-called capital requirements. The commercial banks are required not to fall below a fixed capital ratio. They have to provide a certain percentage on liable equity or "innovative equity instruments" in relation to all their (risk-weighted) assets. The leverage businesses of banks are affected through these requirements. Banks buy swell-money from their customers and paying it with swell-money produced by themselves. This is leverage business, since the customer's swell-money is purchased on tick. The overall leverage is limited by the ratio of liable capital against total assets. The overall leverage cannot be more than this ratio. There is also some regulation and legislation concerning the aspect of liquidity. It is important to mention that all swell-money created from commercial banks is interpreted as debentures to be settled with Central-Bank-money. That is why credit institutions are obliged to have always at least a certain percentage of Central-Bank-money against all their liabilities at their disposal. The ratio depends on the liabilities' time horizon (transactional accounts; cheque accounts; demand accounts: mature daily; money market deposit accounts: mature after 24 hours; savings accounts depending on their concrete specifications mature for instance after three months). There are quite a number of different specifications. A small percentage on Central-Bank-money (or swell-money that could be immediately exchanged against Central-Bank-money when needed) against all these liabilities has to be held under deposit (the so-called minimum required reserve ratio). Capital requirements and minimum reserve requirements are set by legislation. Both criteria are limiting the commercial bank's potentiality of leveraged businesses.

"Joe Bloggs'" family in our example that likes to build a house has the problem that its own created slips of paper are not broadly accepted. The swell-money they create by themselves is not broadly to be seen as good as money – actually there are stores offering goods payable on credit but to pay on credit is not usual for services rendered by craftsman. That is why our family needs to find somebody who accepts its swell-money in exchange for money or swell-money that has broad acceptance. Swell-money of broad acceptance is for instance the swell-money of commercial banks. This swell-money could e.g. be a positive account balance. This money on account is nothing but swell-money - but it is commercial-bank-money. It is a credit that was granted to the commercial bank from their customer. It is a promise on Central-Bank-money; a promise on legal tender to be redeemed upon the customer's request. If the customer really needs Central-Bank-money he can call for redemption.

That is why banks have and are obliged to have at least a small minimum reserve of Central-Bank-money at their disposal. As long as customers make their payments via bank transfers and those transfers are from account to account within a connected banking group there is no Central-Bank-money necessary. It is only the Commercial-bank-money that flows from account to account. It is only the Commercial Bank's obligation that moves from one customer to another. Accepting the customer's swell-money in exchange to own created swell-money is a leveraged business of the commercial bank. On the asset side there is a swell-money of the customer with a higher interest rate than the liability with a lower interest rate on the other side (the commercial bank's liability is newly created swell-money owned as an asset by the customer). From the commercial bank's point of view it obtains a credit to buy the customer's promise on payment. Thus the leverage business is the transformation of solvency, liquidity and supply / demand (value) attached to both involved types of swell-money (promises on payment). This business is of the utmost attractiveness, if the commercial bank can manage to source out the risk contained in this transformation which is the possible default of the customer swell-money. This succeeds if, for example, the risk is sold at a price which is less than the interest margin. What one has to pay to source out the risk should not be more than the difference between the interest paid by the customer and the interest to be paid to the owners of the commercial bank's swell-money. That is where so-called innovative financial products enter the game. These are nothing but special slips of paper securitizing the transformation risk. Let's give an example. A special derivative is a so-called Credit Default Swap (CDS): a promise on money equalling the amount of another promise on money (a credit). The promises on money securitized by the Credit Default Swap only becomes due if the referenced promise on money (the credit) is not kept. Otherwise the swap loses its value. Only if the credit defaults, the issuer of the Credit Default Swap has to redeem the credit instead. The commercial bank intending to insure against a credit default (the insolvency of the customer's swell-money) needs to find another institution willing to emit a Credit Default Swap slip referencing the customer's swell-money. To take out this insurance means to buy the Credit Default Swap and pay for it.

Now we like to discuss the impact of a return on equity target (RoE target, for instance stipulated by the commercial bank owners) on the overall volume of leverage business. First of all we have to clarify the term "equity". What is "equity"? Answer: in principle equity of a company is all that remains available as assets if all liabilities have been redeemed. If I, for example, own 10 Euros in cash and owe 8 Euros, my equity is 2 Euros (10 Euros minus 8 Euros). How does a company get equity? How does it come into the company's book? Corporations could emit shares. Those purchasing the shares own a part of the corporation. What is paid for will be an asset of the corporation. On the liability side of the corporation's balance sheet there is the total shareholder's equity as a special liability of the corporation against its owners. Equity is always the sum total of all assets (the balance sheet total) minus all liabilities (on the liability side) that are not specified as equity – debentures, short term credits and all other liabilities which are not classified as equity. Equity is growing if some profits the corporation makes are retained and not distributed to the shareholder. Those profits expand the asset side of a balance sheet. In consequence the difference between all assets and all liabilities will increase. What does a return on equity target mean? It stipulates that an annual profit should be at least the specified percentage to the value of all equities. How are commercial banks gaining profits? Their main business is to make promises on money, meaning to accept obligations to settle money in the future. They create commercial bank swell-money. This is used to buy promises on money, to buy customer swell-money upon which the customers have to pay more interest than the commercial bank is paying on their own swell-money.

What is the leverage that a commercial bank has to achieve, striving for a return on equity of for example 25 %? The leverage depends on the interest margin as the difference between interest yields on customer swell-money (paid by the customers) and interest on own swell-money (to be paid by the bank). The leverage needs to be at least 25 % divided by this interest margin. (We simplify our contemplation since in reality also all operational costs have to be considered.) Whatsoever, if there is, for example, an equity of 1 Billion Euros and a return on equity target of 25 %, the total volume of leveraged business should gain a profit of at least 250 Million Euros (25 % of 1 Billion Euros). Let us assume the commercial bank pays an interest of 3 % on their own swell-money, which could be savings accounts as an example. If they buy (with their own swell-money) customer swell-money with an interest rate of 4 % (charging 4 % interest to granted credits), they gain an interest margin of 1 %. In consequence, to gain a profit of 250 Million Euros the total volume of leveraged business should be 25 Billion Euros (1 % of 25'000'000'000 = 250'000'000). The commercial bank has to accept at least an amount of 25 Billion Euros customer swell-money and simultaneously, 25 Billion Euros of commercial bank swell-money has to be created and "lend" to the customer. This provides the stipulated return on equity; a fifty-fold of swell-money in relation to the equity has to be created in this economy. One half of it is customer swell-money, the other half of it commercial bank swell-money. Whether gaining this return contains high risks for the bank depends on whether the transfer risks, attached to those leveraged businesses, are successfully outsourced or whether the risks remain at the commercial bank.

The total global volume of debt in the year 2000 was 100'000 Billion US-Dollar. At that time it was the three-fold of the global Gross Domestic Product. In the short period from 2001 to 2007 new issued debentures catapulted the world's indebtedness with further 100'000 Billion US-Dollar up to an amount of 200'000 Billion US-Dollar - doubling the world's indebtedness! In a rough estimation that means, without an increase of equity the banking sector's leverage would have doubled as well. Considering the limitation of leverage as described above, a doubling of equity should have happened to keep the leverage ratio in these years constant. We assume this increase of equity but an open question still remains: Where did this equity came from? Which part of it had come from nowhere (tumbling out of the future by using fair value accounting) and is there even another part drawn from the companies by distributing it to the owners? We have to think about these issues to get an idea of what could have happened.

Does a crash burn or abolish money?

If there is a share market crash and a downward spiral of share prices, newspaper headlines will look like »billions of values are wiped out«. Quite often you can read that »MONEY HAS BEEN BURNT«. Is this really the truth? Does money disappear if there is a crash at the stock exchange? Or, is the real deep truth: no money disappears but has been redistributed. Are losses suffered by the losers the profits made by the winners? We will give short answers to these and similar questions. The key to unriddle the enigmatic world financial system house of cards a little bit further lies in the understanding of tangled up intricacies of indebtedness and illusions of wealth. Further growing indebtedness leads to illusions of wealth. Illusions of wealth drive the society in further growing indebtedness. "Living on tick" can be masked by the illusion of wealth for a while. Society and most of its members live beyond their means but they are not aware of this as long as everybody is addicted to this illusion or accepts it as a truth. It is the future being consumed in times of wealth illusion. Hoped for profits are distributed, feeling certain that the needed growth of value added will be reached since there is so deep a desire.

The magic trick is to create the illusion projecting the desired future values into the present. Not yet existing values or assets were taken to the books and handled as if they were real. That is the way the society assumed itself to be richer at present. At least those who do not know that it is a magic trick and how it is performed consider it as the truth. At the end the exciting question will be: who holds real values and who holds nothing else than empty promises of the times ahead? Irrecoverable claims, securitized by slips of paper swell-money, are becoming worthless.

Promises are turning out to be worth nothing. We describe the principle modus-operandi and will explain some of magic tricks performed within the world financial system. We chose a small example, simplifying the reality. Any similarity to really existing financial institutions, corporations or other market participants would be purely coincidental. We are not at all alleging that some players in the world financial system game have acted intentionally and consciously or with malice aforethought in the described way. It is our firm conviction that lack of rules and structures of the system that should be seen as wrong or problematic could result in such a situation. Even the actors – our conjurers – could not be aware of the occurring consequences. Magic and enchantment emanates from systemic gaps, non conformity and weakness.

Added value tumbling back from the future

Let us assume that in our fictive example there are two asset managers. Two so-called institutional investors having money at their disposal that they intend to invest. We suppose they have Central-Bank-money, they possess actual legal tender and no promises on money and no swell-money. Those two investors are our famous magicians and illusionists. Let us call them Siegfried and Roy. Siegfried and Roy both incorporate their own banks – credit institutions. They capitalize each institution with 5 Billion Euros. The banks start with equity of 5 Billion Euros. In our example this equity consists of Central-Bank-money paid in. Siegfried and Roy purchased with their legal tender at their disposal 5 Billion Euros worth of shares each (with a face amount of 1 Euro per share). Both banks now have 5 Billion Euros of Central-Bank-money at their disposal. Each share is a claim on a five-billionth part of the bank. It is a fractional claim on all the bank's remaining assets after settlement of all liabilities. Since initially the bank does not have any liabilities, each share represents a claim on a value of 1 Euro. The price Siegfried and Roy have to pay for each share with the face value of 1 Euro should be 1 Euro as well. Until now there is absolutely no value added. What are both banks in our example now doing?

> **Remark:**
>
> We'd like to clarify that we only want to illustrate principle effects. Those transactions and dealings described could, at least partially, in the global frame of the world financial system only be performed by the "interposition" of "vehicles for special purposes".
>
> A network of interacting market participants – even not knowing each other because of the anonymity in the capital market – could perform these transactions implicitly.

Both banks grant credits to one another – inter-bank credits. Siegfried's bank is granting a credit to Roy's bank; let us say amounting to 10 Billion Euros. Vice versa, Roy's bank is granting a credit with the same amount of 10 Billion Euros to Siegfried's bank. Roy's bank now owns debentures of Siegfried's bank valuing 10 Billion Euros; Roy's bank has liabilities with the same amount of 10 Billion Euros. The balance sheet of Siegfried's bank looks quite similar: 10 Billion Euros debentures of Roy's bank as assets and 10 Billion Euros as liabilities. For simplification we assume an interest level in the markets of 10 %. The interest payments, that both banks have to make on their debentures, are 10 % of the amount annually. Neither of the banks will make a profit since they have each 10 % interest payments as earnings but as well expenditures of 10 % interest to be paid.

"Drum-roll": now the magic trick is performed! Changes of

the economic situation should help us in the following way: we assume a low or decreasing inflation and the trend of increasing unemployment. An economic situation as it has been for instance in the year 2001. At that time the "New Economy" bubble had burst. The economy was in a downward trend, recession was seen on the horizon. In such a situation the Central Banks could make the decision to give a growth impulse via monetary measures. That was done in 2001. The Central Banks considered that the easy-money politics is necessary to stimulate economies. They lowered the Central Bank's key interest rates. In consequence the whole interest level in the markets was declining. The easy-money politics followed was intended to ease the borrowing of money, as one says. (It can't be emphasized enough: interest is not paid on borrowed money. Interest is paid for granted credits. With easy-money politics not the borrowing of money will be cheaper but the price to be paid for accepting a promise on money.) It should be easier and cheaper to obtain a credit for leveraged investment. We will assume that soon the interest rates on debentures are not 10 % anymore but 5 %. Credits are cheaper now, less interest is necessary on newly created swell-money. How are the banks of Siegfried and Roy affected? Both banks have debentures as their assets. All these debentures have an interest of 10 % attached and an assumed credit period of twenty years.

Let us consider now the whole cash-flow of the debentures and name this total cash-flow the debenture's "future value". The debenture's future value is its redemption amount (10 Billion Euros) plus all interest to be paid annually until maturity. (This simple calculation is used to support easier comprehension. Following the current IAS 39 standardization – the International Accounting Standard for the valuation of financial assets and liabilities – the value of the debentures as assets would be measured "mark-to-market". On the liabilities' side of the balance sheet they could be accounted at depreciated historical costs / amortized costs, if the fair value option has not been chosen.) The sum of the interest, being 10 % of the credit annually, will amount to 200 % after the twenty years of credit duration. That means a debenture with a credit amount of 10 Billion Euros would result in a future value of 30 Billion Euros. It is the redemption amount plus 200 % of interest being paid. One could say it in this way: if one Euro is invested in a debenture with a fixed rate of interest with annually ten cents interest to be paid and the duration is twenty years its future value amounts to three Euros. If now the standard interest rate is only 5 %, the future value of an investment of one Euro to a debenture with a fixed rate of interest now 5 % a year and duration of 20 years is less – it is two Euros (one Euro redemption plus 20 times 5 % = 100 % interest). Let us formulate this again in a little different way: if I would like or wish to buy an asset with a maturity of 20 years, having a future value of 3 Euros, it will cost 1.50 Euros. That is because 100 % interest of 1.50 Euros is paid, which added together with the invested 1.50 Euros is exactly 3 Euros. Following this future value accounting, all the debentures the banks of Siegfried and Roy own as assets suddenly increased by 50 % "in their value". That is now the "fair value" of these debentures. Both banks gain a profit without any kind of further business. There is no business and no transaction involving money. There was absolutely no exchange of money. The profit those banks made is 50 % on all debentures of 10 Billion Euros they own. Both banks do have a book profit of 5 Billion Euros. They gain a return on equity of 100 % – since both banks have 5 Billion Euros of equity each. If these profits are released to the income statement, they can be distributed as dividends. We will assume both banks pay Siegfried and Roy half of the profit as dividends. Both, Siegfried and Roy will get 2.5 Billion Euros each. The dividend will be paid in cash from the legal tender at disposal. WOW! A 100 %-return on equity! That is what successful and capable corporations (and entrepreneurs) look like!

However, there are no real values being created. Neither has swell-money been created – in no form. There is no additional swell-money resulting from this magic trick. There is only the illusion that those promises on payment, made for the future, have been redeemed already today, but that is not the truth. All the promises on money made by the banks of Siegfried and Roy (their debentures) are unchanged. Neither the redemption amounts or the negotiated interest, nor all payment dates have been changed. Consequently this implies that there is no new (or some other) swell-money being created. Only additional promises on payments would represent new swell-money. There are no additional promises on payment made. Nobody made this kind of promises. All promises made by the banks of Siegfried and Roy will be the same as before. All those debentures made are promises on payments in the future of 10 Billion Euros, duration of twenty years and a fixed interest rate of annually 10 %. This swell-money keeps unchanged and no swell-money is added. One only pretends.

With a fair value accounting one assumes in the markets at the observed price level an unlimited demand for debentures that Siegfried and Roy have emitted, respectively that they own. The assumption is: whatever number of those debentures is offered on the market, there will always be enough buyers accepting the fair value price to be paid for these promises on money. Could this really safely be assumed? Could it objectively be expected if the economy is in a worse situation as in our example? Is in such a situation really a potential purchasing power resulting from so many saving that any tendered offering of debentures of Siegfried's and Roy's banks can and will be acquired? Reasonable doubts are in order!

It is nothing else than an illusion – an illusion of wealth. Non-existing Euros are tumbling down from the sky. More precisely one should say: there is added value tumbling back from the future! Added value that does not exist! It is hoped for value added. All that is tumbling back from the future just generates book profits at the banks of Siegfried and Roy. Those book profits constitute an additional liable equity – but the added value behind it does not exist. Without a miracle these profits will vanish because there will be losses in the future of an equal amount. Both banks pay each other only a redemption amount of 10 Billion Euros for all those debentures accounting with 15 Billion Euros in the books when they become due at maturity, after twenty years. Only the face amount of the debentures of 10 Billion Euros is paid back as negotiated, which is another part of this illusion.

To sustain the illusion we need a kind of miracle. What could this miracle be? Answer: there will be market participants cherishing the illusion and they will fall under the spell not being aware that it is a magic trick. How could this be managed? The key to enable the miracle to be performed lies in the reported profits and the pursuit of high yields. In terms of the reported values, the banks of Siegfried and Roy are obviously very successful. The economy is in a worse situation, interest rates and ordinary yields have declined but those two banks have gained high profits – not to say overwhelming profits. The return on equity is about 100 % and half of it has been distributed to the shareholders.

For sure everybody would like to own shares of such successful banks. At the stock exchange there is a tussle to obtain those shares offered for sale by Siegfried and Roy. We will assume that there are only 1.5 Billion shares offered by Siegfried and Roy in each case. Although only 1 Euro is written on that share slip of paper as a face value, they are now traded at 2 Euros. All buyers deluded by illusion and still under the spell believe in the continuation of the previous success story. They calculate as follows: if there is the same alluring dividend of fifty cents for each share the return on the invested capital will be 25 %. Considering the low interest level in the markets this is still highly attractive. Siegfried and Roy are now selling 1.5 Billion shares each at a price of 2 Euros. Their total revenue is about 3 Billion Euros each. They have already received 2.5 Billion Euros as a dividend payment. All their proceeds amount to about 5.5 Billion Euros each. Siegfried and Roy retrieved that which they invested plus a yield of 10 %. They yet own the majority of the shares. They are still the controlling shareholders of their banks. Those who have purchased their shares are, for example, pension funds or insurance companies or other "capital collecting institutions", that invest mainly in best-rated and profitable corporations to achieve high returns. Given a market value of 2 Euros for each share, the so-called market capitalization of both banks of Siegfried and Roy would have reached meanwhile a level of 10 Billion Euros – which started out initially being 5 Billion Euros. Even if Siegfried's and Roy's bank shares would have sold at 5 Euros it could almost be seen as bargains buy. These shares at 2 Euros would be a snip and it can be assumed that their market price will rise in the future, provided that the return on equity will always be 100 %. The illusion of wealth hits twice, because also the market value of the shares is nothing else than a fair value. It reflects an envisaged future, but all expectations already are based on an illusion.

How the rabbit pulls itself out of the hat

There is a modification of the described magic trick that could be performed by issuing new shares in a situation where an economy is not doing well, where the interest level is low. However a special segment of newly created debentures will be equipped with a higher interest rate. This is actually the trick:

Create new debentures with a higher interest and provide them as new funds for equity, purchasing "fresh shares"; buy on tick newly issued shares of those companies with currently a low share quotation.

We experienced this kind of situation at the end of 2008 and the beginning of 2009. Large corporations had to offer higher yields on so-called corporate bonds. These are credits that those companies like to obtain because they required liquidity. Also the banks had problems, since they experienced heavy book-losses due to market values of assets owned being heavily in decline. That is why those banks required urgently fresh funds as equity and also their share quotations were low. Let us play with the following thought experiment. One company, let us say Roy's company, creates swell-money, a corporate bond with 10 % interest. Roy's company gives this swell-money, let us say, to Siegfried's bank in exchange for newly issued shares. Siegfried's bank now has fresh funds as equity. These funds have been paid in as swell-money created from Roy's company. Roy's company holds shares of Siegfried's bank. If now the interest rate usually to be paid on corporate bonds tends to become adjusted and fall to the general low interest level currently in the markets, Siegfried's bank will again make a book profit as previously described. There is success and the equity base has been strengthened twice. This will undoubtedly have positive effects on the share quotation. The price to be paid to purchase a share of Siegfried's bank at the exchange will rise. This has a positive impact on Roy's company. Roy's company owns a share of Siegfried's bank and the fair value of this asset will rise. Roy's company will also make a book profit and is obviously very successful. Can we now allow ourselves to believe that markets a) have bottomed out, beginning to climb out of recession and b) finally made it?

Limits of Money

Any real values being created? No! Has there been any money created? No! There was a money flow. That is right. Money moved from pension funds and insurance companies to Siegfried and Roy. Nothing else happened. Both banks are what they have been before. Two institutes granting credits to each other and that is the only money that initially has been created – swell-money, promises on money. Nothing else! As a debt (liability in the balance sheet) this promise on money is right from the beginning accounted for with its redemption amount. As an asset the promise on money is accounted for at a value reflecting the desired future. This difference in accounting, results in a book profit. What is essentially a book profit? We explained book money as being a promise on money – swell-money. Somebody made the promise to settle money – however in the future. Swell-money is a liability of its issuer. Also swell-money is an asset of its owner. A book profit is also a promise. It is a promise on profit in the future; swell-profit which can be seen as similar to swell-money. A book profit has no corresponding entry on the liability side of any balance sheet as swell-money has. That is the difference. Whoever creates a book profit on the asset side of his balance sheet promises this profit to himself without accounting for it also as a liability. It is expected to realize the book profit in the future, from business with somebody not yet known. Book profit is a fictive debenture of an unknown debtor. One doesn't even know whether this debtor will ever exist. Thus a book profit is not really swell-money. It is only a swell-money illusion. One believes it exists but it doesn't. Nobody has made the obligation to make a corresponding payment or to settle a corresponding added value in the future. That is why it is absolutely open whether these payments will ever be made. A corresponding value added does not exist either. Whether there will ever be a value added in the future is open as well. A book profit is an illusion of value added until the added value is created. Nevertheless, it could be released to the income statement already today. The added value illusion – the profit one promises oneself in the future – can be distributed to the shareholder by using dedicated methods. Or it constitutes fresh liable equity at the banks of Siegfried and Roy. To repeat it again, this new liable equity has, nota bene, not yet really been gained. There is only the hope – veiled by using valid accounting standards – that it really will be gained at some time in the future. That is how profit or equity is created from nothing – tumbling back from the future. If we consider the potentiality of financial institutes to create swell-money we have learned that it depends on the amount of equity they have. Now it becomes obvious, why such book profits are of high attractiveness for those players in the markets. Rising equity increases the potentiality of creating swell-money to the multiple. There is a high risk attached when using this additional potentiality of an equity constituted by book profits. These playing cards in the world financial system house of cards are anything else than secure and stable – those cards are an illusion. They are a magic trick.

What is the situation of the banks of Siegfried and Roy now? They made big bucks, but only by book profits. They granted themselves a credit out of the future, but without making the promise for payment as debtor. That is what an accounted book profit is. These book profits extended the capital bases of the banks as liable equity, but in fact the corresponding returns have yet to be attained in the future from newly created added value to become an added value reality. Otherwise it will be inevitable that a loss of the same amount will occur. That could happen to anybody but not to Siegfried and Roy. Their banks or the banks' new shareholders have to cope with it. A reasonable part of shares is now owned by others – in our example these are pension funds and insurance companies. Siegfried and Roy have already feathered their nest. They lined their own pockets receiving more than their actual wager of 5 Billion Euros each. Half of it was taken out of the banks (2.5 Billion Euros distributed profit each). The other part and more they received from the sales return when selling enough of their initially owned shares (3 Billion Euros). They were paid by all those premium payers and savers buying the shares. There will be no actual loss for Siegfried and Roy. They have already got back more than they had staked. In case of a share market crash, if share quotations fall, those owning the shares would gain less when selling now, than they had originally paid for. Those pension funds and insurance companies experience losses but they gave their money already to Siegfried and Roy when they purchased the shares. In other words: there is no money disappearing, no money will be burnt. Money has moved! It is no longer at the pension funds and insurance companies. Siegfried and Roy have it now.

To avoid possible losses at the pension funds and the insurance companies, the banks of Siegfried and Roy are urged to attain further profits. Profits exceeding those anticipated book profits that have been distributed to Siegfried and Roy are required. These dividends were paid by taking credits out of the future. Somebody who is not yet known has to re-pay (the corresponding added value gap has to be filled by other attained profits or this risk has to be shifted to somebody else). Otherwise the banks and as the banks' shareholders, the pension funds and the insurance companies, will experience losses. Nevertheless, those that have to re-pay the credits out of the future are not yet determined. Maybe it will be the banks themselves, but perhaps it will be governments, bailing out those banks as "systemically important financial institutions" in case of trouble. To attain the required high profits the banks of Siegfried and Roy have to massively enlarge the total volume of their credit business. This means the total volume of all leveraged deals must be increased, irrespective in whatever field and shape. In consequence the banks could grant credits that finance investments: the building and purchasing of buildings, investments in shares, set up of new companies, mergers and acquisitions and whatsoever. For the banks to make enough additional profit, they need to leverage. It is not sufficient enough to only invest the undistributed profit of the past (which is 2.5 Billion Euros). As we stated, the interest level in the markets in our example has fallen to 5 %. To obtain at least what has been distributed to Siegfried and Roy (2.5 Billion Euros, each bank) all the available equity of 7.5 Billion Euros each, should gain a return of more that 33 %. Another ca. 67 % return is required on top of that in a period of twenty years to cover the amount of future money that has been transferred into the present. It has to back the credit taken out from the future (5 Billion Euros, each). In total, the banks would have to gain at least a return of 5 % annually for the next twenty years. This would recover the book profit, meaning to avoid a corresponding loss, but there would be no profit that could be distributed as a dividend at all. However, there will be a strong requirement for the investors to receive a dividend. A return above 5 % is thus a must. Those having capital at stake demand high yields. In each bank there is currently a capital of 6.5 Billion Euros at stake. After selling part of their shares, Siegfried and Roy still own shares denominated at 3.5 Billion Euros, each at stake. Those who purchased the shares of Siegfried and Roy paid 3 Billion Euros, each. Those investors expect and demand a return on equity that should be more than the average 5 % paid ordinarily on the markets. If they could not expect higher yields they would not have invested in company shares; they had better invested in "more secure" investments, for example treasury bonds. In consequence, the overall return on equity, on all equity as it is accounted in the books of Siegfried's and Roy's banks, has to be more than 5 % above the interest level of the markets that commonly is to be expected. That is why those banks have to take correspondingly higher risks. Alternatively to taking these high risks they can make leveraged investments. What does this mean? Answer: The bank creates new swell-money, for instance by emitting bank debentures like certificates of deposit, covered bonds like the German Pfandbrief or any other kind of "securitized" bank obligations. They raise their own indebtedness. They enter into further liabilities to enhance their business: granting credits or purchasing of other kinds of assets. As long as the interest that has to be paid on the bank's debt is below the interest earned from granting credits (respectively below the returns gained by the purchased assets), all these leveraged businesses and investments are attractive. The overall volume of leveraged businesses is limited. There is a leverage ratio on all accountable equity which limits all credits permitted to be granted. Nevertheless, the swell-money bubble is swelling. Credits will be granted in high volumes, for instance to purchase companies, to enhance and expand production capacities, to build or purchase buildings or other real estate. That is easier said than done. In order for the banks to realize all the needed leverage deals requires firstly enough debtors to be found, convinced, captured or persuaded. Further, all these deals have to fit required terms and conditions. There is some help to get this anything but easy job to blow up the overall leverage business to be done: the interest level on the market is comparably low. By inventing the most appropriate legal financial constructions and innovative financial products, it might be possible to get enough customers for instance to stimulate the building and real estate industries. If there is, in addition to that, the possibility and success to conjure up a money illusion, causing possible debtors to cherish the illusion of wealth, it would be more than helpful. There was a lot of creativity in the United States inventing "innovative accounting techniques" to assess the fair value of real estate. The invented "tricks" followed the pattern of the above described magic. A hoped for profit of a suspected and desired positive value performance has been projected from future to present. On these "present values" credits were granted, even credits for consumption (so-called mortgage equity withdrawal). An example of this innovative accounting is a hedonic valuing of real estate.

The hedonic accounting considers, for example, if there is a new shopping mall opened nearby an assessed house. The newly opened store was used as an argument that the "real", the inner value of the house, has increased. The store enhanced the quality of the house's environment and thus it is assumed that a higher price can be obtained if the house is sold. The expected (future) purchasing price attached to the house as its present value is now higher, leading to an increased wealth of its owner, and this higher value of the property can be used to back a newly granted credit – that even can be used for consumption.

The swell-money bubble has been growing. Indebtedness was rising, driven by the broadly cherished illusion of wealth. As long as all the market participants have the true believe that it is no illusion but reality and as long as only a few insist on payment in legal tender when credits become due, this upward spiral can work. Of central importance is: whenever a credit becomes due there will be somebody willing to grant a new credit; the credit can always be rolled-over if required. To get this willingness, the payment of at least all interest is a must. Otherwise the over-indebtedness of the system becomes obvious and transparent for all to see. As explained above, the growth of value added, all the growth of book values, is a must to pay interest or dividends exceeding the level of interest charged for generally in the market. Those high interests obtained are a must to cover already distributed and consumed profits withdrawn from the future. If this therefore required growth of value added – alternatively, respectively in addition, a growth of illusion – cannot be achieved, there is only one last resort: parts of the global Gross Domestic Product, the globally accomplished value added has to be re-allocated. For instance the total sum of all wages (measured in real purchasing power) could sink. The part of value added not allocated to wages anymore can instead then be used to pay interest for yields. The share of value added allocated to serve the yields to be paid, resulting from an always growing swell-money bubble, will be bigger and bigger. The share to pay wages does go down. This type of development can be evidenced by statistics for the past forty years.

Such a house of cards is likely to collapse if the illusion bursts and it becomes clear that not all the promises made will be kept. It could be even impossible to keep all promises. A chain reaction could be the result, as happened in the current world financial crisis beginning in the end of 2007. A number of possible triggers can be considered. Quite often the American Central Bank Federal Reserve (Fed) is mentioned as a trigger due to their scaling up the key interest rates. The swell-money bubble has grown in part through the granting of consumer credits. At the same time, emerging countries like China and India had increasing demand for goods and services. That is why inflation has been seen on the horizon. The consumer price index was rising. That is why Central Banks started to react against it by taking measures of monetary politics, not regarding an important conflict. Those measures aimed at reducing monetary stocks conflicted with the concomitant necessity to enlarge monetary stocks, in order to maintain the illusion of wealth. Only with the increase of swell-money could the necessary and demanded yields be attained. About the same time it became obvious in the real estate segment of the markets that one had falsely cherished an illusion of the wealth. The imputed market values assumed to reflect the real value of property were not achievable in reality. There was absolutely not enough purchasing power and real demand. Considering the rising interest level, it was not even possible to convince enough customers to be willing to take out new credits. The illusion could not be kept alive. It would not be possible to transfer the credits to a sufficient number of market participants. Apart from those indebted there were too many credits granted to members of the economically weak part of the society. There was no other way to further enlarge the indebtedness. The whole society had become over-indebted.

Who are the losers now? How much will be lost? How much money – and what kind of money – will disappear vanishing into thin air? The answer to those questions is: all promises that cannot be fulfilled could vanish. Values are not destroyed since they have not been there. There have only been promises to create added value in the future and these promises will not be fulfilled in total. It is the evaluation, the value assessment that declines. Bursting the illusion only affects such money which vanishes that has never been created. Only those promises on payments disappear that nobody made. Those promises have been taken for granted when accounting assets at their fair value, their future value, desired to be truly achievable. Now it depends on what one owns. What one will get or could get if a promise on money cannot be kept. In case of a mortgage credit the owner of this swell-money, the owner of the slip of paper being the credit contract, will get the mortgage instead of the payment. He will get for instance the building. Those owning unsecured and subordinated debt obligations will get nothing, if this "securitized" promise on money cannot be paid. What does one get when owning a share? There is absolutely no claim on payments being attached to a share. A share represents the ownership of a corresponding part of a corporation's equity, a part of all a company owns when all liabilities are re-paid, and there was only the illusion that the company's net-worth will be worth more. The question is now for which promises on money will there be a chance of fulfilment? Who are those debtors one could trust that they will (and can) keep their promises? Should the granting of credits be reduced at the same time promises on money will become due (it means, credits will mature), the house of cards will collapse. In such a situation only those having Central-Bank-money, having legal tender at their disposal, are able to pay their debt. All the other debtors need to find somebody prepared purchasing whatever assets first even if it is priced below par; alternatively they should be allowed to prolong their credit. The offered assets can only be purchased by those having Central-Bank-money at their disposal because those offering the assets need Central-Bank-money. It is not enough for them to be paid with swell-money; it is not enough to be paid with a promise on Central-Bank-money. They really need Central-Bank-money. Swell-money is losing its liquidity. Swell-money is no longer accepted as a means of payment.

Approaching the limits

Those patterns described came into full operation after the Millennium. What has happened? There were investors, especially big institutional asset managers like pension funds, being the majority owner of a lot of "global actors". Investors are majority owners of market relevant, mostly global active companies. They exert(ed) influence on corporate governance and the business strategy to be followed. They were keen on getting constantly a high and, whenever possible, growing return on all their capital at stake. Even all that part of equity resulting from book profits should gain such a high return. That is why all companies had to scale up their leverage. More and more they ran into debts to make investments on tick. Those loans were created by commercial banks from nothing, based upon equity those banks received from big institutional investors, pension funds and asset managing institutions. Also their equity was partly a result of fair value accounting. Equity which was drawn back from the future! Banks and corporations as well had to cope with an always growing leverage, to gain the requested return on all of their equity. Of course, the result was a growth of the world-wide Gross Domestic Product. The global production of goods and services was growing, but it was debt-ridden. The total amount of debt was growing faster than the total amount of the global Gross Domestic Product. At the same time the companies tried to get a growing share of the value added for themselves by taking over other companies. "Leveraged buy-outs", mergers and acquisitions financed by credits occurred in rising numbers. Not at least this resulted from the fact that the given and growing yield expectations and the wide-open added value gap was no longer sufficiently filled. All the purchasing power of the markets plus all the governmental new indebtedness, adding to the swell-money bubble for forty years, was not enough anymore to bridge the gap. For a short time, the creation of a new illusion of wealth by inventing the "New Economy" provided help. By this illusion asset flows were diverted, a re-distribution of assets took place at the stock exchange. Certainly even this process could not work unlimited. After some time it was perceived as what it is: an illusion! There was utterly not all the value added that would have been necessary to gain a real return on all paid-in equity, a return on all capital saved and a return on all supposed to have capital resulting from the illusion of wealth (fair value accounting). At that point in time the interest and yield level in the markets was comparatively high. Then there was the break-down of the New Economy, but also the horrible terror attack on 9/11/2001. Exchange markets were crashing, revenues and profits declined, partly the markets were collapsing. There was the concrete danger of rising unemployment. The evaluation of assets fell, the book value sank, and the slice of share prices posed severe problems especially on pension funds in the United States, since they hold large portions of shares in their managed asset portfolios. US Government and the American Federal Reserve Bank reacted to this situation by rigorously slashing the interest rates. The interest level of all newly created swell-money sank as a consequence. As a result, all debentures being owned by banks at that time, especially those debentures with long-term maturity and high interest, were rising in value because of the fair value accounting.

Those financial institutions suddenly made huge profits, book profits. Those profits were drawn back from the future. There was actually no chance at all, that all these profits will really be gained in the future from newly created added value. In line with those so-called Basel agreements, negotiated for the international world financial system at the Bank for International Settlements, they were allowed to be accounted as liable equity. And that was not all! Those book profits bear also the potential for (legal) tax circumvention. Clever and smart advisors to financial markets invented and implemented legal strategies transferring those book profits described, to be released as earnings assessable for tax in those countries, with the lowest duties. Here this added value tumbling back from the future has been taxed. Nobody knows whether and where the corresponding creation of value will happen. Nobody knows in which country this added value will actually be produced. There it should be taxed. Its where creation of value actually takes place, where the basis needed to produce an added value has to be financed via taxes. This basis is the Nation's commonwealth, all the publicly provided goods and services. The magic trick performed consists in paying the least taxes on value added that still has not been produced. A part of this self-promised future return transferred into the present was distributed as a dividend. Giving that double taxation agreements are in effect, those dividends distributed to another country were not taxed again on a corporate level. All book profits retained enhanced the companies' liable capital positively. The negative effect however was, that all the companies' shareholders, the owner of the banks, especially those having influence on the corporate strategy, requested to have the same return on this "fresh" capital as they required to get on all the other equity as well. Banks and especially global companies were compelled to further enlarge their leverage. Under this compulsion the banks increased their credit business heavily. Who could be granted credits? It was a big challenge and a necessity for the banks to find and attract new debtors. The sales departments were under heavy pressure, to enlarge the overall volume of leverage investments. Retail banking started to convince even those clients to become credit customers that until now had never been viewed as acceptable. The risks attached to those clients have been much too high. These sales efforts resulted in so-called Ninja-loans. Ninja, the abbreviation means no income, no job and no assets. It was obvious from the outset, that these customers receiving a Ninja-loan would never be able to service such a credit by self-created value added. The banks started to lure those clients with "innovative" offerings like so-called adjustable rate mortgages at extremely low interest rates. However, these low rates were not guaranteed for long. Periodically the interest charged is adjusted to the interest level commonly applied in the markets. The banks tried to outsource and spread the risks by inventing a huge amount of so-called innovative financial products.

As a result of all these efforts, the total sum of all debts worldwide was doubled within a short time period of seven years only. The total volume of debt added was 100'000 Billion Dollar (100 Trillion) in the years of 2001 till 2007. How should the interest ever be paid with real added value? How could all these credits ever be settled and serviced by additionally created added value. How should this essential huge overall volume of added value ever be produced to repay all the debt? Importantly, how long will all these slips of paper be accepted? How long will there be trust, that all these money vouchers, these promises on money, these debentures, this swell-money are repaid or rolled over into new debt, upon their due dates? It was just a question of time, before this gigantic swell-money bubble would release its disastrous and devastating effects. The most crucial factor lighting the fuse to the bomb was the rising liquidity in the added value market and the resulting inflation becoming apparent. The increase of interest rates in effect against inflation ushered in the collapse of the house of cards. The system was approaching its limits. Illusions have kept the system afloat for some time. Illusions were the magic glue which held together the imagination and belief that all the yield expectations will be fulfilled. The public administrations, meanwhile indebted up to their limits, but obligated to price stability, were suffering from the rising interest level. Even more the weakest participants and parts of the house of cards were damaged: those debtors with dodgy creditworthiness were not in the position to meet their debt service obligations. The Sub Prime Crisis in the market was emerging. Defaulting credits by ninjas caused a great stir when the world financial system touched down on the US-markets for those special mortgage loans. The limits had been breached. That was in the winter of 2006/2007.

9. Beyond the Limits: In the Aftermath of the World Financial Crisis 2008

When the music stops in terms of liquidity,
things will get complicated.
But as long as the music is playing,
you've got to get up and dance.
We're still dancing.

Chuck Prince, Citygroup, July 2007

In the current crisis of the world financial system, the world's societies' decisions will set the course of our future. Which future will we have? Which future could we have? Where will we be? To answer these questions, we first of all will explain the most important aspects of the current crisis. It is not our intention to discover who should be brand marked as a culprit of the current crisis of the world financial system and/or the world economy. We do not blemish all those winners of the crisis as con men, hustlers or grifters, and we do not allege that the patterns of operation are of Machiavellian style – it's quiet the opposite. We want to clarify and emphasize the most important systemic problems. Those systemic problems resulted from insufficient and inadequate rules and regulation on a global level. They resulted from disharmony between all Nations different regulations. Those acting in the markets are currently much too often tempted to do what's wrong. They even could be urged to do what's wrong, because the laws and provisions neither demand nor enforce what's right. Doing the right things is even sometimes punished in the markets.

To make this point clear, we will analyse the patterns of operation of the world financial crisis to be seen as problematic. Further we will illustrate an approach for effective political action. We do see a reform of the financial system together with the system of tax and duties, leading to a consistent, sustainable, established world financial system, as an essential component. This could be the key to follow a global path towards a "world in balance", if the required political negotiations and measures are taken simultaneously. If this path to a balanced world is not taken, we will have most probably a further intensifying of a drifting two-class society of haves and have-nots. This could even lead to a total collapse since such a global imbalance is no firm and resilient base for peace. Further we will describe those systemically given patterns of operation leading to winners and losers. We will give hints where the winners could be expected and who will or could be the losers of the world financial crisis.

US Pension Funds alone had to make value adjustments to their managed assets of ca. 2'000 Billion US-Dollar (2 Trillion) and this only happened in the first half of the year 2008. The accumulated write off we expect on all assets of the funds managed as separate assets (all assets that are under management from financial institutions, but not owned by them) is much higher. We expect worldwide at least the five to tenfold of it (5 – 10 Trillion Dollar). In comparison the 1'400 Billion US-Dollar that IMF (International Monetary Fund) expected as a required write off in the banking sector would almost be peanuts. In contrast, there will be those profiteers. A winner will be somebody, who exchanged swell-money owned against Central-Bank-money, Real Estate, commodities or other no-financial properties in the nick of time. The losers will only have securitized claims on money as assets.

If high indebted companies become insolvent and vanish, all jobs they had offered will vanish as well. Also the companies' liabilities will vanish. Those owning the companies liabilities as assets, will in such a case attempt anything to get a grip on something valuable, if there is anything. Values write off at pension funds or insurances will hurt the future purchasing power of those, who own policies or fund shares.

Why do we find ourselves in this situation? Why has the world financial system like a house of cards stood so close to a collapse? The principle reason behind this is the entire world's indebtedness. This high indebtedness can be identified as the wobbly basement of all the current complexity of problems. To give an example, the Germany based bank Hypo Real Estate (HRE) had to be saved, to ensure the further solvency of a couple of other big financial institutes. A failure of HRE and those others financial institutes would have had disastrous impact to Nation and society. And this would have happened not only to Germany, but globally.

Business model of public sector financing

The Hypo Real Estate Group (HRE) calls herself a specialist bank for Real Estate and public finance. A subsidiary is the former German bank "Deutsche Pfandbriefanstalt" (DePfa), interestingly having now its registered business address in Dublin (Ireland). What is the business of this banking for the public sector? It is the granting of credits to public authorities. Those credits are refinanced by creating a special kind of swell-money, denoted and publicly known as Pfandbriefe. Pfandbriefe are a special form of covered debentures / covered bonds. The commodities backing these debentures are mainly treasury bonds, but up to a certain amount, the backing commodities can consist of other debentures like mortgages as well. One has to know, that some countries are not allowed to borrow from Central Banks directly, as for example, US-Government and Great Britain have done, when during the crisis the capital markets did not take over treasury bonds in the amount required. The banking business of public finance takes care, that public authorities will always obtain all the liquidity that is necessary not to become insolvent. There is an interesting and desirable remunerative business sideline. It's the granting of credits to those Nations, having bad ratings, not like, for example, Germany. All those credits with none investment grade and for instance mortgaged loans as well, can be prettified. They can be jazzed up in the following way: As a backing of a Pfandbrief, a bundle of credits of different kinds is used. Credits with investment grade ratings are mixed with credits rated at non investment grades. These bundles are "repackaged" – comparable to what is meanwhile known as "structured products" in the "Sub Prime segment" – and represent the backing of the newly created swell-money Pfandbrief. These repackaged debentures will be partly reinsured by AIG or other so-called monoliners providing a kind of credit default protection. As a result those slips of papers (Pfandbrief) were rated at the best possible investment grade "triple A". They are considered the most secure debentures - reinsured debt obligations - with the highest degree of soundness and solvency. That is why other banks or financial institutions can buy a huge amount of such securitized claims on money, in relation to their equity. They could leverage the equity nearly two hundred fold. They could create two hundred times as much swell-money from almost nothing than they have equity at their disposal, to buy those Pfandbriefe.

Long-term credit assessments according to IRBA

Credit assessment category			risk weight	required equity (8 % · risk weight)
Fitch	Moody's	S&P		
AAA	Aaa	AAA	7 %	0.56 %
AA+ to AA-	Aa1 to Aa3	AA+ to AA-	8 %	0.64 %
A+	A1	A+	10 %	0.80 %
A	A2	A	12 %	0.96 %
A-	A3	A-	20 %	1.60 %
BBB+	Baa1	BBB+	35 %	2.80 %
BBB	Baa2	BBB	60 %	4.80 %
BBB-	Baa3	BBB-	100 %	8 %
BB+	Ba1	BB+	250 %	20 %
BB	Ba2	BB	425 %	34 %
BB-	Ba3	BB-	650 %	52 %
below BB-	below Ba3	below BB-	1250 %	100 %

They create, for instance, credit money and pay the purchase of Pfandbriefe by booking the purchase price to an account. The risk weighting (c.f. Basel/Basel II in the glossary) of those Pfandbriefe as assets, are 7 % only. As a consequence of the required 8 % backing of risk weighted assets, the owning banks need to provide as liable capital 0.56 % (= 7 % • 8 %) of equity only. In consequence having 10 Million Euros of equity would be enough to run a 2 Billion Euros business! DePfa customers will get newly created swell-money from the banks when a credit is granted. The German Central Bank (Deutsche Bundesbank) accepts Pfandbriefe as collateral, making them attractive as banks' assets since they can exchange or swap for Central-Bank-money whenever the need arises.

If however, there is a down-grading of a Pfandbrief (or a down-grading of DePfa respectively the financial intermediate Hypo Real Estate) which could be the case, if the re-insurance company comes under pressure, this has leveraged consequences. Those banks owning Pfandbriefe, are required to provide much more capital. It is the twofold, threefold or more on equity that they need to provide documented proof. Alternatively they have to sell enough of all their

Pfandbriefe in exchange for assets with higher rating. This could be a big problem in situations like the world financial crisis. The financial markets were almost completely dried up. There was neither such a demand for high amounts of Pfandbriefe, nor was it possible, to obtain enough additional equity. As a consequence, those banks focusing on public finance were not able anymore to grant the requested credits to public authorities. Those banks were not anymore able, to take over all those new governmental debentures created day by day. There is a danger, that public authorities will become bankrupt, because of insolvency, if no other buyers, such as banks or public savings banks having enough of equity beyond their statutory capital requirements, can be found to purchase their debentures.

Germany, when taking over risks of more than 100 Billion Euros from HRE, in principle took the role of a reinsurer. Germany reinsured its own credits. This public intervention assured the high rating of this special debentures Pfandbriefe, to prevent the danger of the governments own insolvency.

Governments and public authorities reached an overall indebtedness worldwide of around 40'000 billion US Dollar. They need Government credits at favorable conditions. The interest charged needs to be low. To grant credits with such conditions is not interesting for commercial banks without an opportunity to conduct business side lines connected and based on those credits. Worldwide the entitlements to yield have increased. On such business side lines risky credits are mixed with credits granted to public authorities, and new securitized claims on money are created. Today the resulting swell-money bubble of more than 200'000 Billion US Dollar is in volume more than fifty times as much as the "small Zero" of less than 4'000 Billion US Dollar Central-

Bank-money inside. There are more than fifty times as many securitized claims on legal tender than legal tender exists. New credits cannot be granted by lending money or capital that has been saved, since all worldwide savings are not enough. The capital saved is much less than all those new credits. In the year 2007 the world saved even less than required to fund those credits granted as new to governments and public authorities. There is a needs must that banks create new swell-money to be able to grant all those new credits requested. The swell-money bubble is further swelling. George Soros (2008, pp. 91-105) denotes this as a "super bubble". It is only a question of time before there is nobody left desiring to hold promises on money in ownership. This should be obvious. The Sub Prime crisis beginning in year 2007 could simply be seen as a trigger to the touchdown of the super bubble that had taken off (cf. G. Soros, 2008 pp. 115).

What will be the consequence if there are no successful efforts to increase public earnings worldwide to reach fiscal sustainability? Our future will be either a Brazilianization (cf. the glossary) of the world in an ongoing war on prosperity, value added and taxes, or it will lead us into the total collapse.

Currently there is nothing else than the redistribution of real values and all attractive tangible assets. There will be a governmental guaranteed segment of the world financial markets where public authorities and Governments are guaranteeing the account balances of all the citizens. That means nothing else than all citizens are guaranteeing their own debt. The other segment is where the components of real value are being owned. It is a winner's segment of all those high-net-worth-individuals and those nifty and clever capital gathering and managing institutions that finally made it at the end of the game to get most of all the attractive tangible assets under their ownership. These real values are in the global "game of games" the "pledges" that losers have to give to the winners. Another time we like to quote Johann Wolfgang von Goethe from Faust: The Second Part of the tragedy:

> Fool: »Tonight as a real estate owner I shall sit«
>
> Mephistopheles: »Who still will have a doubt of our fool's wit?«

Is it possible to identify the strongest "gamblers" in this "game"? We should seek them amongst those who together have a dominating influence on the leading "security settlement systems". Security settlement systems are those institutions providing the computer and software platforms where all trades in financial assets are processed. Important companies providing such systems are DTCC/EuroCCP (The Depository Trust & Clearing Corporation and its subsidiary European Central Counterparty), the Euroclear Group and the smaller Clearstream Holding (Clearstream International and subsidiaries), the latter owned by the German stock exchange "Deutsche Börse AG". More than 71 percent of the German stock exchange is owned by institutional investors from the US and Great Britain. All together these few security settlement systems meanwhile dominate the market (cf. W. G. Seifert, 2007). Being in a monopoly position they perform more or less all transactions of shares, debentures and fund shares.

Could there be a correlation between the current world financial system crisis and the growing concentration of managed assets at only a few very big companies? The answer is definitely yes! Big market participants like sovereign wealth funds and the big institutional investors respectively asset management and securities services companies (for instance BNY Mellon, J.P.Morgan, State Street Global, Northern Trust, The Vanguard Group, BlackRock/Barclays, ADIA – Abu Dhabi Investment Authority, GIC/Temasec - Government of Singapore Investment Corporation / Temasec Holding, CIC – China Investment Corp. etc.) manage roughly 40'000 Billion US Dollars of assets actively. Largest part of it is all those securitized claims on money. If those big actors will shift their investment focus from swell-money to legal tender by only ten percent, this will have severe impact on the markets. If parts of the overall amount of credits they grant by holding the swell-money (the slips of paper representing money claims) will not be prolonged when becoming due, the debtors will have to repay the credits with Central-Bank-money as legal tender. If all the Central-Bank-money obtained would be "parked" as liquidity at only a few selected custodians (financial institutions providing Central-Bank-money accounts), a situation would result quite similar to what happened at the world financial crisis in 2008. It is remarkable to mention that there is worldwide a total volume of less than 4'000 Billion US Dollars Central-Bank-money available only. If all those background actors sell ten percent of securitized claims on money they own against Central-Bank-money (which has a higher liquidity) or if they refuse to prolong credits and hoard the liquidity obtained, the financial markets will dry up. A lot of even large banking institutions and investment companies will have solvency problems. They become illiquid and as a consequence more and more companies will have similar problems. What follows will be nearly zero liquidity (Central-Bank-money) available to the common money markets. There will be nearly zero credits granted in the interbank markets. It is since nobody knows who will be a loser. Nobody wants to grant credits because nobody knows who will be able to keep a given promise on money to be settled in the future. As a result those banks (and also other companies) with payment difficulties are urged to sell whatever assets they possess, to obtain liquidity. In consequence the prices for all those assets offered will deteriorate because the supply is rising but the demand is declining. All the amount of so-called fire sales stands helpless in the face of almost zero liquidity (which cripples purchasing power). Those mentioned market participants hoarding excessive liquidity will wait until the most attractive tangible assets will be offered, buying them for very little (Central Bank) money; exchanging the cream of the crops against peanuts. What will be the best? They will get their high valued Central-Bank-money back if those forced under high pressure to offer the fire sales, are their debtors. The assets are sold at very low prices to those insisting on the settlement of Central-Bank-money to repay a debt. Take this as an example: the Banco Santander took over the Sovereign Bancorp paying 1.4 Billion Euros. It was a book value of about 79 Billion US Dollar on assets owned by the Sovereign Bancorp at that time. Who owns Banco Santander? It's more than 65 percent of the shares at institutional investors like State Street and others. Will Sovereign Bancorp now be pulled out of a hole? Or will we see that all the attractive assets are pulled out of Sovereign Bancorp?

How and where will this all end up?

(1) All real values, all tangible assets being purchased through fire sales transactions far below their worth become the property of only a few institutional investors. It's going to be interesting to see which investors this will be. Which of those managed asset pools will contain attractive tangible assets and which will contain nothing other than promises on money? Swell-money, securitized promises on money, are denoted "securities". Mostly they are nothing else than unsecured and subordinated debt obligations.
(2) All those unsecured and subordinated debt obligations remain as assets in those nationalized banks. They serve as backing to the citizens' bank deposits which are now guaranteed by the Nations as has been decided by Governments.

Nations – at least in parts – are nationalizing banks, becoming their owner. But that means: Nations will take this part of the financial market's risks. It's nothing else than the socialization of losses at least in parts. At the same time most insurance companies and pension funds do own claims on money only and not on tangibles.

(3) What happens if the Central Banks don't find and follow a successful "exit strategy"? If they are not able as fast as needed "at the end of the game" to reduce the large amount of legal tender they pumped into the markets? If all the attractive tangible assets are redistributed, all the currently more or less hoarded Central-Bank-money will come into circulation. If not at least the amount of Central-Bank-money becoming active circulating in the market for goods and services cannot be successfully reduced there will be inflation in the consumer segment. Promises on money will lose their value. The purchasing power of money will decrease. However, the returns from tangible assets will increase (nominally) since the prices for goods and services will rise. Even without inflation all those real values, those tangible assets, for instance representing scarce resources, will rise in their (earning capacity) value. It is not the fair value of a tangible asset that is important, it is not important that the (nominal) price that could be realized on the market by selling the asset that is important, since their owners do not want to sell. Why should they sell? What should they do with the money they would receive, if money is loosing continuously its value? Money – now being a hot potato – should be better owned by somebody else. Typical losers will be those who own money and nothing else other than money with diminishing purchasing power. A typical winner will instead own attractive tangible assets. These are attractive possessions with "real" values since they provide for "real" yields. The ear-

nings resulting from the capacities or capabilities of the tangible assets will result from prices that are adjusted according to the inflation. The cash flow of these assets will be "real" cash flows considering the inflation.

(4) If we assume, that the ten largest winners legally circumvent paying taxes on their returns, as it happened for a long time, we could make the following calculation: there are roughly 40'000 Billion US Dollar in value managed as assets. If we assume an average yield of five percent there is an annual return of around 2'000 Billion US Dollar. A tax of twenty percent would give around 400 Billion US Dollar earnings to the public, which is currently not paid globally. What does it mean on a national level? The share of Germany in the world economy has been around 6.1 percent in 2007. Lost earnings from taxation in Germany would account to nearly 25 Billion US Dollar (which is around 17.5 Billion Euros). That is more than all the new indebtedness of federal government, federal states and local authorities in the year 2007. Perhaps this new indebtedness and the circumvented tax payment are somehow interwoven?

The game "musical chairs" as metaphor

There are mainly two types of financial assets in the world financial system. The first kind is Central-Bank-money (banknotes of the Central Banks, coins and other legal tender); the other kind is swell-money (securitized claims on money, respectively promises on money). The debtors are financial institutions, other companies, Governments, public authorities or private persons. The ratio between these two kinds of money currently is about 1:53.5 (or to say 2:107). There is quite much more swell-money of all the above mentioned kind than there is Central-Bank-money. Central-Bank-money is the only legal tender (which holds true even for trades between banks). If the bearer of debentu insist on getting Central-Bank-money at maturity, they go "into liquidity". Severe problems could be the result. There exists less than two percent Central-Bank-money in relation to the overall existing swell-money. What happens if all Central Bank liquidity is hoarded at only a few banks and if banks are not prepared to grant credits to each other anymore; if there will be no interbank credits? In such a case the circulation of Central-Bank-money in the financial markets stops. The liquidity does not vanish from the game, it is lurking. The liquidity is only with a few market participants, looking out for the most attractive investment opportunities.

This situation can be compared with the children's game "musical chairs". In the world financial system it's a game played with 100 "ordinary" participants (the children) and seven gorillas (like those institutional investors as BNY Mellon, J.P.Morgan, State Street Global, The Vanguard Group, BlackRock/Barclays, Fidelity, ADIA, GIC/TEMASEK, CIC and others). All those 107 players in the game are dancing around just two chairs. As long as the music is playing, everybody feels happy; the game is seen to be fun. In the world financial system game "music plays" means everybody accepts promises on money as good as money. There is a rude awakening if the music stops playing. In our metaphor the chairs represent not only Central-Bank-money but alternatively the tangible assets, the real values, as well. If music stops there will be a struggle over the chairs, to acquirer Central-Bank-money and real assets. We can watch all those combats when looking to all these processes in the global market, especially if we observe those parts of the world financial system actually unregulated or deregulated. There are situations optimally supporting the redistribution of tangible assets and other kinds of real values far below those prices that usually have to be paid.

The few possessing high liquidity will get it all from those short in liquidity. All players running into insolvency (those players not getting hold of a chair) have to sell whatever tangible assets or real values they have, to those gorillas, to those institutional investors, with liquidity. All losers have to pawn their properties.

The game "musical chairs" explains figuratively the danger inherently given if there is more than the fifty-fold of swell-money, in the form of securitized claims on money, existing than Central-Bank-money. There is a rising probability that this gigantic swell-money bubble will burst. This process already hit a peak when the Hypo Real Estate fell into trouble. This was the first bubble of medium size which threatened to burst. Actually the burst of the Lehman Brothers' bubble was not prevented. New credits up to the overall necessary total amount demanded in the global economy cannot be granted by lending saved capital only. The worldwide savings ratio and the resulting capital saved is neither sufficient nor has it been for years. The banks have the responsibility to create new swell-money for the purposes of lending. The new granted credits are provided with newly created swell-money. They are served with the commercial banks' newly made promises on money. Newly created swell-money is provided with another newly created swell-money. It is an everlasting growth of the bubble – it is swelling even faster than before. The result is as George Soros said to be a "super bubble". The growth of this super bubble accelerates through the demographic change. In the so-called rich countries, we've seen the trend to get social frameworks following the capital funding principle. More and more Nations asked their citizens to build up capital to take care of their social security at least partly by themselves. One has to consider that financial capital of its bearer is always a debt of somebody else. In consequence with rising capital the share of the returns gained from financial capital and tangible assets as a fraction of the overall Gross Domestic Product (GDP) is permanently increasing. There was never in the last forty years a faster growth of the GDP that would have counteracted this trend. The reasons for the lack in value added are scarcity of (environmental) resources on the one hand. On the other hand there are weaknesses in the valid rules, regulations and deregulations of the globalized economy as well. What is of the most importance is that the basic prerequisites are not stringently and sufficiently implemented. The needed basis to create added value and prosperity is missing for the majority of people on this planet. The basis, the commonwealth, all the institutions, frameworks, networks and much more that we need to achieve globally common good through huge effectual efforts for the necessary immense innovations for a higher value added, are nothing like enough. In consequence we do currently have a large gap in value added.

It is obvious that at some time nobody likes to own promises on money which more and more become worthless. The Sub Prime crisis was only a trigger to this process. Especially all the large institutional investors are moving their capital "into liquidity" or "inflation-proof investments". This dries up the markets since the Central-Bank-money is not in circulation any more. This provokes sudden liquidity bottlenecks at a lot of financial institutions and companies. However, not all are short in liquidity, since the liquidity does not vanish. Liquidity is hoarded or creeps slowly through the market.

What are the consequences now? Governments react in this situation and help those "systemically important financial institutions" against falling into trouble. Those considered too big to fail but close to bankruptcy got into liquidity difficulties and suffered heavy book losses. Governmental action is to buy from those actors all "bad slips of paper", all those debentures becoming illiquid. Alternatively Governments guaranteed those debentures. Troubled assets are losing their character of being a kind of liquidity, since it is not that easy anymore to trade them against Central-Bank-money for instance in the money market. They even lose their value if they are accounted for at their market price (fair value) and their rating is downgraded. That is why banks bearing troubled assets will have increased capital requirements. They need to have more equity than before. To say it in other words: the banks' own potentiality to create new swell-money, which means their potentiality for granting credits, diminishes. Balance sheet total, and thus the absolute amount of all asset accounts are narrowed. If governments jazz up all or part of these troubled assets or exchange them against "bonny bonds" their potentiality widens again. Without enhancing its equity the bank will have as a result of governmental bail-out actions a higher potentiality for creating new (commercial bank) money. This implies: those banks safeguarded will be able to create enough new money to wait for the "pawns" offered by the losers of the game musical chairs. At the right time the bank can start a shopping spree. Those tangible assets and other real values offered then in fire-sales will be purchased at a far lower price. Those selling the assets will be paid by crediting the price to the seller's account. The tangible assets are paid with new swell-money with a bank debenture. As long as there is still the opportunity to make profits with these businesses all the gorillas will participate as bank shareholders of the banks in the background. Right in time they will bail out, taking all the attractive tangible assets. Because of the further rising money bubble, of money and claims on money, inflation could result. Those tangible assets and other assets with real value will increase in (nominal) values, but the returns that can be attained through these assets will increase as well.

What that means is that the game "musical chairs" has not come to an end. Some of those unable to get a chair are relieved from pledging attractive assets (Government and Central Banks are providing them with Central-Bank-money as liquidity). Central Banks try to bring new chairs into the game. To do so Government and public authorities have to take more and more credits. They make more and more promises on money for the future. The swell-money bubble still grows. The final end of the game draws closer. There is a concrete danger of bankruptcy of the Nations.

Those understanding these interwoven patterns of operation can soberly appraise all the governmental measures taken so far. The announcements and promises of politicians that all efforts have been done to overcome the crisis should be considered very carefully. That a balance has been reached by all the actions taken to date after the crisis is less than credible. What's more likely is an accelerated process towards a Brazilianization of the world. It means all the attractive tangible assets and real values will be re-distributed successfully to only a small number of winners. Subsequently an escalating liquidity will lead to inflation or currency reforms. Finally this could lead to an eco-dictatorship: around the year 2050 there could be less than one billion highly privileged people standing face to face with more than nine billion under-privileged. Those "haves", owning the scarce resources and all the attractive tangible assets, and those "have-nots" with no access and owning nothing. However, even in the small privileged group rivalry will be increasing. How much inequality will a society suffer (and how long) without radicalization?

"The monster is still untamed" German president Horst Köhler (former director of IMF) said in October 2009. Currently the government is under enormous pressure to give money to the financial segment of markets. We are facing a financial turmoil, threatening the Nations, threatening all of us. We are in a crisis caused for several reasons, big bank speculations, hedge funds excessive risks and dodgy businesses of other "gambler" (partly being only vanguards of institutional investors) in the "world financial casino". Deregulation, slackening the reins of financial markets, resulted in a global madhouse. There have been irresponsible and unjustifiable speculation and it is still going on. That is why especially those who profited most from this rampant system should be compelled to take a share in financing all these public interventions. In addition, further measures have to be taken – and financed – to give the system back the kind of stability and robustness it badly needs.

We see ourselves in a big dilemma. To solve it, politicians have to face the essential and substantial complexity of problems. Worldwide an increase of public revenues has to be achieved and the course has to be set to bring the global society on the path to reach fair participation on value added and prosperity in the medium term. We badly need a consistent regulatory framework. We need effective rules and regulations, especially for the globalized part of the financial markets and the economy. There is a strong need to get substantial improvements with respect to the harmonization of tax assessment bases. Further actions and measures are necessary to reach a sustainable fiscal balance, which is strongly required worldwide!

The world crisis we suffer in the aftermath of 2007/2008 provides probably a unique chance towards a sustainable future. As important as all those current actions on the political level should be, a financial market tax would be a quite reasonable and a necessary further step into balance. Most appropriately this would be a duty to be negotiated and implemented at an international level. To effectively tackle monetary and fiscal problems the financial market tax should not only be a financial transaction tax as it is already discussed. The important disput would be to levy a direct tax from those doing. Short sales, to tax all kinds of credits when they are granted. It has to be paid by the emitters of new financial products, by those creating swell-money – it should be a swell-money tax (D. Solte (2007) has invented this levy denoting it "leverage money tax"). The swell-money tax could be used to finance all necessary public interventions. That would be a first step focusing on the overall complexity of problems.

The swell-money tax would be a duty providing an effective instrument to face the central problem of the financial crisis. It is to reduce the outsized swell-money bubble or to say it more specifically: to balance the relationship of all securitized claims on money to the Central-Bank-money supply (as the liquidity of last resort). The swell-money tax could be linked in value to the inflation rate. If the swell-money tax increases when inflation rises, it would have limiting effects on the amount of newly created credit money since the emission of new promises on money would be more expensive. As another important detail of its implementation, the swell-money tax could be strictly designed in line with the principle of tax justice and fairness. If the duty is determined from the debtor's rating (higher rating results in a higher tax rate), the swell-money tax could be in accordance with the ability-to-pay principle. Economically stronger subjects should pay a higher duty than economically weaker participants of the markets. This also compensates to some extent the interest burdens for weaker (small) subjects resulting from not having a direct access to the capital markets.

If the tax as described depends on the rating of those creating the swell-money, it would be even an instrument to dampen all these speculative leveraged investments carried to extremes. Those businesses have to a large extent the responsibility that there is a danger that Governments and public authorities could become illiquid. With the swell-money tax, credits would be dearer and in consequence a smaller number of leveraged investments would be profitable. That would reduce the overall volume of leveraged investments. The swell-money bubble would shrink. As a means to finance the necessary public intervention to stabilize the crisis, the swell-money tax could be levied retroactively. To get the acceptance of the market participants to implement the swell-money tax, Government could offer to partly guarantee those levied debentures. Eventually there could be some value protection against inflation. As a compensation and backing of the part of the risk (everything not covered by the capital requirements as defined in accordance to the Basel agreements) those requesting a guarantee should have to pledge some tangible assets. Other assets could be lent against Central-Bank-money at a reasonable cost. This would counteract the threatening fire sales of tangible assets and other real values. Nevertheless the additional liquidity obtained with these transactions would have to be set under strict surveillance to prevent its further speculative utilization.

If such wise and necessary precautionary measures are not taken we will see the progress of redistribution aggravating, a gigantic redistribution of assets. If the music is not starting to play again, gorillas will sit down and keep sitting on the chairs! They will usurp all attractive assets pledged. Will our politicians meet these challenges?

Is a new Great Depression looming?

As we will show next, there are quite principle similarities between the current crisis and the situation in 1929. The fundamental problems and the patterns of operation leading to the Great Depression will be explained simplified in the following. We will not go into the details of the world financial system. We will not explain how several markets are interwoven, since this complexity would rather detract from clarity. That is why we omit to explain all these possibilities to create swell-money in the markets and all the facilities and trading platforms that could be used to exchange types of swell-money and to exchange swell-money against Central-Bank-money. Those readers interested in these special details and those who are interested to follow in detail the deduction of the complexity of problems we refer to D. Solte (2007 2nd edition).

The problem at the center of the today's crisis and the crisis of 1929 is a short fall in liquidity. Money is like blood circulating in the economy. There should be enough blood and blood has to flow, it has to circulate. What does this mean? The economist Irving Fisher has put the interrelationship of money in the economy in his famous equation:

$$\sum_{i=1}^{n} p_i \cdot q_i = u \cdot M$$

On the left side of this equation there is a sum total of all payment transactions. This is the volume of all trades in a well-defined period of time. All trades are summarized that have to be settled in money. The symbol q_i denotes the number of all trades at the same price p_i (e.g. 500 pairs of shoes that have to be paid with 100 Euros each). Enough money is required to pay all these trades. The total volume of money necessary to process all payments is denoted by the symbol M. The required amount of money is not equal to the overall amount of all payments, less money would be enough. The required amount of money depends on the velocity at which the money flows through the market, the so-called circulation velocity of money (u).

Velocity of money: An example

Let us assume that a daughter assists her father in chores and gardening. She will get 100 Euros a month for this aid (which represents newly created value added). With these

> earnings she finances a dancing class (another value added). It costs 100 Euros a month. The dancing master takes investment advice (a third value added) from the father and pays 100 Euros each month. Daughter, dancing master and father got earnings of 100 Euros each a month for their added value services. In total this will be in one year 3 times 100 Euros times 12 equaling to 3'600 Euros of business volume. It is a Gross Domestic Product of 3'600 Euros and the total sum of all payment processes is 3'600 Euros. How much money is required to process all payments? Each month 100 Euros are paid to the daughter. Exactly these 100 Euros the daughter pays to her dancing master. The dancing master as well pays exactly these 100 Euros to the father. 100 Euros are passing through three hands in one month and this process recurs each month, twelve times a year. That means one and the same 100 Euros have been moved 36 times in one year from hand to hand. In this example the velocity of money (u) is 36. It is only 100 Euros Central-Bank-money required to process all the payments made in an overall business volume of 3'600 Euros.

Which money can be used in payment processes? Which money represents "liquidity"? The answer to these questions is twofold. Money that can be used to pay is

(a) fixed by legislation (Central-Bank-money is legal tender)
(b) a question of acceptance (whether for instance credit cards, remittance, "putting on the slate" or other kinds of payments are accepted)

It is set by legislation that Central-Bank-money is legal tender and as such a money with the highest level of liquidity. It is regulated by law that any debt can be settled with Central-Bank-money. If somebody is purchasing something, the price is owed to the seller, it's a debt. As long as nothing deviant has been negotiated and contracted individually, this debt can be settled with Central-Bank-money. The debt can be redeemed with Central-Bank-money. Central-Bank-money as legal tender has by law a so-called debt discharging effect. In contrast a payment with swell-money, the payment with promises on money, is only possible if the counteracting party in a trade accepts this form of payment. It is a question of whether for instance debentures, check money, shares or what so ever are accepted to settle a debt. When settling a debt with swell-money it could even be possible that Central-Bank-money is required in the background. If for instance a payment is done by remitting an amount between accounts in two different banks one account is charged and another account is credited. In such a case the bank debiting an account has to transfer Central-Bank-money to the bank where the account is credited. There is an interbank business transaction in the background where legal tender has to be settled. Alternatively both banks could have individual appointments, concerning the kinds of swell-money they would accept instead of legal tender for their interbank businesses. This could be e.g. bank debentures.

In those years previous to the crisis of 2008 (1929 as well) the overall volume of swell-money was far more than the volume of Central-Bank-money and the volume of the economy (Gross Domestic Product). An enormous amount of swell-money, for instance debentures, securitized claims on money and so on, was existing and accepted as good as money. It was possible to buy companies on credit or with shares. The purchasing price was paid with swell-money. Using the so-called money market as a special part of the market it was possible all the time to exchange swell-money against Central-Bank-money in real time. As long as all credit institutions had faith in each other, they granted interbank credits when ever requested. All commercial-bank-money was as good as Central-Bank-money. That is why the overall amount of money usable to settle debts was enormous. There was a huge amount of swell-money that directly or indirectly could be used for payments in the market for goods and services and in the asset market. There was an abundant liquidity. This liquidity was distributed and active in three markets: (1) goods and services (added value), (2) tangibles (properties and other real values), (3) financial assets. Liquidity not being active in these markets is a liquidity reserve for several reasons, and mainly a liquidity reserve waiting for attractive purchase opportunities.

There is an immense volume of sales transactions in the financial markets. Compared to this volume little money is necessary only for settlement. In this market, debentures, shares and any other kind of financial assets are traded and only a small amount of Central-Bank-money is required. The velocity of money is very high. The annual overall business volume of more than 3 Quadrillion Dollar ($3 \cdot 10^{15}$) in the financial markets is nearly one million times as large as all the Central-Bank-money supply of the whole world. A lot of these trades are just to exchange swell-money against Central-Bank-money. It is to obtain Central-Bank-money whenever it is necessary for payments in other markets. After getting the Central-Bank-money it is re-exchanged in the financial markets against swell-money. As long as a bearer of the Central-Bank-money does not prefer to hoard it as a liquidity reserve, it can be offered in the financial markets in exchange for swell-money, to get a return. No interest is paid to the bearer of Central-Bank-money, which makes it comparatively unattractive as an asset. In consequence and as long as Central-Bank-money is offered, everybody looking for Central-Bank-money and owning swell-money is in principle able to obtain Central-Bank-money whenever required. By the use of a (proper functioning) financial market, swell-money gets the same liquidity characteristic as Central-Bank-money. As long as there is "confidence in the markets", swell-money is thus seen to be as good as money. Swell-money amounted in 2008 to around four times as much as the whole worldwide economic output of that year. Most of this huge liquidity has been mainly active – circulating – in the market of tangibles in the last years. Leverage businesses (leverage buyouts) were a common place; mergers and acquisitions happened frequently all the time. A leverage buyout is a credit financed purchase of real estate, property, company or other. The prices for tangibles were permanently rising. This price bubble burst when it became obvious that the real estate segment of the United States was a bubble. A quite similar event happened 1929 with all those shares, bonds and commercial papers traded on the stock exchange. Meanwhile we have more than fifty times as many promises on money – swell-money – than there is money (legal tender, that means Central-Bank-money). What are those promises on money one can be sure that even in such a situation they can and will be kept? Can one feel certain as a bearer of bank debentures, corporate bonds, consumer credits or mortgages? This growing uncertainty leads suddenly into a flight out of financial assets. Money and the financial market are collapsing. Prices for financial assets are sharply falling and – extremely important to mention – the circulation velocity of money in the financial market heavily drops. In consequence an enormous amount of swell-money loses its character of being liquidity. That happens in a situation where a lot of participants in all markets have payment obligations, credits becoming due, wages, bills and other liabilities at maturity have to be paid etc etc. The circulation velocity of money has decreased in the financial market. Furthermore money has moved to the liquidity reserves, becoming inactive since it is hoarded. That is why now a lot of liquidity is missing in the market of goods and services and also in the market of tangibles. From minute to minute it is more difficult to obtain money. It takes longer as well. The due diligence will take more time; there is a more careful and detailed checking for creditworthiness imposed. More securities or other collateral is requested and on the market of tangibles the prices drop as well. All markets lack in money! There is no acceptance of swell-money as a medium of payment anymore. Even banks do not grant credits to each other anymore. They do not accept swell-money on the interbank market. All the markets dry up because

(1) money / liquidity is missing
(2) the circulation velocity of money in all markets drops

If the circulation velocity of money tends to zero there is market disruption: – rien ne va plus – there are no market activities anymore. Having a circulation velocity of money of one in the market of goods and services the Central Banks would have to flood the markets to keep up the economic level. There should be up to 50'000 Billion (50 Trillion) US Dollar of Central-Bank-money pumped into the markets. That would be the fifteen-fold of the today's available worldwide Central-Bank-money supply. None of it should flow to the liquidity reserves; none of it should enlarge the "overhang liquidity". The latter denotes the part of liquidity lurking to purchase tangibles, e.g. to purchase companies having liquidity problems, if they are offered in fire-sales. There are more than enough examples. In the year 2009 in Germany we can mention all those processes concerning the companies of the Merkle Group (Ratiopharm, HeidelbergCement, Phoenix), Schaeffler / Conti and Porsche.

Meanwhile it should be obvious: enlarging the Central-Bank-money supply is not sufficient to solve the problems. Deflation, recession and even depression cannot be overcome – or however provoking hyper inflation. The focus for action should be the circulation velocities of money, especially the circulation velocity of money in the financial market has to be increased and assured. The hoarding of Central-Bank-money has to be limited.

In 1929 the problem was quite similar. The bottleneck to provide the markets with enough Central-Bank-money was gold. At that time Central-Bank-money was backed by gold. That is why in the United States in 1933 government limited the ownership of gold for all citizens. Before that more and more market participants took Central-Bank-money and exchanged it against gold at the Central Bank. This gold was hoarded as a reserve for bad times, and in consequence the Central-Bank-money supply decreased. That is why from 1933 all citizens had to re-exchange their hoarded gold at the Central Bank. The problems with the circulation of money had not been resolved at that time. Today, in reaction to the current crisis, quite similar limitations should be implemented concerning the hoarding of Central-Bank-money. At the same time the circulation of Central-Bank-money has to be assured at least in the financial market. This could be established via appropriate regulation, stipulating a "maximum permissible reserve ratio" and implementing a "liquidity circulating fund". The latter would be a kind of liquidity bank of all financial market participants. "Overhang liquidity", the amount of Central-Bank-money and other kind of liquidity reserve beyond a level of e.g. one or two percent above the minimum required reserve, has to be paid into that fund in exchange for fund debentures. Every market participant would be on the other hand qualified to take liquidity loans in case of lacking liquidity. That could be the case e.g. if the amount of Central-Bank-money that a commercial bank has on deposit falls below the minimum required reserve. All participants could borrow Central-Bank-money from the liquidity circulation fund against collateral or securities. That would be a crucial component of the overall solution. It would be an effective "exit strategy" for the Central Banks' easy money politics. It would be the effective instrument to avoid and prevent a further drying up of the markets and so prevent deflation and recession turning into a depression.

Do we have a sufficient political reaction?

In the year 2008 governments all over the world decided and implemented huge bailout packages. The German minister of finance, Peer Steinbrück, explained the political view of the crisis and the strategic approach to react to it. He used a vivid metaphorical explanation:

»When something is burning in the global financial markets, it must be doused. Even if it is caused by arson! Afterward, the arsonists must be subsequently prevented from acting in such a manner again. The fanners of the flame must be banned and better fire protection must be provided.«

This metaphorical explanation holds important but relative truths. Unfortunately it does not give an overall analysis of the full problematic. What's missing is a "look behind the curtain", which can be illustrated by the use of the metaphor: firstly you should ask yourself where does water for putting out fires come from? Without an improvement of public revenues an increasing Nation's indebtedness will be the consequence. The Nation must ask the arsonists for the water. Secondly you have to deliberate why the financial markets were drying up, why they catch fire so easily? To solve the complexity of problems it simply does not suffice to protect an increasingly drier forest by only attempting to keep the arsonists at bay. If the fundamental possibilities of irrigation are already there (taxes and tariffs) the trees (community and infrastructure) must be watered regularly. Government and public authorities should gain more public earnings, today and in the future. At least in part these additional earnings should be used to reduce the public indebtedness. All public earnings should be levied fair and balanced. What does "fair" mean? We have to mention that currently on a global level especially all those economically most powerful market participants find legal loopholes to reduce their tax payments. Differences and missing harmonization of the different national tax legislation enable them on a global level to circumvent tax payments. As a result they do not pay their appropriate share up to an amount that all the national legislations have fixed as a fair duty. It should be obvious, that only as long as everybody fairly contributes, can all the necessary bases for education, wealth and social balancing be financed. Only then there is the possibility (without further indebtedness) to invest in all those strongly required infrastructures for social communication, cooperation and coordination. The fair contribution is a must to publically finance the overall necessary infrastructure for the economy, the infrastructure that is a must for value added and prosperity. Our statement that we need more and increased public earnings only means that those that profited most in the global markets should pay their fair share again. It's nothing else necessary than also the biggest profiteers should pay their duties according to the ability-to-pay principle, as all others are doing. If this is reached there is even the possibility to give relief to middle income groups and medium sized businesses, which are up to now taking the largest share. This is of special importance for all those countries like Germany, countries that owe their prosperity to the large number of small and medium sized businesses. Those entrepreneurs, having a high level of commitment and determination, and all those families taking care of the companies they own and manage actively.

The alternative approach to prevent fires, the clear cutting of trees (reduction of public spending through "social dumping" and privatization), is certainly not desired. In the end all that would remain would be a desert (a social system, educational system etc. reduced to the bare minimum for the losing and largest part of the population) with nothing left to burn, but a few oases (the privatized services for the winners). This would be the brazilianization, a two class society of the world. The fire on the financial markets would have been doused, that is true. However, this problem would have been solved at the advantage of the winners only: (a) deserts cannot be set under fire, if there is nothing left to burn; (b) in the few and small oases everything will be abundantly irrigated and in full bloom; hardly anything would catch fire. In those oases (but only there) there would be enough water for irrigation and dousing.

The pestering and agonizing difficulty behind the problems is worldwide public debt. Nations lack in water! The indebtedness stems from the exploitation of the missing and/or non binding (ecological and social) regulations on a global scale. The arsonists cut society off from the water supply and lay waste to the forests transforming them into deserts. This must be stopped! And on the medium term there should be a balancing of social security and commonwealth and their harmonization in essential parts.

Of outmost importance is to solve the problem, how to reach a fair participation on prosperity and value added on a global level? Currently we are on a bad trajectory that does not prevent a future firestorm. The ongoing redistribution that tremendously happens in the crisis has urgently to be stopped. There is the concrete danger that we will see a world probably having the best fire brigades and early warning systems ever seen, but with deserts massively widening and oases retreating. This cannot be a resilient fundament for 10 Billion people living together in peace and dignity.

Currently we see us experiencing a near-chaotic situation.

When if not now should it be possible to set the course into the right direction – a course towards a world in balance? Subsequent to all the previously taken actions against the crisis, we need first and foremost a financial market tax, subject to all leverage! We need a duty on all financial products that should be agreed upon at the international level. It has to be a common duty on all products created on all parts of the global financial markets. Financial products have been invented to camouflage risks. Tremendously rising in number and overall amount, permanently increasing, they contributed massively to the world's mess. There are profiteers countenancing the currently unfair game! They should contribute to the solution even if we prefer to see their behaviour as systemically driven. Their connivance and countenance allots them a share of complicity and responsibility. Most of them have lived off the fat of the land without impeccable behavior and effort, affecting markets and society adversely. For some time they should have been held to account: they have to contribute a fair share in financing reforestation backdated and ongoing. We do not want to have neither a casino economy nor a casino capitalism (W. Sinn, 2009). We desire, deserve and require thick and healthy greenwoods with lush meadows that hardly can be set on fire or wasted.

A poetical contribution for a deliberate reflection can be found again in Goethe's Faust: The second part of the tragedy.

Mephistopheles – certainly in a different context – says:
»I tell you what: your speculative churl
is like a beast which some ill spirit leads,
on barren wilderness, in ceaseless whirl,
while all around lie fair and verdant meads.«

Everybody should read those four lines each and every day. Particularly we recommend it to those who are employed at the banks or consult them to invent, construct or offer all those complicated and structured financial products. Needless to say, it should be deliberately reflected by those speculating with financial products.

Part 3: Outlook

10. Crisis as Opportunity

Facere de necessitate virtutem.
Make a virtue of necessity.

In this book we contemplated the world financial system house of cards from different perspectives. Now it should be evident: besides money that is legal tender, there is a huge amount of swell-money. All credits are swell-money; all promises to make payments in the future are swell-money. All this swell-money finally represents a fortune, it represents a component of wealth, but of what kind? The bearer of swell-money is temporarily abstaining from consumption. Those granting the credits or better to say those bearing swell-money have to wait until the credit is repaid to be able to consume. A bearer of swell-money owns a kind of added value voucher. There is the hope, expectation or belief to get something valuable or something of use in the future in exchange for this voucher. It is this expected but not yet existing value added that represents the added value gap concealed by swell-money. A credit can only be repaid if this missing but expected value added has been gained or created by the debtor. It has to be a newly created added value to decrease the total volume of debt. If a credit is repaid with money or swell-money (instead of newly created added value) only the debtor in charge to fill the gap may change, since money/swell-money is a debt. Those granting the credits respectively those bearing swell-money receive interest from the debtor. All interest to be paid represents a further added value gap, which has to be filled in the future as well. The following is fact: since forty years there has been a faster growth of the swell-money amount than the overall real value added annually (Gross Domestic Product). The amount of financial assets representing debts has grown faster than the worldwide production of goods and services. The added value gap has become bigger and bigger. What caused that development? Why are there so many credits? Is it a lack of judgement? Is it caused by foolishness and speculation? Is it missing regulation to limit the potentiality of creating credits? In our point of view there is more to it than meets the eye. We revealed the fundamental problem. Globally there is an always rising competition on value added. The worldwide potentiality to create goods and services is not sufficient. Nations have designed their systems of taxation to use it as a weapon in the struggle for value added. Tax basis, tax structure and tax rates are geared to allure value added processes or assessable "components" representing virtually a value added. Each government tries to have high volumes of value added declared in the income statement, to be assessable for taxation in the own country, no matter whether this taxed value added is really originating in the own country. Ask yourself for the reason, why the tax rate to corporation earnings is very low e.g. in Ireland and Switzerland? Why has the registered office of the largest German underwriter of public covered bonds, the DePfa bank (the former "Deutsche Pfandbriefanstalt"), been relocated to Ireland? Why do have those British Channel Islands a special status concerning taxation? Why do even all activities within the European Union to harmonize the taxation bases encounter so much resistance from all these protagonists of a single European market? Is there nobody aware that fair value accounting leaves the possibility open to virtually relocate value added for taxation purposes? Does nobody see how subtle constructions allow the release of book profits to be assessable for taxation in those countries with lowest rates? As a result there is a taxation of not yet really created, but only imputed realized future profits. It is not considered in which country the actual value added process to serve these profits will really take place. The taxes should be entitled to this country, since there has the basis for value added be implemented and financed. The key to answer all these questions is the mentioned problem to be seen as focal: globally we have an insufficient level of value added and currently an unfair and imbalanced distribution concerning the participation in wealth and added value. Social frameworks following the funding principle have to amass a fortune to get a share of value added. Pension funds and life insurance companies e.g. invest the gathered premiums in assets. Churches, foundations, charitable trusts and a lot of other institutions wish, need or have to amass a fortune. We tried to make clear how a component of wealth and fortune, how assets in general should be interpreted. It is something with a capability to obtain or gain added value for its bearer. It is not a must that the asset itself can create added value as for instance tangibles like production facilities. Swell-money as well is capable of obtaining added value for its bearer. Interest paid on debentures, or dividends paid on shares, can be used to purchase added value. With the growth of the overall amassed fortune more and more added value is channeled to the holders of big fortunes. Who possess those accumulated fortunes? Who made all these leverage deals to usurp value added? The very rich people in the world own roughly a third of all the world's financial assets. These are the high-net-worth-individuals, the world's millionaires and billionaires. Another third represents leverage business of companies and "ordinary" individuals. Those financial assets are in ownership and under management of companies, private households and institutions. Parts of it are financial assets of foundations and churches as well. The last third is what pension funds, insurance companies and the like manage. It is all the capital that those paying premiums have saved to finance their future living. It's the accumulated fortune of all retirees or pensioners to obtain a share of value added during the autumn of their lives. Particularly a large share of all the world's productive properties and production capacities accumulates at those managing large fortunes. For instance institutional investors own already more than 70% of the shares of all the American top 1'000 companies. The 500 largest companies in the world produce more than half of the global value added (Gross Domestic Product), and they are dominated by institutional investors. Worldwide the overall fortune, the overall amount of financial assets has grown permanently. Correspondingly the overall indebtedness, especially the public debt has grown permanently. Government and public authorities have bridged the added value gap to a large extend by running into new debts. A continuation of this process in the future is impossible. The process already approaches a limit of the world financial system: the bankruptcy of Nations – even the most worthy Nations – caused by excessive indebtedness! "To keep at it" is definitively not possible. Now the question is: which course will the world society take? Will we face the focal economical problem to fill the added value gap? Will we successfully fill the gap with newly created added value, and in doing so, will we solve at the same time the problem of imbalanced participation? It would mean: do we solve the global social problem? Do we solve at the same time the problem of environmental devastation and ecological overexploitation – do we solve the ecological problem? One thing should be crystal clear: economical growth without solving the ecological problem will definitively lead us to a total collapse. Economic growth without answering the question of fair distribution and balanced participation, i.e. without solving the social problem on our planet, holds the disastrous peril of radicalization. This could lead to a total collapse as well. We must not focus our public deliberations and efforts on ostensible and superficial problem dimensions. Is it objectively an effective measure, for instance, to increase the capital requirement for financial institutions, compelling them to obtain more liable equity? Where should additional liable capital come from? What kind of capital is staked? By now, the worldwide volume of new credits granted in one year is more than the seven-fold of the worldwide annual savings. Equity should be seen as a special form of credit. Will further requested equity be "generated" by performing the magic trick of the rabbit pulling itself out of the hat? Will equity be brought into the company by selling new shares against newly created debentures? Will these debentures create further equity by gaining book profits resulting from fair value accounting? All of that will not solve the problem! It will affect the opposite. The added value gap will widen and rupture until it becomes unbridgeable. It would only be a shift of the overall problems into the near future. What about the troubled asset relief program (TARP) or governmental guarantees to outsource "toxic" debentures into so-called bad banks? Will this resolve the credit crunch and safeguard companies and jobs? Let us exemplify this by looking to the bailout package for Opel / General Motors. What offers have we seen from investors? All the investors interested in Opel were willing only to place a small amount of capital at stake. Originally one bidder offered to provide not more than 100 Million Euros of "fresh" equity. As a return service to this "generous courtesy" the investor eagerly anticipated the Government guaranteeing for 4.5 Billion Euros swell-money of Opel. All those credits that Opel badly need would not be granted without governmental guarantee. What it means is that the investor wants Opel to leverage the new equity put at stake to the nearly fifty-fold. The company would have approximately fifty times as much credit than equity.

That is not all, here comes the best: the investor intends to insure the grip on all existing assets of real value. The investor's means are so-called convertible bonds. These are debentures optionally being exchanged against shares in the future. Until this happens those debentures are preferential to equity and all other liabilities. In case of a solvency they take precedence over all other credits that Government has to guarantee. To cut right to the chase of the matter: the "fresh" equity willing to be put at stake should gain high yields by the use of a huge leverage. If it works the investor will take all the returns. If it does not work the Government or better to say all citizens of the guaranteeing Nation are left with the losses. The investor will split with all the attractive real values withdrawn from the heap of the ruins. Do proper solutions look that way, solely because of their alleged safeguarding of jobs? All the attractive tangible and intangible assets are given away and all the risks are taken by Government representing the general public. Does the hope only to preserve a few jobs sanctify this kind of political intervention?

As illustrated, the swell-money bubble has been growing permanently during the last forty years. Hand in hand with the swell-money bubble growing, the income share of returns on capital, as a fraction of the Gross Domestic Product, is growing as well. There is a growing share of value added that has to serve interest and dividends. In consequence, there is a continuous pressure on wages and all remaining jobs. The rising share of interest and dividends leads to a shrinking share of wages and salaries. We have to consider a growing world population and the demographic change; people live longer in wealthy countries. As a result, all those social frameworks that are pay-as-you-go financed will fall into trouble, since payroll deductions decrease. That is why all employees are asked to compensate this upcoming deficiency with individual provisions for their retirement. They are requested to complementary accumulate a fortune capable to provide some added value in the future by themselves. The overall amount of assets as components of wealth and fortune and thus the share of value added for interest and dividends should rise. Could that work?

No! Solutions that have as consequence a further bloating of the swell-money bubble will show no sign of recovery. We need another way; we need a balanced way that considers the given ecological, social and monetary constraints. It can only be a global joint effort, if consensus can be reached. Human individual requirements and mentalities have to be considered. Such a path to the future should appeal to "insightful selfishness". Perhaps it is of most importance, to find a way into balance, where anybody could and will profit. This could be essential to get a broad support. It could be essential to get a chance for an implementation. As problematic as it is, such a way requires probably – for a last time – growth. We have to find a way to attain growth. Fundamentally and of unconditional importance is, that such growth considers and adheres strictly to the social and ecological limits! These given limits have to be enforced to be mandatory. The compliance of economic activities worldwide has to be supervised and assured through effective means. There should be only a growth that is compatible to the ecological restrictions, a growth without ecological problems. This growth has to be distributed fairly to reach a balanced participation on the medium term, thus guaranteeing the poor countries definitely a catch up process. It's the only way that we stand a chance to solve those problems behind all the symptoms we are faced with. It's a complexity of problems, standing behind all currently visible difficulties. The crisis, we experience around the end of the first decade of the new Millennium, sharpened the peoples consciousness for the most important problem domains. People are aware now that we do not have only a financial crisis. There is a social crisis and an environmental crisis as well. We have problems with the climate, energy, water and nutrition, all of these being of crucial dimensions and importance. Burgeon consciousness and the growing perception that the complexity of problems has different facets, open in fact the chance to invent and implement an effective solution. What are the essential characteristics the solution should have? It has to be first of all realistic, even if it follows some visionary aims. The solution has to follow a possible pragmatic way. In the first step the focus should be to show what a way out of all the mess could look like, that has a concrete chance to be followed, based on international and binding commitments. This way out has to stabilize the monetary system, and at the same time it should set the course to a balanced and fair distribution of hopefully more value added in the future. The solution can build on already made agreements and declarations at the international level in politics and non governmental organizations. The solution can build partly on ideas for strategic actions discussed and called for by the general public. Meanwhile there are quiet different groups, organizations and politicians demanding the economy to become "green". They postulate that we must renew the worldwide economy. There is a demand for increased energy efficiency. Alternative and renewable energies are demanded. Enhanced investments to achieve more and better education, construction and renovation for green buildings to gain better resource efficiency, health care reforms for better medical aid and the like are called for. There are already campaigns promoting a Green New Deal or a Marshall Plan to be taken globally. Internationally all systemically important industrialized and developing economies agreed to work out a charter for sustainable economic activity. It has been considered to establish a new global UN Economic Council, similar to the global UN Security Council, at the United Nations. The question is now: how could these well intentioned ideas, concepts and declarations be put together? How could a concrete way be designed to solve the aforementioned complexity of problems behind those problems of the world financial and economic system that are currently visible at the surface? We will sketch such an approach in our outlook. Growing consciousness and awareness are important. To solve the overall complexity of problems one also has to know, which the most appropriate parameters are to achieve effectively the badly needed structural change. If both aspects are recognized, the broad non governmental engagement (for sure governmental engagement as well) could lead us into the right direction.

We depicted already the competition of (national) systems as one crucial aspect. Globally and to a large extent it takes place without rules and regulations.

Metaphorically, it seems as if in history different sports and game clubs – the Nations – were established. They defined their rules of the game on an individual basis for their own narrow partnership. They defined and implemented all the laws, ruling their communal living and their framework for economic activities. As a result we have different "games" played separately in each club. As long as all those individual groups are playing for themselves, everything is fun. Within one group, everybody knows the ropes, regarding them as fair. This only holds true, if we look to a single group of player, a single club and a single game. Now we consider the process of globalization. This process is for several reasons a necessity, for instance we have to manage successfully the "Global Commons" like water and the climate. What happened so far as a consequence of the globalization process? Players of different clubs meet on global playing fields without umpires and referees. Nothing and nobody makes sure, that it will be a fair game with fair play. Although there are a few rules that everybody considers to be important, no referee monitors fair play. The strongest players ruthlessly take that to gain an advantage. They play in a manner that would be unfair, according to the rules valid in a single group. However, with respect to the global game, with the absence of rules and referees, it has to be seen as not prohibited, it's legal. The question of fairness is only answered within all those individual frameworks of national rule settings for the local games. Fairness in the "global game" without rules has a different meaning. On the global playing field all actions and moves that are played are allowed, because there are no rules. What is the aim of the global game? It should not be astonishing, but obvious, since "profit maximization" is the prevailing objective and implicitly the driving mechanism in free markets: the aim in the global game is to win! All players try to capture as much a share of value added and prosperity as possible. The gamblers and players try to gain a victory, triumphing about the losers. That is quiet different from playing the games, organized on a national level. In those plays, the rules for social balancing should take care, that losers of the game will neither be humiliated nor feel humiliated.

This is at the core of the global problem: we need strong and effective efforts to negotiate and set all the rules required to achieve a fair frame for the global part of our market economies. Such a fair frame consists of ecological and social rules and regulations for the world markets. Those common rules and regulations should be mandatory for all or single global markets. All rules, commonly accepted, have to be monitored by umpires and referees. Violations must cause penalties to be inflicted. Who breaks the rules, plays unfair, and is punished. Globally we did not reach such a level yet. Everybody tries to win and be triumphant, and no referees are on the playing field. Fair play is not rewarded, as those playing fair normally will lose. Tough ruffian like and brutal players prevail, they take the ball out of the game and play alone. The losing players remain harried in the playing fields.

World financial system at its limits

Social democracies in wealthy Nations are eroded by market fundamentalism ("free" markets), the currently dominating principle in the globalization process. This conclusion is a result of the comprehensive scientific analysis of the world financial system by D. Solte (2007). In its current organization and alignment the globalization enables the strongest globalized actors to minimize their tariffs and taxes. The result is that global players receive increased total net profits from investments and profitable financial or tangible assets, all the while public income decreases.

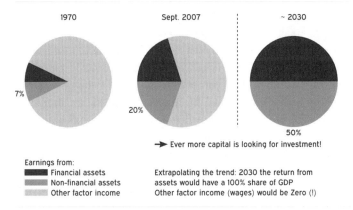

Figure 5: Yield from investments (share of total GDP)

If the total and overall volume of financial assets is growing, means that at the same time the total and overall volume of indebtedness is growing. It is the stretching of the Zero as we figured out in the first part of this book. A granted credit is a debt and the corresponding debenture is a financial asset of its bearer. A claim on money to be settled in the future corresponds to a credit as a liability. It is a liability of those making the promise to settle money in the future. For granting the credit, which means waiting for the money to be settled in the future, an interest is charged. What are credits and saved capital to be used for? To a large extent they finance leveraged investment. Assets of real value, tangible assets like enterprises or real estate are built up, and all these new components of wealth and fortune should generate a yield. A company should sell goods and services, real estate should generate income from renting and leasing. A yield on tangibles is generated either by producing something with them, utilizing them or lending them. Lending is a timely limited relinquishment of a beneficial use to put it on another's temporary disposal.

In the last forty years there is an enduring global trend. The value of financial and tangible property has grown always faster than value added. In consequence a growing share of value added has to be used to service interest and yields. There was already a share of forty percent from GDP in the year 2007. Roughly half of it was used for interest payments on all granted credits. The other half were profits generated from tangibles. An extrapolation of the past is impossible. What would happen if the overall volume of financial and tangible fortune grows always faster than the overall economic output? Already in the year 2030 the world would be in a situation where all the value added, the annual global Gross Domestic Product, would completely be required to serve interest and profits on fortunes. Nothing would be left for instance to pay wages and salaries. It would be obvious that the world is bankrupt. All earnings made would exclusively be used to pay interest or to cover the return on investments in tangibles. This constitutes the ultimate limit of the world financial system! You should compare this situation with a single company having always growing liabilities but a constant turnover. The company's profit on sales should be constant as well. With growing liabilities and thus a growing amount of interest to be paid, wages and salaries have to be reduced. Employees have to be fired until nobody is left, the final end.

A further limitation results, if the total volume of all financial and tangible assets grows faster than the world GDP. The real portion of yields from assets vis-à-vis other (more highly taxed) income becomes ever greater. This is one more reason why public earnings are decreasing. Governments balance these income losses not only through reduction of costs and privatization but also through more and more debts by issuing bonds. In consequence the debt service ratio is increasing. The portion of public earnings that has to be used to pay interest will grow. What would happen if the process of further governmental indebtedness would follow the trend of the last forty years? The governmental part of the economy and the world financial system would approach a limit.

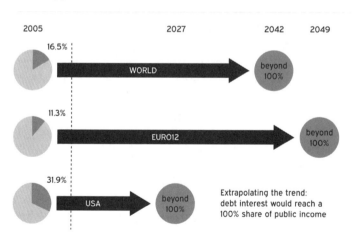

Figure 6: Dramatic pressure on the public side (share of debt service from total public earnings)

If nothing is changed the Nations would run into over-indebtedness. At some point of time in the future public earnings would not even be enough to pay all interests. To cover the debt service with at least a partial payback of credits would be even unthinkable. Consequently it is a "needs must" that something happens. Continuation is impossible! What will happen next? If we deliberate the fact that Federal Government of the United States alone incurred five times as much new debt in 2008 than in the year before, it becomes apparent that the problem of governmental over- indebtedness piles on the pressure. However, over-indebtedness is not the only problem leading to bankruptcy. There will be growing payment difficulties, up to failures to pay, as we experienced already in the current crisis as well. Some Nations had problems to sell governmental bonds in the market. This is not surprising, if we bear in mind that 2008 all the new indebtedness of Governments and public authorities has been more than the overall worldwide annual saving. The granting of credits to Governments cannot anymore mean that saved capital is lent. At least for a part of it, additional swell-money has to be created. Somebody has to go into debt to grant a credit to public authorities. That is one of the reasons why Nations were put under pressure – and are under pressure – to adopt the regulatory framework to this problematic situation. Government had to make sure that all the required new public indebtedness is possible. It has to be assured that markets can produce enough new swell-money to purchase all the newly created public debentures with it.

We can discern dependencies and interdependencies between Governments and markets. The rise in public debts is a result through transactions that have garnered high yields but are subject to few taxes. The deficit of all rich (but highly indebted) countries is almost equal to the amount of taxes that should have been paid but are not paid by the most powerful actors in the globalized economy, particularly in the financial sector. The deal between the financial and the public sector is a complicated lending strategy. One likes to see this deal stemming more from systemic reasons rather than negotiations. What does this deal look like? The few large creditors are allowed to use so-called new innovative financial products to obtain enough equity as a basis for swell-money creation, in order that they are able to create new swell-money so that they can loan it to the Nations. To limit undesirable liquidity effects, government as the main debtor then has to provide reasonable general conditions to ease the collection of this kind of money within the financial markets. This includes rules and regulations for the financial and capital markets, as for instance securitization possibilities, derivatives, REITs, no minimum reserve requirement on foreign currency accounts, no equity requirements when granting credits to best rated Nations etc. Only then the creditors can provide a certain level of stability to the financial system, such as currency stability, and they can make a commitment to purchase all new public debts. The production of fresh money is a must because the global savings rate is not high enough to ensure all needed credits on its own.

Over the years this has led at least to a four-fold increase of the total worldwide debt compared to the global economic performance. The overall volume of the global financial market is the four-fold of the worldwide value added (GDP) achieved in one year. In Europe it has gone up already to five times as large. As stated, all securitized money claims (swell-money) meanwhile constitute a more than fifty-fold claim on the total Central-Bank-money supply. This data stims from official statistics not comprising so calles shadow sampling. "consequences": The truth has to be estimated even worth than we explain.

There is inherently an enormous exposure for high inflation. It's the huge amount of swell-money covering this risk. The dan-

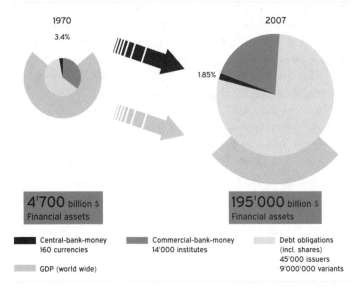

Figure 7: Money and money substitutes ("swell-money")

ger of inflation can be kept away from the market of goods and services as long as swell-money is valued and favoured as a component of wealth and fortune. Enough market participants, especially large asset managers, should be confident that they will get in the future something of value in exchange against swell-money. The system remains comparatively stable, if there is enough confidence that there will be additionally created and real value added in the future to pay back the credits. The situation will become hazardous if the blatant disparity of promises and the real economic performance becomes obvious. Becoming aware of the growing disproportion of all claims on value added being much larger than all the added value that the world is able to produce annually, could negatively affect the willingness to grant credits. A slump in economic activities could be the consequence – as in the current crisis. It could also have an effect on the tendency to save. This could happen especially if the redistribution of all the attractive assets of real value, all those appealing tangibles, comes to its end. What can happen if those originally possessing the largest amount of financial assets (or managing those) will own all the attractive "real" properties? What should one do with money and swell-money if no more attractive assets of "real" value are offered? Instead of saving money it will more and more be used for consumption. There could be a sudden rise in purchasing power being active in the market of goods and services. This could give a short impulse to economic growth, but since ecological resources are limited, can lead to heavy inflation.

To say it precisely in other words: the world financial system is at its limits! The current defaults in the financial markets are not surprising but can be explained (cf. D. Solte, 2007, pp. 129).

A flight from securitized claims on money to real value assets (non-financial assets) was the eventual result. Debt obligations could no longer be sold (Sub Prime crisis). This led as an example to ever increasing demands on commodities and scarce resources (i.e. oil and food), not mainly for consumption but as assets. This first led to an inflation of real value assets and a deflation of financial assets. Resulting liquidity problems will affect a usury deflation since "fire-sales" that were needed to prevent insolvency are induced. Eventually the Nations were forced to interfere in reaction to the subsequent effects on the real economy. Additional public debt mounted as a result. That only further aggravated the complex situation of the financial markets. In such an inconvenient situation and even precarious financial situation, politicians could be tempted to perform a currency reform as an alleged way out. In case of a currency cut the amount of financial assets and financial liabilities is reduced in the following way. In a first step all legal tender is retracted from the markets keeping its value. As a next step all promises on legal tender are devaluated, for instance dividing the notional amount by ten. Next the retracted legal tender is given back to the markets. This procedure tends to keep the given price level and exchange rates. Bearer of swell-money are losing, those owning real value assets will be the winners and afterwards the game will start again with rising indebtedness. This all could and should be avoided. The problem of the monetary system as it became accrued in the world financial crisis 2008 has to be tackled. The core of this problem is two-fold. The first aspect is the circulation velocity of Central-Bank-money which has ground to a halt in the crisis; the second aspect is the enormous swell-money bubble. Swell-money lost its capacity of being an asset of liquidity because of lost confidence. The bubble burst and circulation velocity of Central-Bank-money tends to zero. All the exchange processes of swell-money against Central-Bank-money and vice versa are disrupted. If the circulation velocity of money becomes zero there will be no payment at all - whatever volume of money is out there. To countervail the loss in faith of swell-money's liquidity, it is not enough to inject additional Central-Bank-money by lending it to the commercial banks. If those getting fresh Central-Bank-money are hoarding it, nothing will happen, so it is important that Central-Bank-money circulates. One has to assure a reasonable circulation velocity of Central-Bank-money. Furthermore the leveraging has to be reduced. The ratio of swell-money against Central-Bank-money has to be lowered. The swell-money bubble has to be get under control effectively and the ratio of the total amount of money and swell-money against the real economy has to be lowered. There should be a better ratio on money against all goods and services one can purchase. It's in fact the economic performance that forms the value basis of a monetary system with fiat money. The rest of it is good faith.

What affected such a ballooning swell-money bubble that George Soros (2008, pp. 81) denotes as the super bubble? As we have figured out, an important reason is a permanent new public indebtedness and the dimension of leverage businesses. The world financial crisis made it obvious that even public authorities and Governments could run into payment difficulties. All public debt is swell-money. In consequence further new indebtedness of Governments and public authorities would run counter to the aim to reduce the swell-money bubble. Public earnings must be increased. It's the only chance to keep the basis for value added and prosperity intact. Enough public earnings are needed to provide for all the public goods and services (infrastructures for water, transportation, communication etc., public institutions, education, wealth and much more). If we want to have this provided in the current or hopefully at an improved and enhanced level, a fair share of added value must be dedicated to the commonwealth and common good. An appropriate system of taxes and levies following the principle of tax justice and fairness is needed to channel the needed value added to the commonwealth. We have to consider that until now those most profiting from globalization can and often do evade a fair taxation. Real tax payment today follows a negative ability-to-pay principle. The economically strongest actors pay the lowest real taxes. Missing rules and regulation on a global level and disharmonies of national taxation systems are the reason for this dilemma. There is a competition between Nations, through tax systems and social frameworks, in their struggle on value added. Those benefitting from the game have played and are still playing with the systemic differences. The strongest economic market participants are financing the least share of commonwealth paying the lowest effective tax rates. The utilization of tax havens is the most crucial variant of circumvention. As a conclusion of our deliberations we can state that the worldwide taxation system is topsy-turvy. One has to take measures to bounce it back. As it is fixed in legislation on a national level, the real tax payments have to follow the principle of fairness and tax justice. To avoid legal tax circumvention, an appropriate harmonization of the national tax bases on a global level is necessary.

Up to now there is a competition and rivalry of national systems. The question is who succeeds in an unfair and unregulated global game? Public earnings of a country depend on the volume of the value added, which is taxable in that country. Which added value, proceeds or revenues are taxed depends on the definition of the tax basis. Much depends on methods used which can be applied to channel added value (or proceeds) into their own country for taxation. As explained before even not yet created value added, which is only hoped for in the future, can be relocated to a country's tax base by performing a sleight of hand (cf. chapter 8). Globally acting market participants can utilize the given disharmonies of taxation systems to their advantage. They even exploit the niveau differences in the national commonwealth to gain profits. It is no problem to pool know-how, machines and other capital in our globalized world at any place on earth to set up a company. In consequence jobs are transferred into those countries which stipulate the lowest social and ecological standards. Elaborate but expensive filter technology and other environmentally friendly technologies can thus be avoided. Polluting and devastating the environment is for free. That is why especially those "dirty industries" have been shifted to developing or emerging countries. The know-how is taken from those Nations with the very best research and education. Green cards are used to transfer the brainiest people to where value added should take place. Under these circumstances nothing is provided to cover the cost of education, and as a result the production is much cheaper. Much higher profits can be gained if the production side is not where high ecological and social standards are mandatory.

Those standards would take care of a fair and social cooperation and at the same time assure the right approach to nature. The production of goods and services not having to comply with all these standards is cheaper. That is why ecological and social dumping happens every single day. Even internationally agreed standards are undermined – example: ban on child labor. Ecological and social standards of Nations that we denote as being rich and prosperous are under an immense pressure. In nearly all wealthy Nations – but not only in the wealthy Nations – we have seen the degradation of social standards. In the last years it was partly a smooth degradation, partly it was jerky. Education, wealth, streets, railways, many kinds of infrastructures and more parts of the commonwealth are not provided at a niveau we desire today and in the future. We are living in this situation even though we incur more and more debts since years. We live over the past decades beyond our means. If we ask for the real and genuine reason for these bad developments, we approach the global crisis core problem. Why did the competition on value added and the struggle on resources become more heated? At first it is the overall population on earth permanently growing, in combination with the peoples' demand for more and more consumption. Secondly a finite earth stands vis-à-vis to it. There is only a limited surface on earth available to satisfy our growing desire for consuming goods and services. The surface to be used by living people, the surface to be used to cultivate plants and vegetables, the needed environmental space for all other living creatures, is limited on our mother earth. We do have the severe problem of a fair and balanced distribution or participation! So far we tried to solve it through a cut-throat competition. The earth is at its limits!

Earth at its limits

Today we live in a globalized world. Important driving forces for this process have been innovative information and communication technologies. All those innovations and developments for national and international transportation and logistics have made the world a global village. There is no problem anymore to make phone calls to any point of our planet. In a fraction of a second money and swell-money can be transferred via modern telecommunication networks from any country worldwide. Modern mass media reach all valleys and mountains of the world. Nearly all people of our planet are aware now of our living style, the way of life, in our wealthy Nations. Emerging countries, developing countries and certainly the poorest countries have every right to insist on a fair share in participation. To get the picture of the overall complexity of problems it is important to have a look at the expansion of the human race.

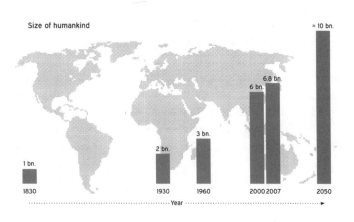

Figure 8: Expansion of the human race (global population)

It is guessed to be four million years ago that the first creature originating the human species – a hominine – came into being. This is the starting point of a growth of humankind with the following stages. Around Nativity the population of our planet in total is comparable to today's population of Brazil (around 200 Million people). Then it took little less than 2'000 years for the number of people living together on earth to reach the first Billion. It was roughly at the time when Johann Wolfgang von Goethe died. The worldwide population then doubled to two Billion people during the next hundred years until 1930. Three Billion people lived already 35 years later on the planet in the year 1965. Another 35 years later in the year 2000 the worldwide population doubled to six Billion. Today there are more than 7 Billion people living on our planet. One estimates that the total amount of people living on earth at 2050 will be 10 Billion. It is assumed that in China and India there will be more people living than lived worldwide in 1965 (3 Billion).

For sure the total amount of people living on earth is not in and of itself that which creates the problem. It is due to the second aspect of globalization: the peoples' production and consumption of goods and services. All the economic activities (over)exploit the resources of our mother earth. How much of nature is occupied by us as humankind? A second question is directly connected: in order to obtain a sustainable world how much environment would humankind need to have, to satisfy all our wishes and desires? All the different problem domains that are directly or indirectly connected to these questions constitute the overall complexity of problems. Each single problem dimension has been described in detail in those already published other "twelve books about the Future of the Earth" of "the sustainability project" (www.forum-fuer-verantwortung.de).

In comparison to European standards 5.6 billion people worldwide today live in poverty. Over ten Million of them, mostly children, die of starvation every year. Millions of others die of AIDS, malaria and other infectious diseases. It is only because each year over 45 Million pregnancies are terminated that an increase of the world population will not go far beyond ten Billion by 2050.

This shattering situation is not sustainable! It violates massively both the fundamental principle of human dignity and the dignity of nature. The question is: how do we deal with this obviously problematic situation? How could we positively exert influence on where we will be? What are the alternatives, what must we do?

The following should be made clear. If we continuously step on the dignity of nature, humankind will come to an inevitable total collapse. If we continue to produce and consume outside of the earth's capacities and if we pile more garbage and toxins into the ecosystem than can be dealt with through a natural cycle, humankind destroys its foundation of existence. We cannot force nature to bear more than it can! Humankind therefore only has one choice: respect the dignity of nature if we want to survive! This is not guaranteed at present.

Future options for the global society

To guarantee the dignity of nature is a must needs! To prevent environmental over-use, given our current level of consumption and production technology for goods and services, there are two alternatives: Brazilianization (neo feudalism) or Balance. The first alternative is to enforce an even more unequal access to consumption and wealth than today. Scarce resources will be set aside for a small elite. The larger portion of people will be limited to just the necessities or even less. There is on the one hand an "exclusive market segment". On the other hand there are discount houses offering poor mass goods and services produced with minimal resources. This is the Brazilianization of the world, the Brazilianization of an increasing human population. We would thus live in a two class society of haves and have-nots where equal rights would not apply. The human dignity of the have-nots would fall to the wayside. Daily displays of hate, force and terror would emerge. In turn that would need to be met with massive interventions as it is already today, including the construction of walls and fences. This is surely not the desired outcome for the majority of people, attractive as it may be for the elite. A structure of few "masters" and many (extremely cheap) servants would become manifest – a global feudal structure. This cannot be a stable fundament for peace!

We discovered in this book that the course of the current crisis could lead into this kind of future. Triggered by the world financial crisis we slide more and more into the abyss of a strong recession. In this process not everybody is a loser. As mentioned, in this unfair "game of games" there are those triumphing. Those, who at the right time exchanged their swell-money against Central-Bank-money, have taken the chairs out of the game. They hoarded all the liquidity in Central-Bank-money to capture all the attractive real value assets at some time for nearly nothing. The losers have to pledge them. Tangible capital transferred as a fortune to those few winners. As a result, the necessary and scarce resources will be owned by a comparatively small group – the elite. In principle this actually would solve the ecologic problem: it would be solved by only having a small group of people using their exclusive access on all scarce resources for themselves only. Those will then produce only as much as technology and all ecological limitations with respect to all scarce resources of the earth would allow. Those owning enough tangible capital would be the only ones that could pay the prices for goods and services requiring scarce resources. The rest of people could pay for indispensables to life only, or even less.

To boost the global economic performance, and to afford the same fair participation as it is in today's wealthy Nations for all, needs enormous innovations first. Based on our current production technologies and their resource-efficiency it is just impossible to produce more goods and services than today and keep within the ecological limits. Currently we would need much more than one earth to provide all required environmental resources sustainably. Mother earth that we only have, could at best be enough if we successfully attain an immense innovative progress. We have to attain a much higher resource-efficiency to produce much more goods and services but at the same time lowering environmental consumption. An economic growth without these innovations is out of the question, the devastation of nature would undoubtedly be the consequence.

A balanced world is the desired future. The big challenge is to reach a fair participation on prosperity and value added for all. For all means we have to assure the dignity of nature. We have to enforce an always responsible utilization of (scarce) environmental resources. A "World in Balance" aims at prosperity for all, prosperity for humans and nature. To achieve such a wealth, we must create a much higher (at best ten-fold) value added than is currently possible, with much fewer environmental resources (at best ten times less – cf. Schmidt-Bleek, 2007). It should facilitate the best possible quality of life, but at the same time assure fair distribution and participation. To distribute fairly what can be produced sustainably today is neither desirable nor probable. All people in the developed countries would need to reduce their consumption by 85%, leaving a consumption-niveau of only 15% of the today's average. Everyone would then have only one third of what we would consider poor (European Union defines having less than 50% of the average as being poor). At the same time all people in currently underdeveloped countries would forfeit a standard of living that we have been enjoying, and that advertising and marketing always propagated through mass media as the lifestyle everybody should strive for. Who of the many and ever increasing number of job-seekers will stand the slightest chance of employment if there is no significant growth of the total value added process? How then can we expect high-skilled labour such as in medicine and with what level of quality? The right kind of growth would ease the answer to these questions. Such a growth should at all means be limited to a resource-sustainable expansion of value creation, and to reach a fair participation an effective transition process of the currently imbalanced global situation into balance has to be assured.

This means however, we have to manage a ten-fold value added with only one earth. In order the resource-efficiency (in relation to the current OECD standard) must be increased by a factor of ten as well. This is the double challenge we are faced with. We have to tackle this challenge successfully to reach a World in Balance! The growth that the world's population could endeavour to reach

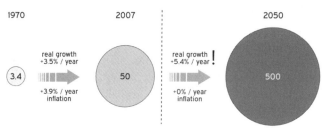

Figure 9: a double challenge for a World in Balance: ten-fold increase of the world's GDP till 2050 with a real annual growth of 5.4%. By all means (ecological) sustainability is a must. To achieve this till 2050 is perhaps possible in a worldwide joint tour de force. A subsequent real growth of that kind, conform to the sustainability requirement, seems to be impossible.

is limited, growth targets should always be viewed through a lens of sustainability. Growth is allowed to that extent only that the attained progress in resource-efficiency admits. The monetary system must allow only such (sustainability conformed) growth. Active money supply should enable a growth in value added if there is a corresponding improvement of resource-efficiency. The monetary system (to be seen as the set of all relevant rules, laws, provisions and agreements) should however also support a balanced wealth distribution to be reached. In consequence, existing peace and wealth promoting balanced distribution patterns of societies should not be undercut but rather enabled to develop. The monetary system should support the necessary transition process to a fair and balanced world. This especially requires an effective control of the money supply, which is active in the tangible asset market. Furthermore the income potential from financial and tangible assets, with its today's imbalanced distribution, has to be examined. There is more balance necessary.

How can prosperity for all be achieved?

History teaches us the following: achieving a desirable level of prosperity for all requires peoples' maximal creativity to be released. For this an adequate global social structure is necessary and a comprehensive set of public goods and services with high quality. The key for creativity is education. Creativity and innovation should be effective and has to consider the complexity of all problems to be solved. This requires a high degree of broad education. To provide this education, enough schools with well-skilled and highly motivated teachers are necessary. Consequently, universities, research and academic teaching is a must. This all has to be considered as an important part of the commonwealth which at the same time is the key for social balance.

Education is much more important than the redistribution of added value provided by governmental measures and social partnership. Education is arduous and expensive. Experience gained in concrete practical work is at least as important as a primary education, which induces a sound health care system as being also of crucial importance. This would assure that all these well-educated and experienced people can develop their creativity having healthiness and a fulfilling life. Prosperous societies with good health care will have consequently more older people. The society has to assure a fair participation of all – those being gainfully employed and those in education, unemployed or retired.

A further need is infrastructure for social communication, coordination and cooperation of people. This comprises a lot of networks, mains, water supply, sewerage, railways, road networks etc., but modern information and communication networks as well. A part of the commonwealth to support motivation and creativity of the society is the development of arts and culture. It is of specially importance to safeguard and develop cultural identities in our globalized multicultural world society. Safeguards for the environment that include the dignity of other beings are essential, a sustainable nature providing liveable space for humans and a broad biological diversity. All this together is the basis for value added and prosperity. It has to be provided to a large extent by corresponding public goods and services. Developed countries gaining prosperity made the following experience: it is important to implement a coherent law and order. This is the system of ecological, social and economical rules and regulations. The market mechanism would then provide competition, achievement and efficiency under the adherence of set rules. The targeted aims, if they are translated into corresponding laws, rules and regulations, will then be reached efficiently through the markets. To be able to comply with all the set rules and regulations and to assure obedience, the basis is needed: infrastructures and all public goods and service as the basis for prosperity and value added. This basis would have a considerable part financed by a fair system of taxes and tariffs. For fairness in taxation, all contributions need to be determined by economic capacity (ability-to-pay principle). This is key. These means of financing have to remain highly efficient and effectively allocated to the aforementioned objective. Permanent public debt is then rendered unnecessary. Hence, reaching fiscal sustainability should and must be the goal. As part of the world financial system, the tariff and tax elements need to be substantiated and implemented. Taxes and tariffs are as well necessary to finance the required "catch-up-process". This should be seen as an essential prerequisite to avoid a total collapse of the system.

The aforementioned system of economical, social and ecological rules must become mandatory in international agreements. This would implement a world wide eco-social market economy. All wealthy countries have, to a certain extent, regulations that follow such a logic. In Germany this is based on Ludwig Erhard's ordoliberal approach of a "social market economy". In the meantime measures and laws are expanded to include regulations for environmental issues. Currently all such ecological and social rules are not anchored in the global market agreements (especially not in the WTO, the World Trade Organization). In fact it is quiet the opposite. In international trade, regulated by the WTO, only quality standards have been taken into account. There are no agreements on valid or non valid process and production methods (PPMs). A social standard, like the ban of child labour, is thus not a matter of current regulation at WTO. Social standards and environmental standards affect the procedure in the manufacturing of products or services and not their quality. So long as quality aspects remain the only standard, the WTO member countries are not allowed to restrict the import of products and services, they could not refuse goods from being sold, that for example, were acquired by child labour or through, as an other example, genetic engineering.

11. Way out of the Crisis

Make everything as simple as possible,
but not simpler.

Albert Einstein

All of life is interrelated. We are all caught in an inescapable network of mutuality, tied to a single garment of destiny. Whatever affects one directly affects all indirectly.

Martin Luther King Jr.

The only limit to our realization of tomorrow will be our doubts of today.

Franklin D.Roosevelt

Witnessing and experiencing the most severe crisis in the last 80 years, the central question is: how to deal with this multidimensional complexity of problems? Are there approaches having a realistic chance for implementation? Do we have to look for isolated solutions for each single problem domain, or will it be the tackling of all problems together in a combined solution approach that stands a chance for success? What are the most important steps to set the course to a fair and balanced world, to avoid the current way to Brasilianization and collapse, to hopefully reach a "World in Balance" within a medium timeframe? Will near-chaotic situations like the current crisis improve the chance for the needed change? Will such near-chaotic situations even be the prerequisite to get a chance for change? We observe that the different dimensions of the mentioned complexity of problems become more and more into focus at public discussions. People and civil organizations, politicians as well, conduct and foster the discourse with growing intensity. This provides hope. More people are aware now of all those different problems, and the world financial crisis, with all those negative effects to the real economy, made it clear to everybody: what's definitely needed is joint and global action! Such crises cannot be resolved individually on the level of Nations. 80 years ago we had so far the most severe world crisis. Everybody reviewing the actions taken at that time has learned the lesson, that protectionism is no solution at all. Escalation will be the most probable outcome. Restraining trade and isolating one's own economy, attempting to find a national solution, will not be effective and successful. Unfortunately within a country, citizens and politicians have difficulties to put aside national interests and give a joint global solution precedence. This is a further dimension of the overall complexity of problems that has to be considered. To cut the Gordian knot, we need a solution approach with a win-win-perspective, given all the different and differing national interests. It should be clear to everybody, that it will be better to work on a joint – global – solution. An approach, that could have a chance of success, has to place emphasis on "insightful selfishness". The insight that only if joint and coordinated actions are taken this will be the best way for everybody, and should motivate the Nations to selfishly commit to a global approach.

A further constraint to be considered is cultural diversity, the diversity of Nations. Subsidiarity is thus a fundamental principle to be followed when formulating a solution. There should be global agreement about rules, regulations and standards; rules and provisions assuring fairness and effectiveness of the world economy to face all global pestering problems. Everybody has to comply with. Jointly agreed aims have to be reached and jointly agreed upon restrictions have to be maintained. The way of implementation has to be decided and processed individually within the Nations. This is the important aspect of national sovereignty.

Such a course to Balance as a jointly taken way out of the currently threatening worldwide disaster should have the following cornerstones:

- Framing common "rules of the game" everybody could and will profit from.
- Establishing those rules as mandatory social and ecological standards worldwide, and the assurance that they are observed.
- Worldwide implementation and provision of all necessary public goods and services, to comply with the social and ecological standards – implement all further parts of the basis for value added and prosperity as well.
- Accelerate an innovation process, aiming to reach a sustainable world economy – ecological, social and economical stability and sustainability.
- Improve value added and prosperity and provide a fair participation of the currently poor, developing and emerging countries. Stipulate a catch-up process for those countries to attain a level on par with developed countries.

It is important to stop immediately the observable process of redistribution of wealth. Currently we are on the way to Brasilianization or total collapse. We have to set the course to a way out of the crisis for everybody's benefit. Recession and a possible depression have effectively to be obviated worldwide with a Global (Green) New Deal: broad investment in education, health, infrastructure, sustainable technologies, energy efficiency and, what is of crucial importance, investment to make alternative energy sources available, or to develop new ways for energy production.

These worldwide investments will lead to a growth in value added. By all means this expanded production of goods and services has to be compatible and in line with environmental and social sustainability. In consequence there must be agreed globally on all the needed ecological and social standards and norms. All economical and social processes in all countries have to comply with these common and global rules. Social and ecological standards should be the guide rails for all economic processes. Corresponding rules define the objectives, which the worldwide market has to achieve. All rules have to be mandatory. Assurance must be ensured, that all economic and social processes comply these global standards. That is why all that is needed to be able to comply with the standards has to be implemented at the national level. This implementation is a most important part of the program to combat recession effectively, without devastating the environment. As it has been quiet so often in history, there are core questions having the most prominent importance and most crucial sensibility. Who shall bare the burden of cost? Where should all the necessary financial means come from?

The blueprint to answer these questions can be found in the European Unions unification process secret of success: co-financing to achieve the acceptance for standards to become mandatory! Like all countries already a part of the European Union, new candidate countries have to comply with a common set of standards and rules. These are defined in the European Union's Acquis Communautaire, the European community law. Its printed version is about 60'000 till 80'000 pages thick. Each member of the European Union has to take care that all these rules and regulations are implemented and observed on the national level. National implementation in its concrete organization is up to the Member States – strictly following the principle of subsidiarity. All Member States have to build up adequate institutions and institutional frameworks to cover all facets of the European Community law. For sure, this is an expensive process requiring resources and money. A candidate country is not left alone, that is the key to achieve the acceptance of all mandatory standards. It's not, that they have to build up everything at their own expense and internal financing only. The European Union provides so-called structural and cohesion funds, which every country is subscribing. These means are used to co-finance implementation in structurally lacking or weak regions. Those regions, where the basis to comply with the standards is lacking or weak, get financial means from the structural funds. Co-financing to achieve standards is key, to gain acceptance and commitments to the European Community law. Applied to the global complexity of problems, the resulting solution approach consists out of a seven item agenda.

12. A Seven-Point-Plan towards Balance

This is the moment when we must come together to save the planet. Let us resolve that we will leave our children a world where the oceans rise and famine spreads and terrible storms devastate our lands.

Barack Obama

We must ensure that the global market is embedded in broadly shared values and practices that reflect global social needs, and that all the world's people share the benefits of globalization.

Kofi Annan

The global financial crisis is perhaps a unique opportunity, to make some important steps towards the vision of a global eco-social market economy. What is needed is an interwoven pragmatic approach to tackle the whole complexity of problems attached to that vision. The principles to be followed jointly in this approach are sketched in the following.

The financial system is and has been used by globally acting companies and individuals to evade adequate taxation. Herein lays the solution for financing and preventing international crises by not allowing or permitting such evasion to take place. In fact this could be key to the establishment of a "Global Contract", a "Global New Deal". The right answer to the global crisis would be a concerted global action. It would be a Seven-Point-Plan "interlacing all slack threads".

The key points are: First, to arrange the environmental standards, within the framework of the Post-Kyoto negotiations (limit the emission of detrimental greenhouse gases). Simultaneously, it has to be agreed upon a demand for alternative energies and their development. That is how we could make a first big step to solve the climate and energy problem. Second, the social standards of the International Labour Organization (ILO) have to be enhanced with all the declared global Millennium Development Goals (an international declaration made at the last millennium year at the United Nations). Special attention should be given to the education of all children, to food, water and health. Much has been accomplished, but there is still a great more to do. Third, we need economic stimulus to tackle the threat of global recession and depression. We need to make the necessary investment so that a global implementation of standards and all needed infrastructures is achieved: new sources of energy, environmental technologies, education, roads, information and communication networks and a lot more. By all means, it has to be assured, that all triggered economic activities comply with the agreed upon ecological and social standards. This is the support program, urgently required by the global economy, to successfully combat recession in all countries on earth and without devastating the environment. It is a "Green Deal". Fourth: it has to be a "Global Deal", a global contract. The mentioned ecological and social standards have to be accepted as binding and should be fixed as mandatory process and production standards (related to PPMs – process and production methods) within the WTO (World Trade Organization). WTO can monitor and provide assurance that all economic activities meet these procedural standards. In order to reach the necessary acceptance to agree, co-financing of implementation has to be offered. Structurally lacking or weak Nations being economically less capable, have to be offered and guaranteed (financial) help. Co-financing would support those economically weaker countries to catch up – as is done in the European Union. Of course, the following question promptly arises: where will the required means for co-finan-

A Seven-Point-Plan towards Balance

cing come from? How to finance the necessary worldwide programme to stimulate the economy? Debt financing would destabilize the monetary system further, That is why additional public earnings are necessary. This could be achieved from fifth: the reform of the financial and the tax-systems. The abolition of tax loopholes and the "containment of tax havens" must be a primary objective. This can be accomplished by a harmonization of the tax systems, world wide. In order to reduce all the currently given opportunities for tax circumvention and evasion, adequate global regulations that synchronize the various national sets of rules are a must. This would restore the taxation fairness, and the highest contributions to public finance will come from those market participants, who have so far successfully managed to defy it to the detriment of the whole of society. Sixth: the effective stabilization of the current financial crisis through measures to keep the money super bubble – the excessive indebtedness – under control. A financial market tax being is strongly required. It should be a direct tax on all newly created debentures and all other financial products, and levied from the issuers. We denote such a levy on financial products more than a financial transaction tax as a swell-money tax – a leverage-money tax as it has been invented in Dirk Solte (2007). This tax would be an effective measure to control leveraging in the markets which has become excessive. The purchasing on credit would become manageable and delimited fairly to a reasonable overall amount. The leverage-money tax could be devised in such a way, as to make precisely those who profit most, to pay more than economically less powerful market participants. Those who contributed to the crisis through their excessive and speculative leverage deals, like the financial institutions and those who up to now exploited disharmonies of national systems to their advantage, have to pay more. Those who invest into capabilities for value added processes, as, for example, the medium sized businesses or the middle-income segment, which already has to pay higher interest rates as debtor, have to pay less. A tax of that kind makes the money super bubble controllable. In the middle-term public debt has to be reduced. Seventh: in order to restore the liquidity of the markets, a kind of "maximum permissible reserve ratio" for financial institutions needs to be introduced. Restoring liquid markets and safeguarding liquidity in the future is urgently needed. The hoarding of cash has to be limited. All market participants should be obliged to pay in all "overhang" liquidity, all means of payment being highly liquid, into a commonly sustained fund. High liquid financial assets going beyond the maximum permissible reserve have to be paid in to a liquidity circulation fund. All market participants are collectively responsible for this fund. Liquidity paid in to the fund could be granted as a loan to those short in liquidity. Debtors of the fund would of course have to meet all required criteria e.g. solvency. Those market participants borrowing liquidity need to have, for example, to meet the requested capital requirements. It would be just partially up to the market participants to plead for stricter criteria if they cast doubt upon the quality of the fund and its debtors.

This is the program for a political solution of the worldwide complexity of problems. It should be put forward in the current G-20-Process "financial markets and world economy". In the following we give a more detailed and structured overview about the Seven-Point-Plan with its core aspects:

(1) **Environmental standards**: The current climate change dialogue could result in a blueprint how to manage Global Commons like the atmosphere, water or energy. The first attempt to limit global greenhouse gas emissions to mitigate global warming is the "Kyoto Protocol" which expires at the end of 2012. The window of opportunity is in the current "Post-Kyoto negotiations" now open to agree to a global

A Seven-Point-Plan towards Balance

"Cap and Trade" regime to manage the climate. The amount of total greenhouse gas emission rights is to be limited globally (Cap) and "trade" between Nations is to be permitted. The allocation of emission rights is the core problem. Environmental pollution and economical participation is today very imbalanced. Developed countries take quiet the biggest share in emitting greenhouse gases and developing countries seek to catch up economically, which makes it difficult to find a consensus. In order to achieve a fair and just basis, a gradual and guaranteed transformation process will need to be negotiated and implemented, leading in the medium-term to equal per-capita emission rights to all peoples world wide and a balanced economical participation.

(2) **Social standards:** It is important to mention, that we can count on already agreed upon international social standards. All Nations have agreed upon the core-standards of the International Labour Organization (ILO). However – as it is the case with environmental standards – no sanction mechanism actually assures observance. Child Labour and pollution, for example, still constitute a competitive advantage in the global markets, since social and environmental standards are so far not considered within the framework of the World Trade Organization.

(3) **World economy:** Preventing a worldwide recession must entail more than a debt-fueled economic stimulus! Global common good should be the focus; ecologically and socially sustainable value added processes should be the aim. In order to achieve this objective, all ecological and social standards have to be mandatory within the World Trade Organization, set as compulsory process and production standards. Only then will there be no more ecological and social dumping for profit maximization. Public investments into the necessary fundamentals (including the entire institu-

tional requirements) result, to comply with all commonly agreed upon standards. The consequence will be a global implementation process of commonwealth, which is necessary for a world wide sustainable development: education and infrastructure, new energies and environmental technologies. The global market will become an eco-social market.

(4) **Global contract:** How can the full deal be accomplished? The answer is: co-financing. For how long have EU-countries already benefited from co-financing? New and weaker Member States receive funds. In turn they are better able to implement European Community laws (the Acquis Communautaire). Such a measure on a global scale is key – the co-financing of standards! We will have then the chance to reach those Millennium Development Goals declared at the United Nations at the beginning of this millennium. Fair and balanced participation is the final aim.

(5) **Financing:** Where do the means for co-financing come from? The answer is: by reforming the financial and tax systems. It could be negotiated within the framework of the international plan for action at the G20-Level ("Financial markets and the world economy"). It is important however, that the reforms negotiated and decided, must not be limited to the financial sector alone. Taxation systems need to be adjusted too, and "tax havens" have to be contained. For only through a harmonization of the tax bases can tax evasion be globally stopped effectively.

(6) **Balance:** In addition, in order to provide the financing and implementation of the transformation processes, it would become necessary to tax financial products and the global transactions including transport, trade and financial flows. Those measures would mix necessities (public earnings) with pleasure (curtailing speculative leverage business in the financial markets). A swell-money tax – a leverage-money tax – would enforce those profiting most, to pay their fair

A Seven-Point-Plan towards Balance

share. It would not place a further burden on the middle class and others, who are already handicapped. As compared to the capacities of large international trusts and financial institutions, the less capable economic participants can not buy in bundles. They are subject to the higher interest that must be paid on a credit (a financial product) and should not be further burdened. Economically strong actors should therefore have a higher tax placed on their own created swell-money, e.g. the credits they take for leveraged investments and speculations. Through the swell-money tax, a fair financial market tax would be formed, that makes the money super bubble containable and controllable.

(7) **Monetary crisis:** In direct response to the global financial crisis, including its effects on the real economy, liquidity bottlenecks must be removed. Liquidity bottlenecks are driving all these bad processes leading to deflation, recession and redistribution of the valuable components of wealth and fortune. It is important that Central-Bank-money must circulate again. To attain this goal, the holding of liquidity reserves of all financial market participants must be limited. An effective means would be the stipulation of a maximum permissible reserve ratio. "Surplus" or "overhang" liquidity would then be made available through a liquidity circulation fund (LCF).

World financial system in balance

The solution of the problems in the world financial system house of cards is a crucial factor to gain broad acceptance of the Seven-Point-Plan. An inherently given problem of the world financial markets is the repercussion of self reinforcing processes, originating from the hoarding of scarce legal tender money. Cash management of Central-Bank-money could dry up markets, if high volumes are concentrated and not circulating. For instance in the years 2008 and 2009 the world economy has been in a situation with a huge amount of financial assets allocated at only a few institutional investors. Besides managing enormous amounts of all the world wide available financial assets, these institutional investors are major shareholders of all relevant financial institutions. Those financial institutions manage another big part of the overall world wide financial assets. In this entwinement the financial assets of the world are concentrated at only a few big actors. They are under management of only a few and those make the investment decisions. In addition there is another huge amount of financial assets under custody. This means those big actors named custodians manage financial assets in bundles on the authority of their owner. What if all or a few of these big actors change the investment or cash management strategy? What if they, for instance, decide to hold a larger share in Central-Bank-money? The result could be that nearly the total amount of Central-Bank-money liquidity, that is available in the world financial system, is concentrated at only a few places. It is "parked" or "hoarded" at only a few financial institutions. Liquidity does not disappear from the system in that case, but liquidity will not be active anymore, it is not in circulation. Liquidity will not be available for others and, for instance, not available to provide loans in the interbank market. The markets dry up. The opposite could happen if the strategy is changed again, if huge amounts of real values are purchased with the hoarded liquidity. This could lead to enormous Central Bank liquidity being suddenly active in the markets. The markets would be flooded.

To solve this problem dimension it would be reasonable to limit the hoarding of Central-Bank-money at all institutions in the world financial system. Besides the already set minimum required reserve ratio ("Not less") there would be a maximum per-

A Seven-Point-Plan towards Balance 243

missible reserve ratio ("Not more") stipulated. We would suggest discussing this measure in the context of China's and Russia's requests for a (new) global key currency. This discussion currently takes place at the United Nations and at the International Monetary Fund about possible reforms as well. The background is that China and Russia (but other countries as well) are creditors for example of the United States. They own Dollar denominated debentures and would like to exchange them against debentures denominated in a global currency (not US Dollars). Foreign currency reserves in Nations have to be seen as a huge amount of "overhang" liquidity. All the actors in the world financial system must participate in a common liquidity circulation fund. Once a previously arranged level of liquidity reserve (signal level) is attained any liquidity that goes beyond would need to be transformed into fund shares (these would be bonds that are guaranteed ultimately by all financial market participants together). The common liquidity circulation fund would thus permit effective interventions through the granting of loans in the event of an imbalanced distribution of liquidity. All actors would be confined by the same conditions. The market would have to bear and safeguard the leverage risk by itself. For their own sake the financial markets' participants would ask for reasonable legal requirements set to financial institutions. Since everybody could become a creditor of the liquidity circulation fund, everybody will demand that the risk for credit defaults becomes minimal. In that way, together with the implementation of a swell-money tax, world financial system crises as we had experienced currently (but other as well) can effectively be countervailed.

The monetary system has to be neatly adjusted. One aspect is the appropriate provision of Central-Bank-money to the economy. Another aspect is to assure a required circulation of Central-Bank-money. The third aspect is an effective control of swell-money creation. Details of the design of a sustainable world financial system and the specification for implementation can be found in D. Solte (2009). The flow of money can be assured, as shown, if all financial market participants are requested to have their liquidity management in conformance with a maximum permissible reserve ratio. You could compare this with the cash management in families. The parents could decide that nobody should have more than 50 Euros carried in the wallet; additional money should be stored at a safe place. It is quiet the same when limiting the cash holding of financial market participants. That can be organized with a common "Money Pot" as we have described. We emphasize again: a maximum permissible reserve rate set fix, is an effective means to limit the hoarding of Central-Bank-money of all market participants. It is the effective means to prevent markets from drying up. If markets dry up those hoarding the liquidity could gain high profits. At the right point in time, if attractive real value assets are offered in fire-sales (since their owners are short in liquidity) they could buy them cheap.

Further, the Central-Bank-money supply should be controlled with respect to a sustainable economy. A growth in money supply triggering economic growth is only allowed if economic growth would not conflict with environmental limits. Growth that leads to excessive use of resources has to be dampened. Limits of maximum allowed resource utilization, for example concerning the emission of carbon dioxide and other detrimental greenhouse gases, should always be maintained. That is why only as much liquidity is allowed to circulate in the markets, so that the total volume of economic activities never exceeds resource limitations and other ecological constraints. Beside Central-Bank-money supply, the total amount of created swell-money has to be effectively controlled. At the same time it is important to assure fairness for all market participants. Measures to control the financial markets should tend to dampen and minimize speculative businesses. Currently the most capable market participants have advantages in speculative and leverage businesses. On swell-money they create, that means for credits they take, they usually have to pay much less interest than economic weaker actors. That is a main reason why especially the economically most capable and strongest actors can make leverage businesses with a very high leverage. That is why they can for example buy capable midsize enterprises comparably cheap. Via mergers and acquisitions they can build up conglomerates even if they do possess only a minimal fraction of all the needed capital. The purchases of companies are highly credit based. That means a redistribution of real value assets against promises. To countervail these processes and to get effectively a grip on the swell-money bubble, a swell-money tax (leverage money tax) would be a reasonable method. It would be a duty on any kind and type of leverage. A swell-money tax is not a financial transaction tax. A financial transaction tax can be compared with the Real Estate transfer tax, which has to be paid whenever the ownership of an already existing property changes. Similar to the VAT, which is levied once if a product is created and sold, the swell-money tax would be levied once from the swell-money creators who are loading instability to the system by going into debt. Actually, every debtor taking out a loan creates a financial product. The certificated or securitized debt, the document evidencing the credit agreement (debt obligation, debenture, promissory note, etc.) is the product. The swell-money tax would be levied on any debts of all debtors, especially those with high or highest ratings. Those paying low interest on their own created swell-money have to pay a higher duty than those, who pay higher interest. The most capable actors would pay higher duties than less capable. This follows the principle of taxation fairness. It follows the ability-to-pay principle, where the duty depends on the economic capability of the tax payer. We have to consider currently a world wide overall volume of at least 200'000 Billion (200 Trillion) US

Dollar in swell-money. These are all the financial assets of the world. A swell-money tax of one percent on the average would raise a financial volume of 2'000 Billion (2 Trillion) US Dollar annually as public earnings. Further financial means can be raised if a harmonization of tax bases and the containment of tax havens takes place. Circumvention of tax payments and tax evasion would be prevented. Its world wide volume can be estimated as being 1'000 to 2'000 Billion US Dollar a year. Both measures together would raise financial means of 3'000 to 4'000 Billion US Dollar a year as public earnings and that is without any further tax increases. That is how the ambitious program "prosperity for all", the Global Green New Deal, the Global Contract, could be financed, and in the middle term public debt can be cleared. Such additional financial means without further indebtedness of Governments and public authorities are essential to co-finance all what is necessary to implement and monitor common standards. A corresponding program to stimulate economic progress around the globe would use this means to build up worldwide the fundamental basis for value added and prosperity. Of course the focus should be related to those countries being "structurally weak". These are all those countries that currently undermine important ecological and social standards. However, even in those so called wealthy Nations there is an acute necessity for additional investments, for modernization and enhancements. The global agreement would apply the European "secret for success" on a worldwide level; worth fighting for not really through wars but debates. All countries would have to accept commonly agreed upon ecological and social standards at the World Trade Organization to become mandatory process and procedural standards. In turn each country will gain advantages by being supported through co-financing. That is how the non-European global part of markets would become an eco-social market as well. Besides co-financing all less developed countries have to be warranted to catch up on a transformation path. At the onset it has to be defined and agreed upon how and when a fair participation on value added and prosperity for all will be reached. Of course it has to be a sustainable path into a balanced future that does not overexploit the resources of our planet. By no means should the foundation of our existence and that of our descendants be destroyed through our economic activities. With respect to the necessary agreement to preserve climate we have to accept and embody the target to come to equal per-capita emission rights. Everybody should be admitted to make the same (small) amount of dirt. Given the current completely imbalanced situation, climate justice for everybody can probably be reached in a smooth transition only. At the moment the status quo of the countries of the world have a quiet unequal greenhouse gas emission per-capita. This cannot be changed abruptly. Step-by-step one has to reach a situation of equal per-capita emission rights.

Common norms for fairness and equity

The issue of "fairness and equity" dominates the current discussions at the international level, e. g. in the context of global order negotiations at WTO (World Trade Organization) and UNEP (United Nations Environment Programme). This issue raises the question, whether a consensus can be reached about a coherent agreement on necessary restrictions of individual freedom and diversity, guaranteeing

(1) fair participation in wealth and value added,
(2) fair participation in Global Commons
while at the same time
(3) preserving a balanced and intact environment ("dignity of nature").

This opens a window of opportunity to negotiate and implement the necessary common ecological and social standards globally.

In 1948 the United Nations proclaimed the Universal Declaration of Human Rights as a common standard of achievement for all peoples and all nations (as it is mentioned in the preamble of the Declaration), forming a mutual basis for regulating the competition between humans for participation. Article 25 is essential with respect to the participation in wealth and value added; »everyone has a right to a standard of living adequate for the health and wellbeing of himself and of his family and the right to security ...«. Article 28 explicitly proclaims, that »everyone is entitled to a social and international order in which the rights and freedoms set forth in this Declaration can be fully realized«. The Declaration contains several norms concerning civil and political, economic, social and cultural rights, but does not take the limited nature into account. Meanwhile, the necessity to preserve the earth can be considered a common understanding and to be mutual interest.

In consequence, the main article 1 of the Declaration, which defines the leading principle of human competition, should be enhanced, e.g. in the following way (changes are set in bold italic):

> ### Article 1
>
> All human beings are born free and equal in dignity and rights, ***and they are committed to preserve the availability of the Global Commons and a balanced environment***. They are endowed with reason and conscience and should act towards one another in the spirit of brotherhood.

The commitment to preserve the availability of the Global Commons and a balanced environment should be clarified by adding a new article to the declaration:

> **Article (new)**
>
> (1) Everyone has the right and duty to protect the environment, to keep the balance of nature intact for current and future generations.
> (2) Everyone has the right to participate equally in all Global Commons.

These enhancements to the Declaration incorporate the environmental aspect: With the obligation to respect human dignity and the dignity of nature, the behaviour of everyone competing for participation should reflect the spirit of brotherhood.

An important aspect is left free for individual interpretation. What does "spirit of brotherhood" actually mean? The Declaration uses further words without explanation like "fair" (article 10), "adequate" (article 25) and "wellbeing" (article 25). This could lead to conflicting interpretations depending upon the attitude and virtuousness of the reader. The question is left open, whether »standard of living adequate for ... wellbeing« has to be interpreted in the virtuous spirit of the "Golden Mean" (Aristotle), the "Doctrine of the Mean" (Confucius), the "Middle Way" (Buddhism), the "Right Path" (Islam) or whether it comprises everything like the "maximization of utility or profit" (hedonistic utilitarianism). Is it virtue, justice and order which have to ensure fairness and equity (wellbeing for everyone), or is this expected from the "invisible hand" of the markets?

If we consider formal logic and decision theories we will have to expect strongly, that the problem of maximizing the overall utility of all the future generations in all dimensions of sustainability - ecological (stability), economical (profit) and social (dignity and peace) – is undecidable. The world is too complex;

there will always be undecidable questions of what is good and pleasure. It is impossible to find any unambiguous and thus unimpeachable "target-function" to maximize ecological, economical and social happiness. Even if a restricted form of the problem in all three dimensions is chosen, the result could only be Pareto solutions.

In consequence, the definition of fairness and equity has to be derived from a consensus how to "balance" the complex and interconnected system of ecological, economical and social aims. This corresponds to a consensus about the leading principle of virtue, between the eco-social "Doctrine of the Mean" and the economic "Doctrine of the Maximum". Could a "Doctrine of Balance" be a compromise for a new model of progress that replaces the current model of growth?

A Doctrine of Balance could be transformed into a "virtue of fairness, equity, conscience and responsibility", meant as the

- leading principle for individual decisions in situations that are not restricted by legislation,
- measure to evaluate and define regulations
- guideline to find common consensus on what is assigned to be a right decision in undecidable situations.

The focal point of the World Order, the Universal Declaration of Human Rights, should fix it, e. g. in article 28, as the leading principle behind the "spirit of brotherhood".

Article 28

Everyone is entitled to a social and international order, ***balancing social, ecological and economical issues, pursuant to the virtue of fairness, equity, conscience and responsibility as the leading principle for brotherhood***, in which the rights and freedoms set forth in this Declaration can be fully realized.

National and international order and legislation that respect Human Rights would have to implement and execute justice that cares for Balance.

An enhanced Universal Declaration of Human Rights could be the starting point to negotiate details within the WTO in close cooperation and coordination with other responsible bodies of the UN. The aim of the negotiations should be to adapt the International Covenant on Civil and Political Rights and the International Covenant on Economic, Social and Cultural Rights, and a third International Covenant on Ecological Rights to be formulated. Co-financing has to be offered, so that these three covenants are accepted in a Global Deal as a Charter for Sustainable Development and as mandatory process and production methods (PPMs) within the WTO. Co-financing was the all important joker in the negotiations of the Montreal Protocol as well as in the European Union, to reach the acceptance of new standards. Co-financing will also be the key to the Global Deal.

The vision's feasibility

Is there a chance to negotiate and implement the Seven-Point-Plan on a worldwide level? What could the organizational process look like – pragmatically and concrete? In the following, we sketch out a pragmatic approach for a global organizational arrangement, proposing the cooperation of already established institutions, multilateral agreements and committees. It will be shown, that with legitimate political will, suitable institutional support is possible. Considering its urgent need, concerted – global - action would be possible.

The G20 process on all issues related to "financial markets and the global economy" is a good starting point. Establishing the implementation process for a sustainable monetary and tax system as a starting point could lead further into the implementation of a global eco-social market economy. Corresponding measures could be agreed to in detail and carried out using the G20 process. At the same time an alliance with the Economic and Social Council (ECOSOC) of the United Nations should be sought. Their role should be strengthened if deemed necessary. In their "World Economic and Social Survey 2008", ECOSOC demanded the world to rethink a "reform of Bretton Woods", the "principles of the Marshall Plan", and the "New Deal" – jointly and globally. A concrete approach for this has been detailed in the "Seven-Point-Plan". Should a new "Global Economic Council" at the United Nations, as proposed by the German Federal Chancellor Angela Merkel, be created, this could replace the G20 as the body for further negotiations. The G20 (or a newly created UN Global Economic Council) would agree on concerted and collective actions in response to the current crisis and its aftermath. They could set up the implementation process of an international framework for harmonizing the monetary and tax system of a globalized economy. Responsibility for the full process would be put to the G20 / UN Global Economic Council. The tasks would then also be delegated to various other institutions in order to agree upon and put into action the full package for a "Global New Deal" as was sketched out in the "Seven-Point-Plan". ECOSOC would be a suitable body to coordinate the implementation process.

Acting on the liquidity shortage, is a short-term measure. The essential driving factor for the global financial crisis and its effects on the real economy has to be eliminated. A maximum permissible reserve ratio has to be agreed upon by all actors in the world financial system. The financial markets participants' liquidity holdings should not exceed permissible maximal reserves. An appropriate "liquidity circulation fund", could be arranged as a collecting point for overflowing liquidity (in particular Central-

Bank-money / legal tender and short term debt obligations, .e.g. treasury bills or sweep accounts). It could be set, for example, under the supervision of the IMF. Details of the "liquidity circulation fund" could be negotiated and arranged in, for example, the Financial Stability Board at the Bank for International Settlements (BIS). Moreover, this liquidity circulation fund could be protected, to some extend, by state guarantees. A precondition for giving guarantees should be that the implementation of a swell-money tax is accepted, in order to set the "money super bubble" under compression pressure.

A "Global Structural and Cohesion Fund" has to be arranged, to provide and put in place means for co-financing a worldwide implementation of accepted standards. Standards regarding ecological and social aspects have to be binding process and production standards in the markets. The "Global Structural and Cohesion Fund" could be anchored to the World Bank. The initial capital of the fund should be raised through the swell-money tax as a Global Stability / Sustainability Contribution and, if necessary, from additionally accepted taxes on global transactions. Also, parts of the additional revenues resulting from a harmonization of the tax bases and the "fenced in" tax havens could be sources of capital. Alternatively these means could be used for national implementation processes and a medium-term reduction of public debt. The tax harmonization should itself be treated as an agreement of standards. This means that a mandated body for negotiation, much like that which exists for dealing with climate change, is necessary in order to delegate responsibilities. Considering its current participating members (the treasury secretaries and finance ministers) the G20 is an optimal body to get such a mandate. For pragmatic reasons the World Trade Organization (WTO) process would be the institutional framework to control compliance to all binding standards. Standards, as agreed upon in the ILO (International Labour Organization), as well as environmental, taxation and financial standards would be anchored, through a WTO process as the valid process and production standards for the global market economy. The already installed conflict resolution and sanction mechanisms would provide means in case of violations.

Will we see this vision becoming a reality? We share the appraisal of Sir Winston Churchill concerning the behaviour of people and politicians: »I cannot forecast to you the action of ... (a Nation)«. Therefore, he said, one has to know as a key their »... national interest«. The question is, whether all relevant currency zones, whether all economies of the world, will have or gain enough "insightful selfishness" to commit themselves to a joint global program of action to avert the real threatening devastating situation on earth. We hope so!

Appendix

Glossary

Abbreviations

ABS	Asset Backed Security
ADR / ADS	American Depositary Receipt / American Depositary Share
BIS	Bank for International Settlements
Bn.	Billion = 1'000 Million = 1'000'000'000
ECB	European Central Bank
Fed	Federal Reserve Bank
GDP	Gross Domestic Product
ILO	International Labour Organization
IMF	International Monetary Fund
OTC	Over The Counter
RePo	Repurchase Agreement
SDR	Special Drawing Right
SPV	Special Purpose Vehicle
Tr.	Trillion = 1'000 Billion = 1'000'000 Million = 1'000'000'000'000
WTO	World Trade Organization

Asset: The term asset is used in business and accounting. An asset denotes the value of anything tangible or intangible that one possesses. In a balance sheet, assets are all the accounts on the left side. Assets could be money or other valuables belonging to its owner. Assets could be for instance real objects like houses, real estate or gold. Assets could as well be receivables (for instance debentures). Financial assets could be seen as claims on money against those making promises on money.

Asset backed Securities: Asset backed securities are a special kind of debt obligations or company shares. As the word indicates, asset backed securities are debentures backed by assets of whatever kind. To create asset backed securities usually a special company is founded, a so-called special purpose vehicle (SPV). This special company emits and sells asset backed securities, buying assets with the return. The assets purchased could be debentures, tangibles or whatever. Those owning the asset backed securities in principle own a share on this special purpose vehicle. Since the SPV has a collection of owned assets, the emitted shares are backed by all the asset positions of the SPV. Asset backed securities could have the form of company shares (fund shares) of the SPV. Asset backed securities could have the form of debentures, emitted by the SPV. Some special legal structures of a SPV are called conduit.

Bad Bank: A severe problem of the world financial crisis is a reduced willingness to hold swell-money as an asset. At the beginning and during the crisis there is, for sure with good cause, doubt being raised, as to which of all those promises on money are to be kept in the future. Nobody knows which payment obligations will and could be settled at maturity. The result in the financial markets is a slump for the demand of swell-money. Those bearers of swell-money are not able anymore to sell these assets in the short term against legal tender. If they need Central-Bank-money, to settle a debt at maturity, they cannot exchange swell-money against legal tender easily. The problem is that there are not enough buyers looking for swell-money, respectively the conditions to sell swell-money are extremely bad. The consequence of fair value accounting is that in such situations assets will be assessed at a lower value. They are assessed with the prices resulting from observed market transactions and since on the market the prices for swell-money has tumbled, all assets seen as equivalent will be evaluated lower. This leads to enormous book losses. Those financial institutions owning swell-money will have reduced equity. Capital requirements set by legislation cannot be fulfilled anymore. To counteract this problem domain, Germany has politically decided and set to law that financial institutes in trouble could outsource troubled assets. "Toxic" assets, swell-money that currently is seen as unsaleable, can be outsourced into a so-called Bad Bank. At a well-defined price financial institutes can sell troubled swell-money they own to the Bad Bank. They are paid with new swell-money created by the Bad Bank. The Bad Bank swell-money gets a governmental guarantee. That is why Bad Bank swell-money is seen to be as good as governmental swell-money. To say it clearly: it is swell-money and it will be swell-money. The advantage of financial institutes using this opportunity to outsource troubled assets results from the evaluation of Bad Bank swell-money. Since it is seen as good as governmental swell-money, fair value accounting will be oriented towards the evaluation of governmental swell-money. That is how further book losses will be avoided. Nevertheless the problem is still open whether there will be enough buyers for Bad Bank swell-money in case of payment difficulties. If one considers that the new indebtedness of governments and public authorities in year 2008 only was more than all worldwide savings, there should be doubts. How could the demand for swell-money as a component for wealth and fortune ever become big enough? That is why there should be reasonable doubts as to whether this solution will be successful. There should be doubts whether the problem of liquidity, whether the problem to assure money circulation, especially to assure the circulation of legal tender in the markets, will successfully be solved with the concept of Bad Banks.

Balance sheet / assets and liabilities: A balance sheet of an economic entity lists all possessions vis-à-vis all claims against the entity. Economic entities could be companies as for instance banks but also Nations, individuals etc. All that an economic entity possesses is listed on the left side of the balance sheet, evaluated in terms of money and called assets. These are structured in several categories like tangibles, intangibles and all (financial) claims against other economic entities. The latter are all "current assets" including money and swell-money that the entity owns. On the right side of the balance sheet are listed all liabilities and the owner's equity. These are all obligations against other economic entities. Liabilities or credit capital are all debts of the economic entity. On the right side of the balance sheet are all promises on money that the economic entity has made. A special form of promise is the entity's equity (as a claim of the owners). The value of the owner's equity is derived by subtracting all liabilities (without owner's equity) from the sum total of all assets. This difference is the net worth of the economic entity. The owners have granted this capital indefinitely. That is why equity is somehow different from other liabilities. Equity has no duration and the owner of equity (like shares) has not the right to demand redemption. Usually equity or shares never become due as long as a company is in operation. The capital paid in when shares are initially emitted and sold will never be paid back to the shareholder. The net worth of an economic entity is distributed to its owner usually only in case of liquidation. In such a case all liabilities have to be settled first if needed. Enough assets have to be sold to obtain the money for settling the debts. What's left will be distributed to all equity owners depending on their share. This is equity and for sure it could also become negative if the value of all what the economic entity possesses falls below the sum total of all liabilities. All accounts on the right side of the balance sheet are always obligations that are listed as assets in balance sheets of some other economic entities.

Balance sheet of a companny
(Financial evaluation of a company's wealth position)

Assets (Receivables, properties)	**Liabilities and equity** (Obligations, debts)
Current Assets	Credit capital = debts to creditors
Fixed Assets	Equity = claims of owners

Bankruptcy: Bankruptcy denotes a specific financial situation of companies or individual persons. It's a situation of inability or impairment of ability to pay its creditors. It is, when obligations to pay can not be fulfilled anymore. Two different kinds of bankruptcy situations are differentiated. The first is illiquidity, the second is over-indebtedness. Illiquidity denotes a situation, where the economic subject does not have and is not able to obtain enough means to settle liabilities, when they become due. It could even be the case, when the entity possesses enough assets, but is not able to sell enough of those to obtain (liquid) money needed. This could be for example the case, if an individual or a company has to pay back a credit that was taken to buy Real Estate. The Real Estate is owned as an asset but if the credit has to be paid back and is not prolonged there could be a problem. If there is not enough cash or other means of payment available, the Real Estate might have to be sold. The question is whether in the short term a buyer can be found, to be able to pay back the credit from the sales-return. Otherwise the situation of illiquidity exists. Over-indebtedness is the situation of an economic entity, having – in the medium term – not enough earnings to service its debts. If for example the wages of an individual or the turnover of a company is not enough to cover all regular obligations. In such situations debts will inevitably rise as long as credits are granted. For the new credits also further interest has to be paid. In consequence the overall debt service is increased. The run into debt would accelerate. If one of the above described situations exists, companies are obliged to file for bankruptcy.

Basel / Basel II: The Bank for International Settlements (BIS) is located in Basel, Switzerland (founded in 1930). Originally this bank BIS was intended to safeguard Germany's ability to pay. BIS had to assure Germany's reparations to pay the damages of World War I. Today the BIS is responsible to coordinate the agreement of international valid principles of financial market regulations. The negotiations are performed at the Basel Committee on Banking Supervision (BCBS) that has been founded in response to the bankruptcy of "Herstatt Bank" (a privately owned bank in the German city Cologne) in the year 1974. Central Banks and supervising bodies of important Nations of the world are working together in this committee. They have negotiated and set for instance the capital requirements for financial institutions. This was done with the intention to stipulate that all banks have a buffer for losses. Financial institutions should have enough equity to be able to cover losses suffering for instance from credit defaults. A bank that grants credits could have the problem that those credits granted will not be paid back. If a credit defaults the bank will suffer a loss. Only with enough equity it is possible to cover this loss if there is no other profit that could be used to compensate the losses (compare in this glossary the explanation of equity). The so-called Basel-Accord from 1988 has been the first agreement specifying the capital requirements. It has been negotiated with the intention to fix the requirements in national legislation. Financial institutes should have at least 8% of equity in relation to all their so-called risk-weighted assets. Credits are claims on money that the financial institutes have against the debtors. All the credits are weighted with their probability of loss, depending on the type of credit and the type of debtor. The sum total of all these weighted risk assets has to be backed with 8% of equity. The weighting factors are of special importance since they influence strongly the amount of equity that a bank needs to have. Of even bigger importance is the question, which of the liabilities can be counted as equity. Could even special bank debentures that the financial institutes create get the equity status? The Basel committee has worked on according refinements and enhancements. All this led to the so-called Basel II-Accord. It has already been transferred into European law in 2007. The United States that triggered the work on Basel II deferred the implementation. Following Basel and Basel II financial institutes invented quite a lot of new so-called "innovative capital instrument" as new financial products. Their main aim is tax optimization. According to Basel guidelines not only shares representing the core equity of a bank will count as equity. If for example debentures are designed to have an infinite maturity (so-called perpetuals) they are accepted to be counted as liable capital. The financial institutes' advantage is that interest to be paid, reduce the tax basis and thus the tax to be paid is lowered. Dividends on shares have to be paid from already taxed profits which make shares a dearer capital instrument than a perpetual.

Basic income: The term "basic income" which is "revenu de base" in French and "Grundeinkommen" in German emerged in the 20th century. Already before, there was the idea of a common minimum income. Bertrand Russell who was awarded the Nobel Prize in literature (1950) argues in his book "roads to freedom" (1918) for a guaranteed income for all »whether working or not«. A couple of further Nobel Prize winners in economy make demands on a minimum income, for instance Samuelson, Friedman and Tobin. In Germany Dahrendorf (1986) advocated a constitutional right to get a guaranteed income. This income should be seen similar to all other basic human rights. No conditions should be made for this right; cf. G.W. Werner (2007), W. Eichhorn and A. Presse (2008) as well. The question how to finance an unconditional basic income is discussed in B. Hardorp (2008) and A. Presse (2009). They argue for using value added tax / tax on consumption for being most appropriate.

Brazilianization: Brazilianization is a term that Ulrich Beck (1999) invented to figuratively describe the foreseeable future of Europe's society. He explains the observed change of Europe towards social imbalance. Brazilianization denotes his forecast of the European society: breakdown in civil society, breakup of the middle class, growing disparity of incomes between rich elites and the impoverished majority of a society as it was observable in Brazil. Franz Josef Radermacher (2002) used this term to describe one of three possible future scenarios to be envisaged globally.

Bretton Woods: It was the village Bretton Woods in New Hampshire, USA that hosted the United Nation's monetary and financial conference in 1944 (commonly known as the Bretton Woods conference).

In this conference all allied Nations agreed on a set of principles to establish an international financial system with fixed currency exchange rates for global trade. On the 26th July of 1944 they signed to set up a general agreement on tariffs and trade (GATT). The US Dollar was agreed to be the world reserve currency. To get this status the United Stated were committed to redeem dollar with gold at a fixed exchange ratio of 35 US Dollar per ounce of gold. This contracted agreement fell apart when the United States were not able anymore to fulfil their commitment to exchange the US Dollar against gold. They unilaterally cancelled their contracted obligation in 1971. In consequence the fixed exchange rate regime was transferred to a system of flexible exchange rates since 1973. Following the Bretton Woods agreement the international institutions IMF – International Monetary Fund – and World Bank have been constituted and they are still in operation.

Certificate: A certificate is a special debenture. Certificates are derivatives referencing to something as the so-called underlying instrument. This could be a financial instrument like a share but it could as well be a share index or any other kind of index. Meanwhile there is a huge amount of quite different certificates. Usually the value attached to a certificate is derived from the underlying instrument. That means the value performance of a certificate is somehow connected to the value performance of the referenced object. This connection does not have to be one to one, it could be very complicated. A certificate can be traded vicariously instead of trading the referenced object directly. Those vicarious trades will not affect the market value of the referenced object (trading of share certificates do not influence the share prices). Nevertheless it is important to mention that a bearer of a certificate usually has no claim on the referenced objects (it does not comprise a purchase option). If, for example, owning a gold certificate one does not get gold upon request. A certificate usually is an unsecured debenture. Buying a certificate does not mean buying the referenced object, and a certificate does not comprise the claim to the referenced object to be settled upon request.

Glossary

Credit Default Swap: Credit Default Swaps are so-called credit derivatives. They are debentures enabling one to trade the risk of a credit default. The underlying instrument of the Credit Default Swap is a receivable, a financial asset (a credit). In case of a loss of receivables which means that the debtor is not able to settle the debt, the Credit Default Swap completely loses its value. The bearer of the Credit Default Swap loses the money set at stake. The bearer will not get back what has been paid when purchasing the Credit Default Swap (which will be more or less the credit amount).

Cross Border Leasing: There are a lot of opportunities to press home an advantage from differences of the Nations' tax systems. The given disharmonies enable different ways to circumvent or evade taxes. Cross Border Leasing is an example with a very special design of a contract that utilizes the given potential for tax evasion. In a Cross Border Leasing deal all contracting partners from different countries attempt to profit. In the United States the broker mediating the arrangement make profits, the banks and assurance companies get advantages and for instance in Germany governments and public authorities expected to make profits. They agreed on Cross Border Leasing contracts with public infrastructures. What is the core of a Cross Border Leasing deal? It is a dedicated construction that transferred public properties into an exclusive ownership but of two parties at the same time. For instance municipal sewage, plants and networks, water supply and others have been at the same time in American and German ownership with respect to taxation. It's somehow tricky. From the perspective of German law the property was lent. That is why the loan was constructed in the way that from an American judicial view it was given the status of a purchase. That is why, following American legislation, depreciations on the property were tax deductible. In principle, lease holds with very long maturities were contracted, but that was the German view point only. At the American side the contract was interpreted as a kind of repurchase agreement. It means a property was purchased and at the same time a repurchase at a later point of time was contracted upon. The purchased properties were paid with newly created swell-money and it was intended that this swell-money can later be used to purchase the property back. This can only work, if the swell-money does not lose its value. That was the aspect that was not assured anymore when the world financial crisis hit. The newly created swell-money – now in German ownership – lost its value. There is the danger, that they will not be able, to purchase back their real value properties. That is how the true character of cross boarder leasing became obvious. The German contracting partner has guaranteed a credit granted to the US American partner. The German partner was liable for the payment of this debt. The credit guaranteed to the American partner was secured with German property. The monetary benefit for the German partner resulted from absorbing this risk.

Currency / Foreign Currencies: Currency can be seen as a term denoting the legislation of the financial system in one currency zone. It is used as well to denote a currency zone's legal tender and swell-money denominated in legal tender. It is not that easy to define precisely the constituent parts of foreign currency. There are two types of tokens used as currencies: Legal tender (Central-Bank-money) and securitized claims on money, which means all swell-money. Foreign currencies comprise foreign Central-Bank-money. Usually, all money claims against foreign banks (whether they are denominated in the own or the foreign currency) and all claims on money (denominated in foreign currencies) against domestic banks are also comprised as foreign currency. That means foreign currency is not necessarily a claim against a foreigner.

Debenture: Debenture is a term to be used for "securitized credits". Securitization does mean that the credit is evidenced by a document. In principle the document evidencing the credit can be seen as a paper that could be traded. Meanwhile those documents are not really a paper. They are nothing else than an entry in database systems. In former times they were physical documents. A debenture is thus a tradable credit. It is a promise on money that matures at some future point of time.

Derivative: Derivatives are financial products whose value is derived from other products (so-called underlying instruments). A derivative is derived from the underlying instrument. Examples of derivatives are so-called swaps, options and futures. Those derivatives contract special rights, related to the underlying instrument. A call-option, for example, defines the right, but not the obligation, to buy the underlying instrument at a specified price (called exercise price), in the negotiated period of time, from the issuer of the option. Meanwhile there are so many different types of derivatives that they become unmanageable. All certificates, meaning all debentures deriving their value from underlying instruments, are derivatives as well.

Equity: A balance sheet of a company lists all the company's properties, receivables and all liabilities, especially all debt. The difference between all monetary evaluated asset components one possesses and the monetary assessment of all liabilities is the net worth. The net worth of a company can be seen as its stock value adjusted by all debt. It depends on the used accounting standard whether the assessment of assets and liabilities considers somehow the estimated future earnings and payments as well. However, a positive net worth represents the so-called equity of a company. Equity belongs to the company owners. The net worth is distributed to all owners in case of the company's liquidation. If the company goes out of business, all liabilities have to be cleared. Everything the company owns afterwards is equity. That can be distributed to all shareholders depending on their share. As long as a company is in operation, equity is more or less the company's ability to bear losses. If for example a company incurs al loss in one business year, this loss reduces inevitably the company's net worth. A loss reduces the equity. And in case a company has more liabilities than assets there is equity missing – negative equity. In such a case the company has to make future profits, in order to reach again a status of positive net worth. That is why equity can be used as an indicator assessing the so-called solvency of a company. It indicates the capability of a company to bear losses without the need to run into new indebtedness. Positive equity means, the company could in principle sell assets, to absorb a loss. If no net worth, meaning no equity, is available, any loss has to be covered by taking new credits. In consequence the whole debt service will increase (cf. the explanations about insolvency).

Fiat Money: The term "Fiat Money" makes a reference to the Latin phrase "Fiat Lux" ("let there be light"). Fiat Money does mean "let there be money". Fiat Money denotes any kind of unbacked money, slips of paper that should be seen as having a value but in fact, there is nothing of value stored under deposit. The backing of money with gold as it was agreed upon internationally, in the Bretton-Woods-Agreements, has been cancelled since 1971. At that time, the word financial system consisted of different currencies, but with fixed exchange rates. Today more or less any money created by commercial banks or whatever other issuer is of the kind Fiat Money. Central-Bank-money and legal tender is also more or less unbacked. Even Central Banks that do have some gold reserves under deposit or in ownership do not have any obligation to exchange banknotes against gold. Instead of being backed by gold, Central-Bank-money receives some well defined value, because of legislation. The value attached to legal tender originates from its legally fixed debt discharging effect. As long as nothing else has been negotiated and contracted, legal tender cannot be refused by the creditor in a settlement of a debt. Legislation of this kind is restricted to legal tender only. That means other Fiat Money like commercial-bank-money (for instance "check-money") could be refused in a settlement of a debt. That is why for instance somebody having a positive checking account balance could insist on the redemption in cash.

Financial Instruments / Financial Assets: Financial Instruments / Financial Assets are all money or claims on money that an economic entity possesses. A financial instrument is in and of itself the slip of paper evidencing money or a claim on money. A financial asset denotes the monetary evaluation of a financial instrument. Whatever financial instrument is owned as an asset is a liability of somebody else. This holds true for any kind of money and swell-money, for instance shares or debentures as well. Central-Bank-money coming in the form of banknotes or sight deposits at the Central Bank is created from nothing. It comes into circulation when the Central Bank purchases something paying with the newly created money. Alternatively it comes into circulation, if the Central Bank lends the newly created money when granting a credit. All that money is denoted as Fiat Money since it is created out of nothing. Central-Bank-money is a liability of the Central Bank and a financial asset of its owner. In the same way, commercial-bank-money is created. It comes into circulation, if a commercial bank purchases something from a non-bank, paying with the newly created commercial-bank-money. The sale proceeds are credited to the seller's bank account. Another possibility is to grant a customer a credit and crediting the customer's bank account with the credit amount. New commercial-bank-money is created when the bank account is credited. Commercial-bank-money is a liability of the commercial bank issuing that money. By granting a credit, the commercial bank does not lend money that somebody else has paid in. What the bank instead does is to grant a claim on Central-Bank-money. The customer gets a promise of her bank to get Central-Bank-money up to the granted amount, if needed and requested. Usually one does not require Central-Bank-money to settle payment processes.

G 20: G 20 is the abbreviation of Group Twenty. It denotes the group of twenty major economies. It is an economic but unofficial forum consisting of the twenty largest industrialized and emerging economies: Argentina, Australia, Brazil, Canada, China, France, Germany, India,

Indonesia, Italy, Japan, Mexico, Russia, Saudi Arabia, South Africa, South Korea, Turkey, United Kingdom, United States and the European Union. The establishment of the G 20 was in reaction to the financial crisis in the late Nineties. The main issue discussed at G 20 are the key-aspects of global economy, especially the global financial system. Representatives of the member countries usually meet annually. In reaction to the financial crisis that began 2007 they met more frequently. In their declarations they argue for joint and concerted actions to face the financial and economic crisis. Even though those declarations are legally not binding, they emphasise strongly a sound willingness for cooperation. Currently most relevant declarations have been made on the so-called G 20 Summit in Washington (November 2008), London (April 2009) and Pittsburgh (September 2009). The representatives participating at these meetings are the countries finance ministers and Central Bank governors, the Presidency of the Council of the European Union, the president of the European Central Bank, chairman and managing director of the International Monetary Fund, president of the World Bank and the chairman of the World Bank's development committee.

GDP: GDP calculates the overall economic productivity of a country in one year. GDP is used as an indicator to measure the creation of value inside a country. It calculates the amount of all produced goods and services meant for consumption. Those produced goods and services being partial and preliminary performances are not counted. There are three different approaches to calculate (nominal) value added. First there is a value added approach (approach evaluating the production). The value added approach calculates the GDP by subtracting all intermediate inputs from the market value of all produced goods and services (production value). Added are all taxes on all goods and services not deductible (for instance value added tax or petroleum tax). Subtracted are granted subsidies on goods and services. When using the expenditure's approach, the total spending on all goods and services (consumption of private household, non-profit organisations, government and public authorities) is the starting point. All gross investment and exports are added, imports are subtracted and the result is corrected by considering inventory changes. The third possibility to calculate the gross domestic product is the income approach. Firstly the national income is evaluated. It consists of employee compensation, corporate profits, rental income, net interest and proprietor's income (the so-called factor income of all factors of production in an economy). Production and import duties to the Nation's government, amortization and depreciation, are added, granted subsidies are subtracted. The resulting value is adjusted by the primary income balance which is the difference from all primary incomes derived from abroad and all domestic incomes of foreigners.

Good Faith Backing: Legal tender and Central-Bank-money of today is not backed by gold or any other precious metal. There is no component of a real value under deposit at the Central Bank that secures the value of legal tender. Instead this kind of today's Fiat Money is backed by good faith only. It is the good faith that government and Central Banks are maintaining the money supply to keep the money's attractiveness stable. The other aspect of faith is that it will be accepted in payment of taxes. A bearer of money has confidence, that others will see the same value attached to the money. As long as everybody has this confidence, it can be used as a medium of exchange for goods, services, tangibles etc. The money can be used as long as there is acceptance. In general there is no statutory obligation for acceptance. The only body who is obliged is the Government, to accept legal tender to settle payments of taxes.

Hedge Funds: Hedge funds denote special investment companies. Usually hedge funds are characterized as companies trying to make high profits with leveraging, a lot of other strategies and the use of financial products of a very different kind. Partly hedge funds have developed their own and new strategies. An example of such a strategy is a long/short strategy. It's an example how hedge funds take advantage by using whatever legally is not forbidden. In a long/short strategy hedge funds sell something short, with the obligation to deliver it at a fixed agreed upon point in time in the future. That what is sold today and which has to be delivered in the future the hedge fund does not own. It's a speculative selling. Hedge funds make a bet that they will be able to purchase that at a lesser price, than they have sold with a future delivery date, before they have to deliver it. Form a general point of view this means: They go into debt by owing somebody something (could be money or oil, commodities, shares and whatever) by selling it. In return, they get the sales price immediately. At least shortly before they have to deliver what they have sold, they have to purchase it somewhere. If at that time they have to pay a lower prize they gain a profit, otherwise they suffer a loss. Short position denotes the credit they took. It is not necessarily a money credit. It is what they owe to somebody. They owe something they have sold short. They owe that which they have sold, but not having possession. A long position denotes the ownership of this thing.

Hedonic Accounting: Usually when measuring the value added of a country, the market prices of the goods and services traded are taken as a measure. Some countries apply a different approach. The United States calculate their national gross domestic product by using the Hedonic Accounting; since a few years Europe applies this measure for some categories of goods as well. Hedonic Accounting is an evaluation measure that takes into account the qualitative changes of a product or services within a period of time. For instance if an ordinary computer of today is twice as powerful as that which could have been bought for the same price a year ago, the Hedonic Accounting observes a decrease of the "real" price. Hedonic Accounting argues that a customer will get today twice as much for the money, than a year ago. The "inner" ("real") value of the computer has increased. This means no inflation but a price cutting (deflation) for this special good or goods. Hedonic Accounting for Real Estate takes into account for instance changes in the surroundings for the object. If for example close to a residential building a new school or a shopping mall has opened, a rising inner "real" value of the building is argued. Following this argumentation, one assumes that a higher price could be achieved when purchasing the object on the market. The price of the object, its nominal value, is assumed to have risen, even if it is not offered for selling (c.f. real GDP in this glossary).

Housing Bubble: In the US the market prices of residential buildings have grown permanently from 2000 to 2006. When this price bubble burst in winter 2006/2007 Real Estate prices fell sharply. Their owners became victims of their high mortgaging to built or buy a house. They took a lot of credits very often at adjustable rates to finance. A lot of those indebted house owners were thrown into bankruptcy.

Hybrid Financial Instruments: National and international legislation in financial accounting differentiate usually between own capital and borrowed capital. For instance in taxation both types of capital are treated differently. Own capital is usually liable to cover losses. If capital is borrowed, the result is a corresponding liability and interest has to be paid for. Interest payable is treated as a company's expenditure reducing the taxable profit. Dividend payments to own capital do not reduce the taxable profit. Hybrid Financial Instruments are special debentures, trying to combine both aspects. Hybrid Financial Instruments do have both, the characteristics of own capital and of borrowed capital. Financial institutes for example, are allowed to count Hybrid Capital to fulfil the capital requirements as they are allowed to count all equity. Since interest to be paid is tax-deductible makes hybrid capital cheaper than equity. Interest to be paid on Hybrid Financial Instruments are in the same way tax-deductible than interest to be paid on any other kind of borrowed capital.

Investment Funds / Investment Trusts: Investment Funds / Investment Trusts are special financial institutes. They are economic entities that participate in the world financial markets acting on behalf of investors. Investment Funds are managing the assets brought in from investors. All investors receive fund chairs (fund swell-money). All assets that the fund manages are not owned by the fund, which makes this institute different from a normal company. The managed assets are so-called special property or separate assets. The fund is actively managing these assets. It means they can be used for investments, for example to purchase debentures or shares. There are funds as well that invest their special assets in Real Estate only, for instance, Real Estate Investment Trusts (REITs). The profits from the investments are partly used to cover all operating expenses of the fund. The remaining profit should be distributed to the investors (and taxed there).

Leverage: Let us assume somebody would like to make an investment. He likes to purchase something, but does not have enough capital (for instance money that has been saved). To make the purchase there is the need to take credits. Since the investment cannot be made with saved capital only, part of the investment is made "on tick". If for instance one has saved 100'000 Euros and wants to purchase a building to the value of 500'000 Euros there is the need to take 400'000 Euros as a credit. The ratio between the saved capital and taken credit is called leverage. In the above example the leverage is four. The investor took the fourfold of credits compared to saved capital. A leveraged investment means a purchase partly on credit.

Leveraging: Leverage investment strategies are investments that are partially done on credit. Besides saved capital one takes new debt to supplement the investment. Leveraged investments are reasonable and profitable if the investment yields a better return than the interest to be paid on the debt. A special form of a purchase on credit concerns merger and acquisitions of companies. Often the purchased company or a part of the company's assets are used to collateralize the credit taken (Leveraged Buy Out).

Money Stocks / Money Supply: Monetary economics differentiates several monetary aggregates. For instance, the European Central Bank (ECB) denotes all created Central-Bank-money in circulation (banknotes and Central Bank deposits) with M0. If all the swell-money created from commercial banks (with a-day-to-day maturity) is added, this is denoted as M1. M2 comprises M1 plus all claims on money, with fixed durations up to two years or in up to three months notice (time and saving deposits). Besides those three monetary aggregates there are several others, for example monetary stocks comprising debentures and quiet different claims on Central-Bank-money with very different maturities or terms. The classification of money and monetary aggregates is not standardized. That is why monetary aggregates having the same identifier could be different. Above we described how the European Central Bank (ECB) defines deliberated sets of money. The German Central Bank (Deutsche Bundesbank) for instance, comprises saving accounts with a three month legal period of notice not in M2, as ECB is doing, but in M3.

Nominal / real: When assessing the value of economic objects, a distinction is made between their real value and their nominal value. Economic objects are for instance tangibles, intangibles, goods and services. The nominal value of an object is its price denominated in currency units. If there is inflation in an economy one could assume that this (nominal) price of goods and services will increase from year to year. The prices are rising but the goods keep the same. Butter still will be butter next year. That means the value of use attached to butter does not change over the time. That is why nominal value and real value are distinguished. The real value is adjusted for the effect of inflation. Usually one starts from a reference year. Referencing to this year an annual inflation index is calculated for subsequent years. Real values of objects are calculated by adjusting their nominal value (prices) by this inflation index. Does for instance a pound of butter cost 2.20 Euros today (2009) and the calculated inflation rate (reference year 2005) is ten percent the real value of butter today (in terms of 2005 prices) would be 2.00 Euros. This is only one form to calculate real values. There are other calculation methods that do not use an inflation index. An example is the so-called hedonic accounting (cf. the explanation in this glossary).

OTC markets: Trading of debentures, shares and whatever securities that do not take place at exchanges are called Over The Counter (OTC) markets. The term denotes that two trading partners arrange a deal among themselves. They can make a deal in a phone call or in whatever kind. It could as well be by meeting together at a counter undersigning a contract. OTC is the abbreviation of Over The Counter.

Real GDP: Economic growth rates are usually not referred to a nominal GDP. Most often a real GDP is calculated first. The nominal values (prices) of all goods and services produced in a year will be inflation corrected. The important question is how this inflation correction is performed. What is the inflation index that is considered? Alternatively there is another approach to calculate the real values of goods and services as well. It is the hedonic accounting that is increasingly been used. This is an evaluation method aimed to consider qualitative improvements of goods and services as well. As an example let's assume the inflation basket, which is the basket of goods considered to calculate the inflation index, contains one "standard" computer. In the reference year a standard computer would have cost 1'000 Euros. If today a standard computer costs 1'100 Euros this would mean an inflation of ten percent. Using hedonic accounting, qualitative improvements, e.g. computer power, would be considered. Would a standard computer of today for instance be equipped with twice as much main memory and a doubled clock frequency means one gets more paying 1'100 Euros. One gets today a computer being twice as powerful as a standard computer in the reference year. It is assumed that a twice as powerful computer would have cost in that year twice as much. It would have cost 2'000 Euros. Actually one gets today such a computer at a price of 1'100 Euros. That means there is a drastic deflation for this item in the inflation basket. Instead of costing 2'000 Euros it costs 1'100 Euros only. It means the price decreased by 45% (deflation). This small and simplified example should have made clear how much "potential for creative use" exists when applying hedonic accounting. In the US, hedonic accounting is already in use since a long time (since 1996) but has originally not been used e.g. in Germany. To gain more significance when comparing with other economies, the European Member States meanwhile have introduced hedonic accounting for some segments of goods and services as well. In Germany the accordant revision of the national account system took place in the year 2005.

REIT: A Real Estate Investment Trust is a corporation dedicated to a very special business segment. The focus of its business should be the management of real estate as assets. The REIT's income thus results from operating, letting and trading real estate. Such corporations are exempted from usually applied corporate taxation. All profits gained are taxed at the owners of the REIT only. This is important since it means that taxation depends on the owner's residence. It's the taxation system of the country of the owner's residence, which determines how much tax has to be paid and where it has to be paid.

RePo: RePo is the abbreviation for sale and repurchase agreement. These are purchases where at the same time the contracting partners agreed a repurchase in the future. That means the first agreed upon transaction is for instance the purchase of a share today. At the same time it has been agreed upon that the party who sold the share will repurchase it in the future. In principle this would mean that the share is lent out for a certain period of time. However, both agreements combined in a RePo are treated as separate deals, to camouflage this lending. They are treated legally independent to gain (taxation) benefits. RePos have mainly been invented for "tax optimization". For instance a share was sold the day before dividends were paid. The purchaser of the share was somebody residing in a country levying very low tax on dividends. The price to be paid to repurchase the share considers the reduced tax payment. The one who owns the share at the day of dividend payment and taxation receives a part of the circumvented tax for his effort. The other part of the circumvented tax reduces the repurchase price of the share. The RePo "re-qualified" dividend payments into trading profits. In a RePo the legal ownership is transferred to the purchaser for the agreed upon period of time, whereas the economic ownership is left at the seller (the re-purchaser in the future). All earnings gathered (especially the dividend paid) over the entire term of the contract, resulting from the ownership (legal ownership), are transferred to the original owner by adjusting the re-purchase price (some allowances are left to the purchaser). This procedure is denoted manufactured payment.

Reserve requirement: For liquidity reasons commercial banks need to have access to enough legal tender. Legislation has set so-called minimum reserve requirements to ensure the commercial banks' liquidity up to a certain amount. E.g. in the Euro zone a credit institution is required to have a certain percentage of all its sight deposits (short time liabilities) in Central-Bank-money under deposit (usually as sight deposits at the Central Bank). The European regulation (EC)No1745/2003(ECB/2003/9) sets this minimum required reserve ratio to two percent of all customer deposits and emitted bank debentures with maturities of less than two years. In 2012 the ratio has been lowered to one percent. There is no minimum reserve requirement for customer deposits with longer durations (for instance saving accounts) and all other debentures with longer maturities. RePo businesses are exempted from minimum reserve requirements as well. Credit institutions are obliged to have at least the required minimum reserve amount of Central-Bank-money on account at the Central Bank. Reserve balances receive interest at a level defined for the so-called deposit facility of the Central Bank. Credit institutions are offered the facility to lend Central-Bank-money if needed by using lending facilities that the Central Bank provides. The cost for commercial banks to have Central-Bank-money under deposit are thus not more than the set key interest rate to be paid for a credit minus the interest paid at the deposit facility. Currently (October 2009) this difference amounts to 0.75%. The key interest rate for credits (main refinancing) is 1%, interest paid at the deposit facility is 0.25%.

It is important to consider that e.g. market money funds do have no minimum reserve requirement. That means customer accounts that are exchanged "overnight" against shares of market money funds reduce the reserve requirements of the customer's bank. It is because the balance of the customer account is decreased before the minimum required reserve is calculated (at the end of a trading day). That is one example how credit institutions have possibilities to influence the amount of minimum reserves they are required to have on deposit. In the US this possibility is heavily used. It is called account sweeping.

Possibilities to influence the required amount of reserves to be hold are of special relevance. The minimum reserve limits the banks' possibility to create swell-money. A higher minimum reserve ratio restricts the potential to create swell-money. If for instance a minimum reserve ratio of two percent is set fix, the total amount of created check money (commercial-bank-money) and bank debentures with less than two years maturity can be not more than the fiftyfold of all Central-Bank-money in circulation (if the commercial banks have all that Central-Bank-money on deposit). Exceptions, e.g. exempting money market funds from minimum reserve requirements, give commercial banks a lot of opportunities to circumvent these limitations. Today the limiting effect of a minimum required reserve ratio has to be seen only as theoretically given. For instance the European Central Bank offers a special facility for so-called marginal lending where commercial banks can get unlimited credits. As long as commercial banks have eligible collateral, they can borrow Central-Bank-money overnight. That means the minimum reserve requirement does not really limit the potential of commercial banks to create swell-money. Currently the minimum reserve requirements can basically always be fulfilled as long as confidence is in the markets. One more aspect has to be considered. A few countries (for instance Canada and Great Britain) have no minimum reserve requirements anymore. The United States have fixed the minimum reserve requirements for special deposits (eurocurrency liabilities, non-personal time deposits) at zero percent since 1990. Eurocurrencies are denoted all foreign currencies (this should not be confused with the Euro currency, the currency of the Euro zone).

SDR (Special Drawing Right): As long as the Bretton Woods agreement was valid, the exchange rates of currencies were fixed. Countries having liabilities at other countries had to settle foreign currency or gold. When those liabilities become due the backing of currencies – gold – could supplement the settlement of foreign currency reserves available. When bottlenecks in the availability of gold in some countries became apparent (1969) the currency zones jointly decided to invent an artificial reserve replacing gold in international transactions. That means they replaced the currency backing with gold by a currency backing with something that could be created from nothing (fiat money). The new invented structure has been denoted Special Drawing Right (SDR). Internationally the currency zones take shares in the International Monetary Fund. According to their share they were allowed to create Special Drawing Rights. These SDRs could be used to settle foreign debts. Special Drawing Rights are thus somehow a kind of global currency. All currency zones participating at IMF decide on the amount to be created and its allotment. This is very similar to the organization of Central-Bank-money supply in the Euro zone. SDRs however, are currently not legal tender, especially not global legal tender. That means the acceptance of SDRs with debt discharging effect is voluntarily. To some extent the IMF agreements assure this acceptance. Participants being short in foreign currency liquidity are allowed to exchange a certain amount of SDRs to participants, selected from IMF, against free convertible currencies (US Dollar, Euro, pound sterling, Yen). When the Bretton Woods agreement was abandoned and the US Dollar was no longer backed with gold, the world financial system changed to a regime of flexible exchange rates. Since that time the value of a Special Drawing Right is the weighted sum of the four most important currencies in global trade (US Dollar, Yen, pound sterling and Euro). The weighting reflects the export proportion of these currency zones as a first aspect. The second aspect is how much these currencies are used as currency reserves of countries.

Securities: "Security" it is the broadest term given to all fungible (meaning individual units are capable of mutual substitution), negotiable instruments representing a financial value. Roughly, one could say, securities are all slips of paper evidencing the ownership of a claim. If we look to it from the other side, securities are all slips of paper evidencing the promise, which the creator of the security has made. The slip of paper is in and of itself the security. It does not mean that it is backed with something. Banknotes, debentures, bonds, Pfandbriefe, shares, certificates, derivatives and much more are securities. The term "security" or "debt securities" is used in most official statistics. It comprises of all kinds of debentures. However, a security, a collateral, (something tangible or intangible with value) does not have to be deposited in. Real value assets like tangibles as collateral are rather an exception. There is quite a much bigger volume of unsecured debentures. One could say "unsecured securities" are the rule. The securitized debt is only backed with "good faith". Even in the case of so-called asset backed securities it does not mean that the assets are tangibles or other real value assets. That which could back the security could be a security as well or it could be any kind of receivable or another claim on money. There are existing asset backed securities for instance that are backed by sales proceeds hoped for in the future but not yet certain. Thus, more fittingly would be the term "debt obligation" instead of "security", meaning something that obligates a debt. That would denote something tradable which evidences a claim on the redemption of a granted credit.

Securities Depositories: All securities, which mean all electronically tradable debentures, are managed as entries in database management systems. All information about the kind of debenture, the volume, the ownership, the issuer etc. is managed as a dataset in special databases. These databases are called Securities Depositories. Depending on size and scope of the managed securities, the depositories are distinguished as National, Central or International Security Depository. Depositories are a kind of file for a specific scope and volume of debentures.

Security Settlement Systems: Security Settlement Systems are information and communication platforms. They serve as depositary and provide all necessary services to process security trades (payment and settlement / transfer of ownership).

Stock index / Share index: Stock exchanges publish so-called stock indices / share indices (plural of index) that consider different groups of companies. Those companies considered in one group have usually more or less the same characteristics. E.g. the so-called DAX 30, a German stock index, relates to the share quotation of the thirty largest German companies. The companies selected in the DAX 30 have to comply with some well-defined characteristics. To give a few examples e.g. one selection criteria defines that at least ten percent of the company's shares should be in free float (shares that are not held by large owners and have no sales restrictions). The company's domicile should be Germany or at least the amount of share trades in Germany should dominate. The weighting of the company's share quotation in a stock index follows as well a number of criteria. There are quite a lot of different stock indices. Well-known are for instance the Standard & Poor's S&P500 (500 largest US corporations), the British FTSE Group (a joint company of the Financial Times and the London Stock Exchange) FTSE Global 100 (top 100 multinational companies) or the Japanese Nikkei Inc.'s NIKKEI 225 (225 selected Japanese companies). There are indices trying to reflect special investment strategies concerning risk and chances. The higher the risk of losses the higher the chance for profits and vice versa. Based on those indices there are financial institutions that create so-called index certificates which are derivative debentures. Those derivatives' value follow the price performance of the weighted share portfolio considered in the referenced, the underlying index. It is important to mention that an index certificate is a derivative. It is usually an unsecured debenture. When buying such a certificate one does not own the referenced shares. All one possesses is a debenture. It is a securitized but unsecured promise on money with a volatile value following the price performance of all shares considered in the index.

Sub Prime crisis: The Sub Prime crisis is the crisis of Sub Prime markets. The crisis began when the housing bubble in the US burst in winter 2006 / 2007.

Sub Prime market: This denotes the US market of special mortgage credits. It is a market of all credits granted to customers with poor creditworthiness.

Sustainability / Ecological footprint: The ecological dimension of the term sustainability comprises requirements with respect to the exploitation of nature. The living generation should use only as much raw materials and ecological resources that are renewable or regenerative within a reasonable period of time. If we ask "how much resources do we need" the answer depends on our level of consumption and the "resource-efficiency" of our technologies. We can calculate then how much raw materials and resources are needed to produce all the desired products, goods and services. Sustainability aims to provide all future generations the same abilities to meet their needs as the present. The question then is: "how much raw materials and resources is a living generation allowed to utilize"? To answer we can generalize the concept of sustainable forestry. Sustainable forestry means the following: if there is a given surface of forest land, it is allowed to take out only an amount of trees that duly can re-grow. The number of trees allowed to be cut down consistent with sustainable forestry, is basically limited through the available surface of forest land. If we consider the actual consumption of trees, we could ask the other way around: "how much surface of forest land would be necessary to provide this amount of trees through a sustainable forestry?" How much surface of our planet should be dedicated to forestry in order to a sustained provision of this raw material in the requested amount to produce our products? If we answer this type of question for all kind of raw materials and environmental resources which we exploit to produce all consumed goods and services, the result will be the so-called "ecological footprint". The ecological footprint calculates how much surface of earth humankind would need to have (considering the given level of consumption) in order to create all value added through a sustainable economy. The ecological footprint sums up: How much surface would be necessary to have enough grass to feed all the animals we eat? How much surface would we need to have for agriculture? How much surface would be necessary to have enough plants so that all the detrimental greenhouse gas emissions can be converted into organic matters back again through photosynthesis, how much surface to obtain wood, how much for water and how much surface for regenerative raw materials which we could utilize to produce energy etc.? Adding all these numbers together, the result is the overall surface we as humankind would need to have in order that all the economic operation is sustainable. Needless to say, the question is: do we have this surface on our mother earth?

Swap: A Swap denotes a special derivative. Swaps are contracts to exchange cash flows in different currencies or with different payment intervals. Swaps are referencing two underlying instruments. In case of a currency Swap for instance the owner of a US Dollar denominated debenture will get the interest payments connected to a Euro denominated debenture and vice versa. In case of an interest Swap somebody who has a monthly payment obligation could swap it with somebody who has an annual payment obligation (and vice versa). There are quite different possibilities of Swaps. In case of a Credit Default Swap (CDS) for instance the risk that a credit is not paid back at maturity, is swapped against payments of premiums. In such a case the Credit Default Swap represents an insurance (but has not the legal status of an insurance). The insurer gets a series of payments but has in case of a credit default the obligation to pay the credit amount to the insured one.

(Circulation) Velocity of money: Let us assume that a daughter assists her father in chores and gardening. She will get 100 Euros a month for this aid (which represents newly created value added). With these earnings she finances a dancing class (another value added). It costs 100 Euros a month. The dancing master takes investment advice (a third value added) from the father and pays 100 Euros each month. Daughter, dancing master and father got earnings of 100 Euros each a month for their added value services. In total this will be in one year 3 times 100 Euros times 12 equaling to 3'600 Euros of business volume. It is a Gross Domestic Product of 3'600 Euros and the total sum of all payment processes is 3'600 Euros. Hoe much money is required to process all payments? Each month 100 Euros are paid to the daughter. Exactly these 100 Euros the daughter pays to her dancing master. The dancing master as well pays exactly these 100 Euros to the father. 100 Euros are passing through three hands in one month and this process recurs each month, twelve times a year. That means one and the same 100 Euros have been moved 36 times in one year from hand to hand. In this example the velocity of money (u) is 36. It is only 100 Euros Central-Bank-money required to process all the payments made in an overall business volume of 3'600 Euros.

Further Readings:

Abelshauser, Werner (2004): Deutsche Wirtschaftsgeschichte seit 1945. München: Verlag C. H. Beck

Akerlof, George A./Schiller, Robert J. (2009): Animal spirits. How Human Psychology drives the Economy and why it matters for global capitalism. Princeton University Press

Anders, Peter E. (Hg. 1991): Betriebswirtschaftslehre humoris causa. Wiesbaden: Gabler Verlag

Anders, Peter E. (Hg. 1993): Betriebswirtschaftliche Bonbons. Wiesbaden: Gabler Verlag

Anders, Peter E. (Hg. 1995): Betriebswirtschaft non olet. Wiesbaden: Gabler Verlag

Beck, Ulrich (1999): Schöne neue Arbeitswelt. Vision: Weltbürgergesellschaft. Frankfurt am Main: Campus

Beise, Marc/Schäfer, Ulrich (Hg. 2009): Kapitalismus in der Krise. Wie es zur großen Krise kam, wie erneut die Gefahr wirklich ist und wie sich die Probleme lösen lassen. München: Süddeutsche Zeitung Edition

Binswanger, Hans Christoph (2005): Geld und Magie. Eine ökonomische Deutung von Goethes Faust. Hamburg: Murmann-Verlag

Bloss, Michael/Ernst, Dietmar/Häcker, Joachim/Eil, Nadine (2009): Von der Subprime-Krise zur Finanzkrise. Immobilienblase: Ursachen, Auswirkungen, Handlungsempfehlungen. München: Oldenbourg Wissenschaftsverlag

Boolstuber, Richard (2008): Teufelskreis der Finanzmärkte. Märkte, Hegdefonds und die Risiken von Finanzinnovationen. Kulmbach

Burghof, Hans-Peter (2009): Zur Diskussion gestellt: Krise des Bankensystems: Zu viel Finanzinnovationen, zu wenig Regulierung? Vortragsmanuskript, Lehrstuhl für Bankwirtschaft und Finanzdienstleistungen, Fakultät Wirtschafts- und Sozialwissenschaften, Universität Hohenheim

Creutz, Helmut (2004): Die 29 Irrtümer rund ums Geld. München – Wien: Signum Wirtschaftsverlag

Dahrendorf, Ralf (1986): Ein garantiertes Mindesteinkommen als konstitutionelles Anrecht. In: Schmid, Thomas (Hg.): Befreiung von falscher Arbeit, Thesen zum garantierten Mindesteinkommen. Berlin

Diamond, Jared (2005): Collapse: How Societies Choose to Fail or Succeed. Viking Press

Diekmann, Karl (2007): Der große Selbstbetrug. Wie wir um unsere Zukunft gebracht werden. München: Piper Verlag

Dohmen, Caspar (2008): Let's make Money. Was macht die Bank mit unserem Geld? Freiburg: orange-press

Drugen, Thomas (2007): Goldkinder. Die Welt des Vermögens. Hamburg: Murmann Verlag

Dueck, Gunter (2008): Abschied vom Homo Oeconomicus. Warum wir eine ökonomische Vernunft brauchen. Frankfurt am Main: Eichborn Verlag

Eichhorn, Peter (2009): Von der Finanzkrise zur Staatskrise? Diskussionspapier, Fakultät für Betriebswirtschaftslehre, Lehrstuhl für Allgemeine BWL, Public & Nonprofit Management, Universität Mannheim

Eichhorn, Wolfgang/Presse, André (2007): Grundrechte und Grundeinkommen. In: Werner, Götz W./Presse, André (Hg.): Grundeinkommen und Konsumsteuer. Karlsruhe: Universitätsverlag

Ekardt, Felix (2007): Wird die Demokratie ungerecht? Politik in Zeiten der Globalisierung. München: C. H. Beck Verlag

Ferguson, Niall (2008): The Ascent of Money. New York: The Penguin Press

Fisher, Irving (1935): 100 Percent Money. New York: Adelphi Company

Fisher, Irving (1933): The Debt Deflation Theory of Great Depressions. Econometrica, October 1933, 1, pp. 337–57

Flassbeck, Heiner (2006): 50 einfache Dinge, die Sie über unsere Wirtschaft wissen sollten. Frankfurt am Main: Westend Verlag

Flassbeck, Heiner (2009): Gescheitert. Warum die Politik vor der Wirtschaft kapituliert. Frankfurt am Main: Westend Verlag

Flassbeck, Heiner/Spiecker, Friederike (2007): Das Ende der Massenarbeitslosigkeit. Mit richtiger Wirtschaftspolitik die Zukunft gewinnen. Frankfurt am Main: Westend Verlag

Friedmann, Thomas L. (2006): Die Welt ist flach. Eine kurze Geschichte des 21. Jahrhunderts. Frankfurt am Main: Suhrkamp Verlag

Fromm, Erich (1976): Haben oder Sein. München: Deutsche Verlags- Anstalt

Galbraith, John Kenneth (1954): The Great Crash 1929. London: Penguin

Gburek, Manfred (2007): Geld und Gold klipp und klar von A bis Z. München: Verlag Litera-Tour

Global Marshall Plan Initiative (2004): Global Marshall Plan. Stuttgart: Horizonte Verlag

Global Marshall Plan Initiative (2006): Solidarität, die ankommt. Ziel-effiziente Mittelverwendung in der Entwicklungszusammenarbeit. Ulm: Ebner & Spiegel

Gottwald, Franz-Theo/ Fischler, Franz (Hg., 2007): Ernährung sichern – weltweit. Ökosoziale Gestaltungs-Perspektiven. Hamburg: Murmann Verlag

Hagelüken, Alexander / Freiberger, Harald (Hg., 2009): Die großen Spekulanten. Märchenhafte Gewinne und gigantische Verluste. München: Süddeutsche Zeitungs Edition

Hahlbrock, Klaus (2007): Feeding the Planet. Environmental Protection through Sustainable Agriculture. Hg. Klaus Wiegandt. London: Haus Publishing

Hardorp Benediktus (2008): Arbeit und Kapital als schöpferische Kräfte. Einkommensbildung und Besteuerung als gesellschaftliches Teilungsverfahren. Karlsruhe: Universitätsverlag

Hardorp, Benediktus (2009): Elemente einer Neubestimmung des Geldes und ihre Bedeutung für die Finanzwirtschaft der Unternehmung. Freiburg im Breisgau 1958, zweite Auflage: Heidelberg 1971, dritte Auflage: Karlsruhe 2009: Universitätsverlag Karlsruhe

Hartmann-Wendels, Thomas/ Pfingsten, Andreas/Weber, Martin (1998): Bankbetriebslehre. Berlin–Heidelberg–New York: Springer- Verlag

Hellwig, Martin (2008): Systemic Risk in the Financial Sector: An Analysis of the subprime-Mortgage Financial Crisis. Preprints of the Max Planck Institute for Research on Collective Goods, November 2008. Bonn

Heuser, Uwe Jean (2000): Das Unbehagen im Kapitalismus. Die neue Wirtschaft und ihre Folgen. Berlin: Berlin Verlag

Heuser, Uwe Jean (2008): Humanomics. Die Entdeckung des Menschen in der Wirtschaft. Frankfurt am Main: Campus Verlag

Horx, Matthias (2001): Smart Capitalism. Das Ende der Ausbeutung. Frankfurt am Main: Eichborn

Institut der deutschen Wirtschaft Köln (Hg., 2004): Perspektive 2050. Ökonomie des demographischen Wandels. Köln: Deutscher Instituts Verlag

Institute of International Finance (2008): Final Report of the IIF Committee on Market Best Practices. Principles of Conduct and Best Practice Recommendation

IPOC, WMO/UNEP (2007): Intergovernment Panel of Climate Change: Climate Change 2007. Synthesis Report

Issing, Otmar (2007): Einführung in die Geldtheorie. 14.Auflage. München: Vahlen GmbH

Issing, Otmar (2008): New Financial Order. Recommendations by the Issing Committee/Preparing G-20 – Washington, November 15th.

Jarass, Lorenz/Obermair, Gustav M. (2008): Tax on EBIT instead of profit. EC Tac Review

Jarass, Lorenz/Obermair, Gustav M. (2006): Jeder sollte Steuern zahlen – Ein Beitrag zur Unternehmenssteuerreform 2008. Ulm: CPI-Books

Jäger, Jill (2007): Our Planet. How Much More Can Earth Take? Hg. Klaus Wiegandt. London: Haus Publishing

Kapitza, Sergey P. (2005): Global Population Blow-Up and After. Demographic Revolution and Information Society. Hamburg: Report to the Club of Rome and the Global Marshall Plan Initiative

Karmann, Alexander / Klose, Joachim (Hg., 2006): Geld regiert die Welt? Wirtschaftliche Reflexionen. Marburg: Metropolis-Verlag

Kaufmann, Stefan E. (2007): The New Plagues. Pandemics and Poverty in a Globalized World. Hg. Klaus Wiegandt. London: Haus Publishing

Kämpke, Thomas/Pestel, Robert/Radermacher, Franz Josef (2003): A competional concept for normative equity. European Journal of Law and Economics

Kindleberger, Charles P. (2001): Mania, Panics, and Crashes. A History of Financial Crises. Macmillan Press Ltd. 1st. ed. 1978

Klinger, Nadja / König, Jens (2006): Einfach abgehängt. Ein wahrer Bericht über die neue Armut in Deutschland. Berlin: Rowohlt

Krugman, Paul (2008): The return of depression economics and the crisis of 2008. London: Penguin Books

Latif, Mojib (2007): Climate Change. The Point of No Return Hg. Klaus Wiegandt. London: Haus Publishing

Marx, Reinhard (2008): Das Kapital. Ein Plädoyer für den Menschen. München: Pattloch Verlag

Mauser, Wolfram (2007): Water Resources. Efficient, Sustainable and Equitable. Hg. Klaus Wiegandt. London: Haus Publishing

Meyer, Bernd (2007): Costing The Earth. Perspectives of sustainable development. Hg. Klaus Wiegandt. London: Haus Publishing

Merz, Friedrich (2008): Mehr Kapitalismus wagen. Wege zu einer gerechten Gesellschaft. München: Piper Verlag

Müller, Dirk (2009): Crashkurs Weltwirtschaftskrise oder Jahrhundertchance? Wie Sie das Beste aus Ihrem Geld machen. München: Droemer Verlag

Müller, Harald (2007): Building A New World Order. Sustainable Policies for the Future. Hg. Klaus Wiegandt. London: Haus Publishing

Müller, Leo (2006): Ackermanns Welt. Ein Tatsachenbericht. Reinbek bei Hamburg: Rowohlt Verlag

Münchau, Wolfgang (2008): Kernschmelze im Finanzsystem. München: Carl Hanser Verlag

Münz, Rainer/Reiterer, Albert F. (2007): Overgrowdes World. Global Population and International Migration. Hg. Klaus Wiegandt. London: Haus Publishing

Neirynck, Jacques (1998): Der göttliche Ingenieur – Die Evolution der Technik. Renningen Malmsheim: Expert-Verlag

North, Michael (Hg. 2000): Deutsche Wirtschaftsgeschichte. Ein Jahrtausend im Überblick. München: C. H. Beck Verlag

North, Michael (1994): Das Geld und seine Geschichte. Vom Mittelalter bis zur Gegenwart. München: C. H. Beck Verlag

Opielka, Michael (2004): Sozialpolitik. Grundlagen und vergleichende Perspektiven. Reinbeck bei Hamburg: Rowohlt Verlag

Otte, Max (2009): Der Crash kommt. Die neue Weltwirtschaftskrise und was Sie jetzt tun können. Berlin: Ullstein Verlag

Paál, Gábor (2009): Die Erde am Limit. Hörbuch. Forum für Verantwortung

Pfingsten, Andreas (2009): Das Sub-Prime-Virus: Ursachen und Folgen der Finanzkrise. Vierteljahreshefte zur Wirtschaftsforschung 2009, S. 14–24, Deutsches Institut für Wirtschaftsforschung, Berlin

Poitras, Geoffrey (2000): The Early History of Financial Economics. 1478–1776. From Commercial Arithmetic to Life Annuities and Joint Stocks. Cheltenham UK, Northkampton USA: Edward Elgar

Presse, André (2009): Grundeinkommen. Dissertation, Universität Karlsruhe (TH), Fakultät für Wirtschaftswissenschaften

Racek, Alfred (2001): Befreiungsphilosophie des Geldes, Thaur, Druck- und Verlagshaus

Radermacher, Franz Josef (2006): Globalisierung gestalten. Die neue zentrale Aufgabe der Politik. Berlin: Terra Media Verlag

Radermacher, Franz Josef / Beyers, Bert (2007): Welt mit Zukunft. Überleben im 21. Jahrhundert. Hamburg: Murmann Verlag

Radermacher, Franz Josef (2002): Die neue Zukunftsformel. Bild der Wissenschaft, Heft 4 / 2002, S. 78–86

Radermacher, Franz Josef (2004): Global Marshall Plan – A Planetary Contract

Radermacher, Franz Josef (english 2004): Balance or Destruction – Ecosocial market Economy as the key to global sustainable development. Wien: Ökosoziales Forum Europa

Rahmstorf, Stefan/Richardson, Katherine (2007): Our Threatened Oceans. Hg. Klaus Wiegandt. London: Haus Publishing

Rawls, J. (1978): A Theory of Justice. London: Oxford University Press

Reich, Robert (2008): Superkapitalismus. Wie die Wirtschaft unsere Demokratie untergräbt. Frankfurt am Main: Campus Verlag

Reichholf, Josef H. (2007): The Demise of Diversity. Loss and Extinction. Hg. Klaus Wiegandt. London: Haus Publishing

Reinhart Carmen M./Rogoff, Kenneth S. (2009): The Aftermath of Financial Crisis. Paper prepared for presentation at the American Economic Association meetings in San Francisco, January 3, 2009

Reinhart, Carmen M./Rogoff, Kenneth S. (2008): This time is different: A panoramic view of eight centuries of financial crisis. NBER Working Paper No. 13 882, Issued in March 2008

Reinhart, Carmen M./Rogoff, Kenneth S. (2008 a): Is the 2007 U. S. Subprime Crisis so different? An international historical comparison. American Economic Review, 98, 2, S. 339–344.

Riegler, Josef (1990): Antworten auf die Zukunft. Ökosoziale Marktwirtschaft. Wien: Adolf Holzhausens NfG

Roeper, Hans /Weimer, Wolfram (1996): Die D-Mark. Eine deutsche Wirtschaftsgeschichte. Frankfurt am Main: Sozietäts-Verlag

Rudolph, Bernd (2008): Lehren aus den Ursachen und dem Verlauf der internationalen Finanzkrise. Schmalenbachs Zeitschrift für betriebswirtschaftliche Forschung, zfbf, 60, 713–741

Sabet, Huschmand (2005): Globale Maßlosigkeit. Der (un)aufhaltsame Zusammenbruch des weltweiten Mittelstands. Düsseldorf: Patmos Verlag

Schäfer, Ulrich (2009): Der Crash des Kapitalismus. Warum die entfesselte Marktwirtschaft scheiterte. Frankfurt am Main: Campus Verlag

Scherhorn, Gerhard (2008): Geld soll dienen, nicht herrschen. Die aufhaltsame Expansion des Finanzkapitals. Wien: Picus Verlag

Scherhorn, Gerhard (2009): Verstärkt die Finanzkrise die Klimakrise? Forum Wissenschaft des BDWi, Ausgabe 2

Schmidt-Bleek, Friedrich (1998): Das MIPS-Konzept. Weniger Naturverbrauch, mehr Lebensqualität durch Faktor 10. München

Schmidt-Bleek, Friedrich (2007): The Earth. Natural Resources and Human Intervention. Hg. Klaus Wiegandt. London: Haus Publishing

Schumacher, Hajo (2005): Kopf hoch, Deutschland. Optimistische Geschichten aus einer verzagten Republik. München: Karl Blessing Verlag

Schumann, Harald / Grefe, Christiane (2008): Der globale Countdown. Gerechtigkeit oder Selbstzerstörung – die Zukunft der Globalisierung. Köln: Kiepenheuer & Witsch

Schumpeter, Joseph A. (1970): Das Wesen des Geldes. Aus dem Nachlass herausgegeben und mit einer Einführung versehen von Fritz Karl Mann. Göttingen: Vandenhoeck & Ruprecht

Seifert, Werner G., mit Voth, Hans-Joachim (2007): Invasion der Heuschrecken. Intrigen – Machtkämpfe – Marktmanipulation. Wie Hegdefonds die Deutschland AG attackieren. Berlin: Ullstein Buchverlage

Sinn, Hans-Werner (2005): Die Basar-Ökonomie Deutschland: Exportweltmeister oder Schlusslicht? Berlin: Econ Verlag

Sinn, Hans-Werner (2009): Risk-Taking, Limited Liability and the Banking Crisis. München: Ifo Institute for Economic Research

Sinn, Hans-Werner (2003): Ist Deutschland noch zu retten? Econ Verlag

Sinn, Hans-Werner (2009): Kasinokapitalismus. Wie es zur Finanzkrise kam, und was jetzt zu tun ist. Berlin: Econ Verlag

Solte, Dirk (2007): Weltfinanzsystem am Limit – Einblicke in den »Heiligen Gral« der Globalisierung. Berlin: Terra Media Verlag

Solte, Dirk (2009): Global Financial System in Balance – Crisis as opportunity for a sustainable future. Berlin: Terra Media Verlag

Soros, George (2008): The New Paradigm for Financial Markets. The Credit Crisis of 2008 and what it means. New York: Public Affairs.

Sowell, Thomas (2008): Economic Facts and Fallacies. New York: Basic Books

Spahn, P. B. (2002): Zur Durchführbarkeit einer Devisentransaktionssteuer. Gutachten im Auftrag des Bundesministeriums für Wirtschaftliche Zusammenarbeit und Entwicklung. Bonn, Frankfurt am Main

Steingart, Gabor (2007): Weltkrieg um Wohlstand. Wie Macht und Reichtum neu verteilt werden. München: Piper Verlag

T. Anne (2009): Die Gier war grenzenlos. Berlin: Econ Verlag

Taleb, Nassim Nicholas (2007): The Black Swan: The Impact of the Highly Improbable. New York: Random House

The Technical Committee of the International Organization of Securities Commissions (2008): Code of Conduct Fundamentals for Credit Rating Agencies

Wackernagel, Mathis, et al. (2002): Tracking the ecological overshoot of the human economy. PNAS, Vol. 99, No. 14, 9266–9271

Wackernagel, Mathis/Rees, William (1997): Unser ökologischer Fußabdruck. Wie der Mensch Einfluss auf die Umwelt nimmt. Basel

Wagner, Hermann-Josef (2007): Energy. The World's Race for Resources in the 21st Century. Hg. Klaus Wiegandt. London: Haus Publishing

Weber, Andreas (2008): Biokapital, die Verschwörung von Ökonomie, Natur und Menschlichkeit. Berlin: Berlin Verlag

Werner, Götz W. (2008): Einkommen für alle. Köln (2007): Verlag Kiepenheuer & Witsch. Taschenbuchausgabe: Bergisch Gladbach: Verlagsgruppe Lübbe

Werner, Götz W. /Presse, André (Hg. 2007): Grundeinkommen und Konsumsteuer. Impulse für Unternimm die Zukunft. Karlsruher Symposium Grundeinkommen: bedingungslos. Karlsruher Universitätsverlag

Wicke, L./Spiegel, P. /Wieke-Thüs B. (2006): Kyoto-Plus – so gelingt der Klimawandel. München

Wigger, Berthold U. (2009): Der überforderte Staat und die kommende Haushaltskrise. Kommentar, Institut für Wirtschaftspolitik und Wirtschaftsforschung, Lehrstuhl Finanzwissenschaften, Fakultät für Wirtschaftswissenschaften, Universität Karlsruhe (TH)

Willenbrandt, Harald (2006): Das Dagobert-Dilemma. Wie die Jagd nach Geld unser Leben bestimmt. München: Wilhelm Heyne Verlag

Ziegler, Jean (2005): Das Imperium der Schande. Der Kampf gegen Armut und Unterdrückung. München: C. Bertelsmann

Global Marshall Plan
balance the world
with an Eco-Social Market Economy

The Global Marshall Plan Initiative is aiming for a "World in Balance". To achieve this we need a better design of globalization and the global economic processes – a worldwide Eco-Social Market Economy, an Inclusive Green Economy. This is a matter of an improved global structural framework, sustainable development, the eradication of poverty, environmental protection and equity, altogether resulting in a new global 'economic miracle'.

Please support our work for a World in Balance with your donation. The Global Marshall Plan Foundation has a tax-deductible status in Germany.

Global Marshall Plan Foundation	Tel.: +49 (0) 822 90 420
Rosenstr. 2	Fax: +49 (0) 822 90 421
20095 Hamburg - Germany	Donation Account:
info@globalmarshallplan.org	IBAN DE88 2512 0510 0000 0002 12
www.globalmarshallplan.org	SWIFT (BIC) BFSWDE33HAN